PROFESSIONAL COMMUNICATION ETHICS

Matthew Reavy
The University of Scranton

WAVELAND

PRESS, INC.

Long Grove, Illinois

For more information about this book, contact:
Waveland Press, Inc.
4180 IL Route 83, Suite 101
Long Grove, IL 60047-9580
(847) 634-0081
info@waveland.com
www.waveland.com

Printed in the United States of America

7   6   5   4   3   2   1

Contents

Preface

The best communication ethics courses encourage growth not just as professionals but also as individuals. Students in mass communication fields sometimes expect to learn existing standards and practices that tell them what they should and should not do. Ethical dilemmas, however, frequently are situations in which people might differ on what constitutes right or wrong action. Learning to reason through problems ethically is an essential foundation for making difficult decisions. The purpose is not to make the right decision but rather to make a right decision—one that can be defended with reason. The toughest ethical problems are those where a decision must be made when multiple parties disagree.

The first five chapters review the philosophical foundations of ethics, discussing the subject matter at a level appropriate for an audience with no formal training in philosophy. The next chapter focuses on the benefits of and problems with professional codes of ethics. Chapter 7 offers models for ethical decision making. Ideally, readers will learn how to analyze an ethical conflict and evaluate issues more objectively, identify values at the root of ethical conflicts, recognize the importance of loyalty and obligation in ethics, and select a specific ethical principle to decide the best course of action. Students need an understanding of basic philosophical principles, but they also need to apply those principles to real-world situations.

Chapters 8 through 13 examine ethics using issues, not professions, as the organizing principle. Areas covered include public interest, truth, conflicts of interest, privacy, confidentiality, and visual ethics. Each issue chapter is accompanied by a case study. Readers assume the role of a communication professional—an editor, a reporter, a public relations associate, an advertising executive, or a marketing director—working through the cases and offering solutions they can defend.

The presentation of the complicated topic of ethics is intentionally succinct, the result of feedback from students over many years. While brief, the text provides sufficient background to explore difficult issues—both practical and philosophical. The goal is not only to introduce existing norms of ethics in professional communication but also to prepare individuals for conflicts of value, duty, and loyalty—and to emphasize that communication professionals make decisions that impact people's lives.

1

Ethics, Morality, and the Law

In this chapter, you will learn about:
- Defining ethics
- Similarities and differences between ethics and morality
- The rationale and context of decision-making systems
- Law as an enforced civic morality
- Three dimensions of "right" and "wrong" conduct

Do you know the difference between right and wrong? Given that most people reading this book are adults, one would hope the answer is "yes."[1] Then why study ethics? The answer to that question is simple as well—because ethics rarely deals with deciding between a clearly "right" action and a clearly "wrong" one. Instead, ethics usually involves a *dilemma*—a difficult choice between alternatives. A good, moral person in such situations may find determining an ethically defensible course of action very challenging.

Take, for example, the basic concept of truth. Most of us were raised to understand that it is right and proper to tell the truth. Professional organizations in the various fields of mass communication recognize this as well. Indeed, the first precept of the Society of Professional Journalists' Code of Ethics is "Seek Truth and Report It."[2] Likewise, the Public Relations Society of America Code of Ethics states: "We adhere to the highest standards of accuracy and truth in advancing the interests of those we represent and in communicating with the public."[3] Leaving aside for now the complexities

1

involved in identifying "truth," should journalists and other communication professionals *always* report the truth?

As a young reporter, slightly more than a year out of college, I once covered a car accident in which a group of local teenagers were killed. The car left the road and burst into flames. According to the first witness on the scene, the teens could be heard screaming inside the burning wreckage. Should I have reported that "truth" in an article that would no doubt be read by the parents, family, and friends of the two teenagers? Suddenly many readers would jump to the opposite side and, instead of defending truth-telling, would oppose it. "Don't lie, but don't tell the whole truth either," they might say. But suppose that article was to result in one teenager driving a bit more cautiously, thus possibly avoiding a similar fate. Suppose not one teenager but two or ten were saved. Should I have told an excruciating truth in the hope of doing some public good? Or, in this case, would telling the truth do more harm than good? You can see that there are no clearly right or wrong answers.[4] That is the realm of ethics.

What Is Ethics?

Before we can start to discuss ethics, we must first come to some understanding of what exactly we are talking about. What is ethics? That question is not so easily answered as it might first appear. While it might be trite to fall back on dictionary definitions, doing so illustrates the problem we face. For example, Merriam-Webster's defines *ethics* as "the discipline dealing with what is good and bad and with *moral* duty and obligation [emphasis added]."[5] It further defines *moral* as "of or relating to principles of right and wrong in behavior: ethical."[6] So, are ethics and morality essentially the same?

While the two terms possess a similar heritage, they have become differentiated in the minds of many today. For example, philosophers frequently describe issues or decisions as both ethical *and* moral, with the difference between those terms either expressed or implied.[7] If the two terms were truly indistinct, such a description would be redundant, like saying something is "ethical and ethical" or "moral and moral." The terms must therefore have different connotations, at the least. Thus, we begin by explaining precisely how we intend to differentiate them.

Ethics and Morality

Ethics and morality are both systems that deal with human conduct, typically with the rightness or wrongness of that conduct.

An act that is moral and ethical is deemed to be a "right" act. Conversely, an act that is immoral and unethical is considered "wrong." Yet, if the two terms are differentiated, there must be situations in which, at least theoretically, an action can be moral but unethical or ethical but immoral. The distinction lies primarily in two areas: rationale and context.[8]

Rationale refers to the foundation of the ethical or moral system. Ethical decision making relies on reason as its foundation. Any ethical judgment *must* be based in reason and justified through reason alone. By contrast, morality can be argued as having an extra-rational foundation—one that does not necessarily rely on reason. For example, morality could grow out of one's upbringing or personal experience. One's moral decision making could be based on faith, on a "gut reaction," or on intuition.[9] That is not to say that morality cannot arise from reason or be defended with reason. However, unlike ethics, morality does not, of necessity, rely on reason alone.[10]

For many, the difference between ethics and morality does not involve rationale so much as *context*. Morality is an intrapersonal (within the person) duty to pursue right conduct. By contrast, ethics is an interpersonal (between persons) duty to do so.[11] Morality thus refers to the individual's perception of the rightness of an act, while ethics involves or includes the perception of others, usually within a profession, an organization, or some other communal group. One might thus describe morality as one's "personal ethics." Likewise, ethics could be viewed as a kind of "civic morality."

Both morality and ethics serve important roles in civil society. As Bertrand Russell wrote: "Without civic morality, communities perish; without personal morality, their survival has no value. Therefore, civic and personal morality are equally necessary to a good world."[12] But they are not one and the same. Given the distinction recognized here, it is in fact possible for something to be moral but unethical or ethical but immoral.

Imagine, for example, that you work for a public relations firm that agrees to take on an abortion clinic as a client. The public relations profession and your firm have no ethical problem with representing an abortion clinic. Some might even argue that refusing the clinic your firm's public relations services would itself constitute an unethical act.[13] But imagine also that you—because of faith, upbringing, or reason—believe that abortion is immoral and, therefore, that promoting the clinic's service is also immoral. In this situation, agreeing to represent the abortion clinic could constitute an action that is simultaneously ethical and immoral.

At the same time, what is moral for one person might not be moral for another. A scene from the 1966 film *A Man for All Seasons* illustrates this concept. In the movie, Thomas More takes a moral stand against King Henry VIII's decision to ignore orders from the Roman Catholic Church so that he can obtain a divorce and remarry in hopes of producing an heir to the throne.

> *Norfolk:* I'm not a scholar. I don't know whether the marriage was lawful or not—but damn it Thomas, look at these names! Why can't you do as I did and come with us for fellowship?
>
> *More:* And when we die, and you are sent to Heaven for doing your conscience, and I am sent to hell for not doing mine, will you come with me for fellowship?[14]

Morality dictates what individuals must do. They must act in accord with their own beliefs if they are to be moral. As More says elsewhere in the film: "What matters is that I believe it or rather, no, not that I believe but that *I* believe it."[15] One might be convinced, albeit with some difficulty, to change one's own beliefs. However, a moral person should not act against his or her own beliefs no matter how great the temptation, the promised reward, or the feared punishment.

Ethics can also conflict between professions as illustrated in a famous, or infamous, episode of the PBS series *Ethics in America*. The episode, titled "Under Order, Under Fire" dealt primarily with former military personnel discussing ethics as it pertained to their service. Two legendary television journalists, Peter Jennings of ABC and Mike Wallace of CBS, were also on the panel. The show's host posed a hypothetical situation to the journalists involving a fictional war between the imaginary country North Kosan and a coalition including the United States, which served as home to both of the journalists' networks. Given permission to move with the North Kosanese army, the journalists were asked what they would do if they witnessed the North Kosanese setting up an ambush that would result in the death of a platoon of American soldiers. Jennings initially said he would warn the Americans, even if it meant his own death. But Wallace had a different take. He said he considered it a "higher duty" to preserve his journalistic integrity by recording and reporting the ambush. Jennings then agreed with him, much to the shock of the military personnel in the room. The action may well have been ethical from a journalistic standpoint, but it was shockingly unethical in the eyes of the military.[16]

Ethics and the Law

If ethics can be called civic morality, then law represents that civic morality enforced with the threat of punishment. When you follow the posted speed limit on a highway, you are obeying the law. Failure to do so will result in a fine, imprisonment or both. The fear of punishment dictates that you act in a certain manner, even if your conscience does not compel you to do so. As Terry Ray notes, "The element of coercion is what distinguishes law from both ethics and morality."[17] Worrying about whether something is legal involves questions of *"Will I get caught?"* or *"Will I be punished?"* rather than *"Is this a good act?"* or similar moral concerns. Violating a law could also raise both legal and moral concerns simultaneously. Driving 20 mph over the speed limit on an empty freeway raises a legal issue, but going 20 mph over the speed limit in an active school zone also raises moral issues.

A scene from the movie *Absence of Malice* starkly illustrates the difference between ethics and the law. A lawyer for a newspaper reviews an unattributed story written by a reporter. He counsels the reporter that he's only concerned with the law—what protection the newspaper has if the story about a suspected racketeer proves to be false. The reporter isn't sure what he means. He responds that as a matter of law, the truth is irrelevant. Without any knowledge that the story is false, the newspaper is "absent malice" If the reporter has been both reasonable and prudent, then the newspaper is not negligent. The reporter can write whatever she likes, and the subject cannot harm the newspaper

Because it grows out of civic morality, law is an expression of our collective sense of right and wrong. The law sets limitations on individual morality and thereby provides some direction for moral choice. You may act according to your conscience, but you will be punished if you go beyond the confines set by society. Law does more than simply restrict bad behavior though. The English philosopher John Locke argued that the rule of law actually makes people more free because it protects them from violence and restraint, thereby enhancing their liberty.[18] Society thus requires law, and some measure of willing adherence to that law, in order to function.

While law may be an expression of civic morality, following the law does not, in and of itself, constitute a moral act. Blind adherence to law—adherence born of habit or fear rather than conscious reflection—is at best amoral (without morals) and at worst immoral (morally wrong). Indeed, the theory of civil disobedience holds that a moral person must at times deliberately disobey a law if conscience so dictates. Thoreau wrote that free people had not only the right but the duty to follow their own moral compass rather than have morality dictated to them by law:

> Must the citizen ever for a moment, or in the least degree, resign his conscience to the legislator? Why has every man a conscience, then? I think that we should be men first, and subjects afterward. It is not desirable to cultivate a respect for the law, so much as for the right. The only obligation which I have a right to assume is to do at any time what I think right. It is truly

enough said that a corporation has no conscience; but a corporation of conscientious men is a corporation with a conscience. Law never made men a whit more just; and, by means of their respect for it, even the well-disposed are daily made the agents of injustice.[19]

Laws can be moral, but they can be immoral as well (cf. the Fugitive Slave Act of 1850). Take for example a judge who orders a journalist to divulge the name of an anonymous source. The judge might have the legal right to demand that the journalist reveal the source's name; however, the journalist might at the same time have an ethical obligation to keep it secret. Journalists have at times gone to jail for violating the law rather than violate the ethics of their profession. For example, a judge jailed *New York Times* reporter Judith Miller in 2005 after she refused to name the source who leaked the identity of a CIA operative, a move that prompted many journalists to defend Miller's actions on ethical grounds.[20] She spent nearly three months in jail before testifying with the permission of her previously anonymous source.

The Conduct Cube

Morality, ethics, and the law can be said to form three dimensions of individuals' *conduct*—their personal behavior. Imagine a cube with six sides (see figure 1.1). Each face of the cube represents one of the six "good" or "bad" facets of an action: moral or immoral, ethical or unethical, legal or illegal. Each of the individual 27 blocks represents some combination of those dimensions (e.g., moral/ethical/legal, immoral/unethical/illegal, etc.). Acts can also be neutral in respect to any or all of these dimensions. Indeed, the center (invisible) block of the cube would represent an act that is purely neutral—amoral, nonethical, and extralegal. Many of our actions fall into this category. For example, selecting which pair of socks to wear to class on a given day rarely involves questions of morality, ethics, or the law. However, actions that could be deemed "good" or "bad" almost always involve considerations of law, ethics, and morality.

The conduct cube illustrates the differences between law, ethics, and morality by allowing us to visualize individual actions in three dimensions, to draw distinctions among the three characteristics of conduct, and to identify where an issue falls in relation to these concerns. For example, an advertiser who wants to put up a billboard selling malt liquor in a poor neighborhood with an extremely high rate of alcoholism may not be committing an illegal act, but some would say that action is immoral and possibly unethical. It might "make good business" sense, but you will note that being good for business doesn't appear within the cube. One could argue

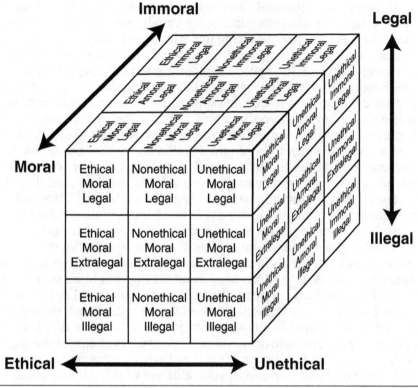

Figure 1.1   The Conduct Cube.

an ethical responsibility to one's business, a legal obligation to one's stockholders, or a moral duty to one's coworkers. But the fact that something will be "good for business" does not, in isolation, make it good or bad in a moral, ethical, or legal sense.

Why Study Ethics?

Ethics and the need for more ethical discussion are in the news daily. Google the term and you will find hundreds or even thousands of news articles dealing with ethical problems in politics, law enforcement, medicine, business, education, and, communication. Should journalists be able to make paid speeches to public relations professionals? How far can an advertiser go in airbrushing youth onto an attractive but aging celebrity? Is it even possible to run an ethical political campaign in a close congressional race? These examples present ethical problems and are the sources of interesting, informative, and often influential ethical discussions.

What you will probably also notice in your search is that many of the articles dealing with ethics don't really involve ethical dilemmas. They involve people acting unethically—deliberately violating ethics and, usually, doing something their own consciences tell them is wrong. Why? Well, there is typically a strong temptation to act unethically. Often the lure is financial. Imagine that you are writing a stock column for a major newspaper. In tomorrow's column, you will write about a tip you received that the Pear Corporation will acquire the up-and-coming streaming video service, Wulu. Anyone who buys Wulu stock today could double their money tomorrow. It's a strong temptation to buy some of that stock today or to tell your friends and relatives to do so. It's also highly unethical (and illegal).

Sometimes a simple desire to keep one's job can entice one to act unethically. Imagine instead that you handle Wulu's public relations. Your boss approaches you and says that a good friend of hers is an executive for the Pear Corporation. She would like to know if you have any private information that might make the proposed sale dangerous for Pear. You have information that might be of interest to the Pear executive, but you know that it is unethical to divulge a client's private information. On the other hand, failure to provide the information could endanger your job. Now imagine that instead of being a young, single professional, you are a mid-career manager with a family that relies on your paycheck to survive. If you lose your job, you must move, pull your kids out of school, and possibly ask your spouse to make a career change as well. You can see that the temptation to act unethically can be quite strong.

Of course, sometimes people act unethically simply because they don't recognize that an action raises ethical concerns. Author Jennifer Belle hired actors with "compelling and infectious laughs" to read her book in public places around New York.[21] Creative? Absolutely. But it blurred the line between advertising and genuine opinion. Was the laughter while reading a testimonial? The American Advertising Federation Principles of American Business states: "Advertising containing testimonials shall be limited to those of competent witnesses who are reflecting a real and honest opinion or experience."[22] One wonders whether Belle ever considered the publicity stunt from an ethical perspective. But that doesn't make it okay. As Jack Marshall wrote on the blog Ethics Alarms:

> It was creative, clever, aggressive, proactive; it was effective, obviously; and it gave some starving actresses, of which there are many in New York (600 women responded to Belle's ad), some much-needed work. It was still a dishonest method of publicizing the book, no less so than fake rave reviews in a press release and planted "reader reviews" on Amazon.com.[23]

While Belle's actions may have been amoral or nonethical from her perspective—because she did not consider the moral/ethical implications of those actions—many professionals would still say that the actions themselves were deceptive and therefore unethical.

Summary

We study ethics not only to resolve ethical problems but also to recognize them in the first place. This book addresses making ethical choices in various professions. In addition to covering philosophical foundations of ethics as well as existing standards and practices, it provides a foundation for ethical reasoning to help readers grow both individually and professionally. Among the goals of the book are promoting a better understanding of how to examine ethical issues objectively, identifying value at the root of ethical conflicts, recognizing the importance of obligation in ethics, and applying those principles in reaching an ethical decision.

NOTES

[1] Then again, perhaps we are being overly optimistic here. Justin McBrayer argues that while U.S. public school children are taught rules (law), they are also taught that all morality is a matter of opinion and that there are no moral facts. McBrayer, J. (2015, March 2). Why our children don't think there are moral facts. *The New York Times*.

[2] Society of Professional Journalists. (2014, September 6). SPJ code of ethics. http://spj.org/ethicscode.asp

[3] Public Relations Society of America (PRSA) (n.d.) PRSA code of ethics. https://www.prsa.org/about/ethics/prsa-code-of-ethics

[4] Ethical discussions often breed curiosity. For the curious, let me say that I did not report the fate of those teenagers. As far as I know, other than my editor, no one familiar with the case learned "the truth" from myself or my newspaper. Nor, decades later, do I regret that ethical decision.

[5] Ethic. (2022, November 27). *Merriam-webster.com Dictionary*, Merriam Webster. http://www.merriam-webster.com/dictionary/ethic

[6] Moral. (2022, December 4). *Merriam-webster.com*, Merriam Webster. http://www.merriam-webster.com/dictionary/moral

[7] For example, Leininger, M. M (Ed.). 1990. *Ethical and moral dimensions of care*. Wayne State University Press; Piercy, N. F., and Lane, N. (2007). Ethical and moral dilemmas associated with strategic relationships between business-to-business buyers and sellers. *Journal of Business Ethics* 72(1), 87–102; Luttenberg, J. Hermans, C. and Bergen, T. (2004). Pragmatic, ethical and moral: towards a refinement of the discourse approach. *Journal of Moral Education* 33(1), 35–55.

[8] Ray, T. T. (1996). Differentiating the related concepts of ethics, morality, law and justice. *New Directions for Teaching and Learning, 66*, 47–53.

[9] In fact, research indicates that some moral principles might not even be available to conscious reasoning. Cushman, F., Young, L. and Hauser, M. (2006). The role of conscious reasoning and intuition in moral judgment: testing three principles of harm. *Psychological Science, 17*(12), 1082–89.

[10] Many philosophers oppose such a distinction, most notably Kurt Baier, who argued that all matters involving the rightness or wrongness of human conduct, moral or ethical, must stem from and be justified by reason. Baier, K. (1958). *The moral point of view: A rational basis of ethics.* Cornell University Press.

[11] Again, this position is certainly not without its critics. For example, William Frankena argues that any definition of morality must include a positive social morality. Robert Ewin goes further to eschew a strict line between morality and ethics. Frankena, W. K. (1978). Is morality a purely personal matter? *Midwest Studies in Philosophy, 3*, 122–132; Ewin, R. E. (1991). Personal morality and professional ethics: The lawyer's duty of zeal. *International Journal of Applied Philosophy, 6*(2), 35–45

[12] Russell, B. (2009). *The basic writings of Bertrand Russell.* Routledge, p. 336.

[13] Michael Cherenson, a former chair of the Public Relations Society of America, cites the advocacy function in the PRSA code of ethic: "We serve the public interest by acting as responsible advocates for those we represent. We provide a voice in the marketplace of ideas, facts, and viewpoints to aid informed public debate." Cherenson, M. (2009, February 5). Ministers, moms and public relations ethics. Message posted to http://prsay.prsa.org/index.php/2009/02/05/ministers-moms-and-public-relations-ethics/

[14] Graf, W., Zinneman, F. (Producers) & Zinneman, F. (Director). (1966). *A man for all seasons* [Motion Picture]. United Kingdom: Columbia Pictures.

[15] Ibid.

[16] The incident is detailed in Fallows, J. (1996, February). Why Americans hate the media. *The Atlantic.* A portion of the video is available online at: http://www.youtube.com/watch?v=HGg_dpGhlf0

[17] Ray (1996). p. 50.

[18] Locke, J. (1764). *The two treatises of civil government* (Thomas Hollis, Ed.) A. Millar et al. https://oll.libertyfund.org/title/hollis-the-two-treatises-of-civil-government-hollis-ed

[19] Thoreau, H. D. (1849). *On the duty of civil disobedience,* pp. 4–5. Elegant Ebooks. http://www.ibiblio.org/ebooks/Thoreau/Civil%20Disobedience.pdf

[20] See, for example, Editorial. (2005, July 7). A journalist jailed. *The Washington Post.* http://www.washingtonpost.com/wp-dyn/content/article/2005/07/06/AR2005070601964.html

[21] Belle, J. (2010, August 2). I paid them to read my book: Jennifer Belle's "the laughter project" pays dividends. *PublishingPerspectives.* http://publishingperspectives.com/2010/08/i-paid-them-to-read-my-book-jennifer-belles-the-laughter-project-pays-dividends/

[22] American Advertising Federation. (1984, March 2). The advertising principles of American business. https://www.aaf.org/common/Uploaded%20files/Club%20Resources/CLB_Resources_Advertising_Principles.pdf

[23] Marshall, J. (2010, August 6). Book publicity ethics. *Ethics alarms.* http://ethicsalarms.com/2010/08/06/book-publicity-ethics/

2

Metaethics

In this chapter, you will learn about:
- The primary three branches of ethics
- What metaethics is and what it studies
- Semantics as it relates to metaethics
- Ontology as it relates to metaethics
- How all of this relates to ethics in professional communication

When we talk about ethics, we are discussing a vast field of knowledge and debate that spans cultures and time, likely going back before recorded human history. Scholars tend to divide the discipline into three general areas: metaethics, normative ethics, and applied ethics.

Applied ethics entails the use of ethical principles to address real world situations, including actual and hypothetical case studies. Often these involve ethics within a career field, such as medical ethics, business ethics, or professional communication ethics. Indeed, a "profession" requires training and formal qualification that generally includes ethical standards.

Normative ethics refers to how we determine the principles that constitute norms of ethical behavior. For example, should a public relations executive tell the complete truth about a client that would place the client in a bad light? On the one hand, we usually view telling the truth as a good. But a public relations executive also has a duty to serve the client, which constitutes another good. Do we place truth above duty or duty above truth in this situation? Normative ethics offers principles that can help us make and defend our ethical decisions.

Operating at an even more basic level, *metaethics* bridges morality and ethics, exploring the very nature of "good and bad" or "right and wrong." What does it mean to do good? To be good? To lead a good life? What is "good" anyway? Is good the same for everyone across all cultures and time periods? Does it endure independent of human understanding, or does it rely on a determination by humans? Does "good" even really exist, or are we just fooling ourselves? Those questions, and your answers, constitute the focus of this chapter.[1]

Metaethics in
Professional Communication

When Swedish photographer Paul Hansen won the prestigious World Press Photo contest, his work drew a huge amount of attention. The winning image depicted a group of men carrying the bodies of two young Palestinians in a funeral procession after the children and their father had been killed in an Israeli airstrike. Tech multimedia publication *The Verge* praised Hansen's "harrowing" photograph, noting that "its visceral power is virtually impossible to deny, or even describe."[2] But critics pointed out that the image seemed "almost too perfect to be true."[3] *ExtremeTech* Senior Editor Sebastian Anthony went so far as to call it a "fake," citing evidence from a forensic analyst that the image had been digitally altered and was more aptly described as a composite than an actual photograph.[4] In short, he said the image did not depict the truth.

Hansen countered that he did not alter the photograph but rather simply adjusted the tonal range of the raw image in an effort to recreate the reality he saw on the ground:

> In the post-process toning and balancing of the uneven light in the alleyway, I developed the raw file with different density to use the natural light instead of dodging and burning. In effect to recreate what the eye sees and get a larger dynamic range.[5]

Because the eye sometimes sees things that the camera does not (and vice versa), editing served merely to restore the image to what the eyes of observers would have seen. Thus, although Hansen edited the image, he said he did so in an effort to depict the truth more accurately.[6]

So, who is right? Does a photograph depict truth? Many photographers would argue that their images represent the closest one can come to an objective portrayal of reality—to truth. As André Bazin once said, "the impassive lens" removes all subjectivity from an image and captures it more purely than any art.[7] Others disagree. For famed photographer Richard Avedon, the first staff photographer at the *New Yorker*, all photographs are accurate, but none of them is the truth.[8] Rather than being a fact, he argued, a photograph is an opinion. But is an image accurate once it has been edited? How much editing does it take to transform a photograph from at least a somewhat objective view of reality into purely art or opinion? Given that people will view the same image or even the same reality many different ways, depending on everything from their eyesight to their life experience, can humans actually experience truth? And, if not, how can we be certain that what we call truth even exists?

That is the realm of metaethics.

Ethics and Moral Semantics

In the previous chapter, we observed that ethics and morality have similar roots but distinct meanings. When examining concepts that encompass and even transcend both areas, scholars of meta-ethics often use the words "moral" and "morality" as a more funda-mental way to express meaning that encompasses our definitions of both morality and ethics.

Metaethics can be broadly divided into two areas: ontology and semantics. *Ontology* considers the nature of being (of existence). *Semantics* is the study of meaning, especially meaning in language. For example, imagine that you have to explain the meaning of the word "dog" to someone who has never seen one. You might decide to discuss why a Chihuahua and a Saint Bernard are both dogs, but a cat, a fox, or even a wolf are not. If we cannot explain a thing, do we really know what it is? How much more difficult is it then to define more abstract concepts such as truth, integrity, fairness, or good? These fall into the area of *moral semantics*, the study of meaning in the areas of ethics and morality—specifically, the study of what are we doing when we make a moral statement (e.g., "it is right to tell the truth"). When we talk about moral semantics, we are talking about the meaning of statements about morality, what we think about morality. For moral semanticists, ethics is "the logical study of the *language* of morals" [emphasis added][9] not necessarily of morality itself.

Just as we divided metaethics into two areas, we can divide moral semantics into two broad areas as well: cognitivism and non-cognitivism. Cognition refers to how we know or understand things. *Moral cognitivism* asserts that when we speak about morality, we make statements that are capable of being true or false (i.e., they are "truth-apt"). In other words, it is at least possible that "moral-ity" exists, and we can theoretically know or understand moral con-cepts. By contrast, *moral non-cognitivism* contends that morality does not exist, at least not in the way that moral statements seem to imply, and so any statements about morality are incapable of being true or false. They are, as some might say, "not even wrong." Moral non-cognitivism does not argue the point, because it's not discussing morality per se. Instead, it takes the nonexistence of morality as a premise to its positions about meaning in moral statements.

Moral Non-cognitivism

If morality does not really exist, then what are we doing when we talk about things like right and wrong? Non-cognitivism addresses that in a variety of ways, each constituting its own branch of thought. For example, *emotivism*, as a non-cognitivist theory, asserts that moral statements are not statements about reality and therefore cannot be proven true or false. Instead, it suggests that moral statements are nothing more than expressions of an individual's emotions about the subject, often constituting attempts to persuade others to agree.

For emotivists such as the theory's founder, A. J. Ayer, ethical statements are "mere pseudo-concepts" that add nothing to the facts of a situation.[10] Take confidentiality as an example. Suppose I said, "It was wrong when those communication managers used confidential business information for their own personal benefit." Ayer would argue that all I really said was "those communication managers used confidential business information for their own personal benefit." Saying "it was wrong" added nothing to the original facts. I did not even say that I disapproved of it. It was as though I had said, "Those communication managers used confidential business information for their own personal benefit. Boo!" It is a base expression of emotion, and perhaps a kind of appeal for others to feel the same emotion. If I were to say it was right, it would be the same as saying "Hurrah." For this reason, emotivism is sometimes referred to as a "boo-hurrah theory." For emotivists, all statements about morality amount to little more than expressions of emotion like "boo" and "hurrah."

Some non-cognitivists contend that moral statements are more than simply emotions. They are commands. *Moral prescriptivism* holds that ethical/moral statements constitute prescriptions for right behavior, effectively telling us how to act. As a non-cognitivist theory, prescriptivism rejects the idea that moral statements reflect any kind of moral reality. Rather, those statements simply constitute imperatives—commands to do or not do something. If I were to say, "Good journalists should be accountable," prescriptivists would argue that all I am really saying is "Journalists . . . be accountable!" That sentence does not contain any facts, and so it is not really capable of being true or false.

One problem with theories like emotivism and prescriptivism is that they fail to account for the way we sometimes use moral statements, especially in what philosopher Simon Blackburn terms the "if-construction."[11] Blackburn observes that we often employ moral statements in "if/then" sentences in such a way that they could not be simply imperatives or expressions of emotion. For example, consider the following: "If serving the public is the highest good, then sometimes sharing confidential information is good." Emotivism would have us read this statement as, if hurray "serving the public," then hurray "sometimes sharing confidential information." Emotions don't lend themselves to the kind of if/then thinking involved in moral reasoning. Neither do imperative statements. It makes little sense to say, "If 'serve the public,' then 'sometimes share confidential information.'"

Given the problems with emotivism and prescriptivism, Blackburn argued for a new approach, which he called quasi-realism. *Quasi-realism* is a non-cognitivist theory that attempts to bridge the gap with cognitivism by asserting that, while moral statements are nonfactual, they nonetheless act like factual statements. As a non-cognitive theory, quasi-realism maintains that morality does not exist in any real sense. Thus, statements about reality are not "truth-apt." However, Blackburn said that people making moral statements do so as though they were talking about real things. It starts, he said,

> with an emotivist, a fundamental expressionist, account of the fundamental elements of what we are doing when we moralize. And that is a particular activity, a particular thing you do, which is basically to express attitudes, to put pressure on plans, intentions, conducts. It's something practical. But we talk as if there were a truth in that talk, that's why the quasi. We talk as if there were a reality, a normative reality, the kind of reality Plato believed in.[12]

Even though morality does not exist, individuals talking about morality do so in a way that suggests it is real. Therefore, Blackburn argues, statements about morality represent a kind of quasi-realism.

Moral Cognitivism

Imagine two individuals who believe in a monotheistic God are arguing about whether God is male, female, neither, both, or more. To both of those individuals, God is a reality even though they might disagree about God's sex/gender. Now imagine an atheist enters the conversation and is asked to determine who is correct. The atheist asserts that "God does not exist," and so the question cannot have a "true" answer. To the atheist, it's nonsense. That atheist's position is essentially one of non-cognitivism. The believers, though they might disagree with one another, both assert God's existence. They are cognitivists for whom the question has a true answer, even though they might never know what that answer is.

But what does the atheist mean by saying, "God does not exist?" When non-cognitivists argue that morality does not exist, what do they mean by morality? It must have some kind of existence, even a theoretical or purely linguistic existence, for them to be speaking about it. Now imagine that a second atheist comes along and says that the believers are not uttering nonsense. They are simply saying things that are not true. The second atheist asserts that when the believers suggest that God has a gender, any gender, they are arguing based on a false premise (i.e., "God exists."). As a result, all their statements are false. The second atheist is a cognitivist, holding that the believers' statements are truth-apt—that they are at least capable of being true linguistically. However, the second atheist maintains that the statements are nonetheless false because God does not exist. This position is known as *error theory*, a cognitivist theory of moral semantics acknowledging that moral statements are fundamentally truth-apt but that they are all false because morality does not exist.

For error theorists such as John Mackie, "there are no objective moral values"[13]—no "rightness or wrongness" that simply exists within the world. But neither are those who talk about such values simply expressing their own feelings or attitudes. They are making *assertions*, statements of fact or belief strong enough to be akin to fact for the individual making the assertion. This led Mackie to coin the term "error theory," which he explained as "admitting that a belief in objective values is built into ordinary moral thought and language, but holding that this ingrained belief is false."[14] Because the belief is an assertion, it can theoretically be true or false. But because error theory holds that moral values do not exist, all such assertions must be false.

Error theory stands virtually alone among the cognitivist theories in denying that moral values exist as anything other than a false premise for moral statements. We place it among the cognitivist theories solely because it holds that moral statements are truth-apt. Remember, we are discussing moral semantics, the meaning of moral statements. Non-cognitivists hold that moral statements cannot be true or false. They are expressions of emotions, commands, or quasi-realistic feelings. On the other hand, cognitivists maintain that moral statements can be true or false. They are assertions. Error theorists agree with that position, even though they believe all such assertions are false.

Other cognitivist positions are perhaps easier to understand because they share a view that moral statements express facts about morality that can be true or false. As such, they reflect what many ordinary people tend to believe they are doing when they engage in moral or ethical conversations. Philosophers sometimes refer to the empirical study of such conversations as "folk metaethics."[15] Most cognitivist theories agree with the commonplace notion that ethical/moral values are indeed real, existing either subjectively in the human mind or objectively in the fabric of the universe.

In metaethics, the term *subjectivism* broadly refers to the idea that moral values depend on the human mind for their existence. Firth provided a straightforward way of identifying subjectivism:

> a proposed analysis of ethical statements is subjectivist if it construes ethical statements in such a way that they would all be false by definition if there existed no experiencing subjects (past, present, or future).[16]

Morality is not nothing. But, like beauty, it lies in the eye of the beholder. There is no such thing as beauty if no one exists to judge it so.

Moral subjectivism suggests that every person develops individual moral values, usually prioritizing them against one another in a way that facilitates personal decision making in matters of right and wrong.[17] While this seems to be demonstrably true, there is a problem. If you adhere to your own moral values, one might say that you are a moral person. But what if your own moral values differ dramatically from those of others in your society? Suppose, for example, that you believe your company has an unfairly large amount of money, and so you personally judge it acceptable for you to steal some of that money for your own benefit. Stakeholders in your company—your boss, stock owners, fellow employees, customers, and so forth—would likely think you were doing something wrong. On the one hand, you might be acting in such a way that you believed what you were doing was good. But many people would be uncomfortable saying that you are a "moral person," at least the way we generally mean that term.

Ethical subjectivism looks at moral values from the perspective of humanity as a whole.[18] Firth argued that one might look at moral values as though seen through the eyes of an "*ideal* observer—an observer who is conceivable but whose existence or nonexistence is logically irrelevant to the truth or falsity of ethical statements."[19] If a truly ideal observer were to view a moral value in a certain way, Firth reasoned that multiple ideal observers would all view that value the same way. In such a case, their estimation of that moral value could effectively be considered to be true. In this way, we could construct a set of moral values that are at once dependent on human perspective—the perspective of the ideal observer—but at the same time absolute and capable of being analyzed or serving as a subject of meaningful ethical discussion.

Subjectivism holds that moral statements constitute statements of fact, at least some of which can be true. Taking this idea even further, *moral objectivism* maintains that moral statements involve values that exist independent of humanity, much in the way that scientific facts exist. Moral values are an objective reality. Where subjectivism sees humans as defining moral values, objectivism envisions humans as discovering those values. But if moral values exist, where do they exist? How do they operate? Where do they come from? To what kind of reality do our moral statements refer? Moral objectivists fall into one of two general schools of thought on this issue: naturalism and non-naturalism.

Moral naturalism is a branch of moral objectivism asserting that moral values represent facts of nature, much the same as scientific facts. For example, Charles Darwin said in *The Descent of Man* that morality is a natural end for intelligent, social animals such as humans:

> "[A]ny animal whatever, endowed with well-marked social instincts, would inevitably acquire a moral sense or conscience, as soon as its intellectual powers had become as well developed, or nearly as well developed."[20]

For Darwin, the ultimate good for humans and other social animals is the good of the group, the tribe, or the species. Humans evolved to know that the welfare of the group sometimes called for individual sacrifice and so deemed this "good." At the same time, other actions were deemed "bad," especially when adversely affecting members of the same tribe. As Darwin said, "No tribe could hold together if murder, robbery, treachery . . . were common."[21] These moral values are not limited to or merely conceived by humans; rather, they accrue to all social animals and therefore exist independently within nature.

The other school in objectivism is *moral non-naturalism*, the branch of moral objectivism that views moral values as facts—but facts not emanating from nature. Even though moral values are effectively non-natural, they are not necessarily of divine origin. As G.E. Moore wrote in his *Principia Ethica*, it simply means that moral values do exist, but do not exist in nature. He preferred the term "metaphysical" to non-natural, referring to a "supersensible reality."[22] Of course, a number of philosophers have connected morality to the existence of God. For example, the philosophers Augustine and Aquinas asserted that morality is grounded in God. Thus, when one makes a moral statement, it is based on moral reality grounded in the existence of God.

Ethics and Moral Ontology

Metaethical semantics focuses on meaning in moral statements. *Moral ontology* explores the nature of morality itself—whether it exists and, if so, whether it is relative or universal. Thus, when we discuss moral ontology, we focus on the scope of morality as well as arguments related to its existence. We have spent time exploring the way we ascribe meaning to our statements about morality. These statements can be said to be indicative of our understanding of moral reality. Thus, moral ontology corresponds loosely with the various semantic theories,[23] and we will use that overlap to help better understand discussions about the nature of moral reality. However, take care to remember that semantics and ontology are two separate concepts. Semantics focuses on meaning in statements about morality. Ontology focuses on the nature of morality.

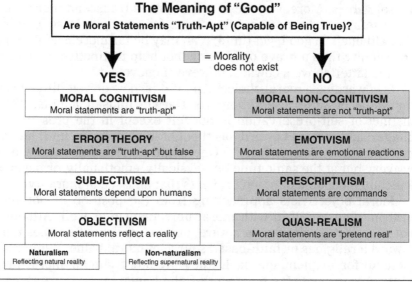

Figure 2.1   The Meaning of "Good"

We break moral ontology into three separate areas: relativism, universalism, and nihilism. *Nihilism* rejects the existence of moral reality. Nihilists argue that traditional moral values have no basis. Most of the non-cognitivist approaches, along with the cognitivist error theory, would tend to fall broadly into the area of nihilism, because they reject the existence of moral values. Nihilism, however, goes beyond rejecting moral values—asserting that life and the whole of reality are entirely without meaning. This leads many to think of nihilists as depressed pessimists, but Nolen Gertz argues that "pessimism is the opposite of nihilism."[24] Indeed, nihilism has sometimes manifested in popular culture as an optimistic approach that frees humanity from imposed moral values and allows us to dictate the purpose of the universe, ultimately whatever makes us happy.[25] Of course, one might ask whether self-created value is true nihilism or more in line with the semantic concept of moral subjectivism, which you might recall suggests that people develop their own individual moral values. The rejection of all moral values can, in itself, be seen as a kind of value. If this is true, can any human fully be a nihilist?[26]

At the opposite end of the spectrum from nihilism is *moral universalism*, the idea that moral values are real and comprehensive, applying to everyone at all times in all cultures and all religions. This is what objectivists would point to as the basis for meaning when people make moral statements. For example, Darwin's moral naturalism would argue that moral values such as self-sacrifice evolve in all intelligent, social species. In that sense, they are universal values. Moreover, these moral values transcend mere societal usefulness. In the case of courage, for example, Darwin noted that although "a good, yet timid, man may be far more useful to the community than a brave one, we cannot help instinctively honouring the latter above a coward, however benevolent."[27]

Is cowardice a moral choice? And if it is, how does it differ from the value of self-preservation? As Darwin himself admits, "The instinct of self-preservation is not felt except in the presence of danger; and many a coward has thought himself brave until he has met his enemy face to face."[28] One might be rationally inclined to bravery but at the same time be physically, emotionally, or psychologically incapable of being brave. Is that an issue of morality?

Moral objectivists approaching from the position of non-naturalism tend to fall in with moral universalism as well. Although not necessarily religious in nature, non-naturalism often does tend toward a religious or faith-based source of moral value. While religions differ in their approach, they lay down similar moral precepts. According to the fourteenth Dalai Lama:

> I maintain that every major religion of the world—Buddhism, Christianity, Confucianism, Hinduism, Islam, Jainism, Judaism, Sikhism, Taoism, Zoroastrianism—has similar ideals of love, the same goal of benefiting humanity through spiritual practice, and the same effect of making their followers into better human beings. All religions teach moral precepts for perfecting the functions of mind, body, and speech. All teach us not to lie or steal or take others' lives, and so on. The common goal of all moral precepts laid down by the great teachers of humanity is unselfishness.[29]

Note that these religions share, with naturalism, the value of benefiting others and the group over oneself. In addition, psychological research indicates that "All world religions defend some version of the Golden Rule, a doctrine that reflects evolved inclinations toward fairness and reciprocity."[30] However, as with naturalism, they may or may not extend these values to members outside the group, members of other religions, or even branches of the same religion.

Philosophers and other thinkers from Immanuel Kant to Noam Chomsky have asserted a basic universalism in morality—at least to the extent that if one believes an action to be acceptable for oneself, then it must be acceptable for others and vice versa. On the other hand, we are hard-pressed to find specific moral values existing across all cultures, in all times, and applying to all people. The non-universalists would argue that if universal values exist in the real world, like scientific facts, then universalists should point to them. Show us where these universal facts are and how they got there, they would say. Universalists might reply by pointing out that gravity is a scientific fact, yet no one can show us precisely what it is or tell us how it got there.[31] Like gravity, the universalists might say, we can describe morality and see its effects—acknowledging its reality without necessarily needing to explain exactly what it is or why it works the way it does.

One particularly difficult problem for moral universalism is that one would think universal morals would apply not only to all cultures but also to all time periods. Take for example the Catholic Church—one of the oldest and largest institutions in the world—and its views on capital punishment.[32] In its earliest days, the Church officially favored capital punishment to avenge or deter crime. During the time of inquisitions, heresy became a capital crime. Clerics, though themselves forbidden to kill, turned over the guilty to secular authorities for execution. But over time the Church became more averse to capital punishment. In 2018, Pope Francis ordered a change in the Catechism of the Catholic Church and deemed the death penalty "inadmissible."[33] In 2020, he committed the Church to "calling for its abolition worldwide."[34] For absolute moral universalists, right and wrong exist immutably. From the universalist point of view the Church was morally right at one point and morally wrong at another, even if we do not know which was which.

Non-universalists approach the answer differently. For example, *moral relativism* asserts that morality exists relative to a number of factors. What might be morally acceptable for one group, in one place and time might not be morally acceptable for another group in another place and time. Moral relativists would judge people and their actions according to their time, culture, laws, and other factors contributing to their view of the world.

Consider people who have pets. Most pet owners view themselves as good people, and they view their relationship with their nonhuman housemates positively. They provide the animals with love, food, shelter, warmth, exercise, and medical care. They often go to great expense to ensure happy, healthy lives for their companions. They recognize that there are also bad pet owners—people who neglect, abuse, or otherwise mistreat their animals. Many would demand that these people be condemned and punished for their actions. Some would question the morality of certain practices, such as leaving a cat outside overnight or chronically overfeeding a pet, but they wouldn't argue that there is anything inherently wrong with owning a pet.

Now imagine a future in which pet ownership is denounced as something akin to animal slavery. That's not as far-fetched as you might think.[35] Regardless of how one treats a pet, the pet is property. The vast majority of pet owners partially or wholly deny their pets freedom. They control everything from where the pet sleeps to what and how much it eats. They and society can also decide when the pet dies, even in the case of healthy, young animals. In this future, these facts could lead society to conclude that owning pets is wholly immoral.

For most moral universalists, owning a pet would be inherently either moral or immoral, but not both. They might not know which was the correct answer, but they would assert nonetheless that a correct answer exists. For most moral relativists, the answer would be more fluid. A moral relativist in the future might argue that while pet ownership is undeniably wrong in that time, pet owners from the past should not be condemned as "bad" or "evil." Rather, they would argue that pet owners should be judged, or at least understood, in the context of their time and society.

Cultural relativism suggests that ethics and morality should be understood relative to one's culture in terms of time, place, people, religion, law, and other considerations. An action that might be morally acceptable in one culture might not be acceptable in another. Cultural relativism encourages a range of possible responses to a situation. We can divide that continuum imperfectly into strong cultural relativism and weak cultural relativism.[36] *Strong cultural relativism* at its extreme might suggest that morality emerges from culture and the two cultures in our previous example would both be correct. *Weak cultural relativism* at the opposite extreme might argue that cultures inform our understanding of morality within that culture, but they do not by themselves constitute morality. Thus, one culture might be morally right and another morally wrong, even though we might recognize that culture could mitigate the immorality of actions taken by individuals within that culture.

A kind of cultural relativism can be seen in professional communication as well. Most fields of professional communication voice shared values such as independence, truth, social responsibility, privacy, confidentiality, and so on. However, those values often must be understood relative to each profession rather than universally, varying based on the nature of the profession, the nature of the communication, and the expectations of the audience. For example, Principle 1 of the Institute for Advertising Ethics' Principles and Practices states that "Advertising, public relations, marketing communications, news, and editorial all share a common objective of truth and high ethical standards in serving the public."[37] But is truth the same for all areas of professional communication? Certainly, most would share the value of truth as factually accurate information. But do traditional journalists covering an election attempt to portray politicians in factually the same way as those politicians' speechwriters, or their public relations representatives, or the creative personnel working on their advertising campaigns? All might serve the truth, but they do so in accordance with the accepted values of their respective professions. All might claim to be working ethically for the good of society, but they play different roles and accept different ethical responsibilities in doing so. We will discuss this at greater length when examining applied ethics.

Summary

Metaethics bridges morality and ethics, exploring the very nature of good/bad or right/wrong. It can be broadly divided into two areas: ontology and semantics. Moral semantics studies meaning in the areas of ethics and morality—specifically, what we are doing when we make a moral statement.

Moral non-cognitivism contends that morality does not exist, so any statements about morality are incapable of being true or false (they are not "truth-apt"). Emotivism suggests that moral statements are nothing more than expressions of an individual's emotions about the subject, often constituting attempts to persuade others to agree. Moral prescriptivism holds that moral statements constitute prescriptions for right behavior, effectively telling us how to act. Quasi-realism says that people making moral statements do so as though they were talking about real things even though morality does not exist.

Moral cognitivism asserts that when we speak about morality, we make statements that are at least capable of being true or false. Subjectivism broadly refers to the idea that moral values depend on the human mind for their existence. Moral subjectivism suggests

that every person develops individual moral values, usually prioritizing them against one another in a way that facilitates personal
decision making in matters of right and wrong. Ethical subjectivism
looks at moral values from the perspective of humanity as a whole.

Moral objectivism maintains that moral statements involve
values that exist independent of humanity. Moral naturalism asserts
that moral values represent facts of nature, much like scientific
facts. Moral non-naturalism also views moral values as facts but
not emanating from nature.

Moral semantics focuses on what we mean when we make moral
statements. Moral ontology explores the nature of morality itself—
whether it exists and, if so, whether it is relative or universal. Nihilism rejects the existence of moral reality. Moral universalism lies
at the opposite end of the ontological spectrum, arguing that moral
values are real and comprehensive, applying to everyone at all
times in all cultures and all religions.

Cultural relativism suggests that while ethics and morality are
real, they should be understood relative to one's culture in terms of
time, place, people, religion, law, and other considerations. Positions
within cultural relativism can range from an understanding that
cultures have an influence on the moral actions of their members
to the concept that cultures are the sole source of morality for their
people. Ethics in professional communication represents a kind of
cultural relativism, with communicators sharing a common understanding of moral values but at the same time framing those values
differently depending on the nature of the profession, the nature of
the communication, and the expectations of the audience.

NOTES

1 Metaethics is a deep philosophical well into which many individuals have poured
lifetimes of study and thought. It is a well that we will but walk around and glance
into here, realizing that the surface we see imperfectly gives only the barest hint
of what lies beneath. The deeper one goes, the more disagreement can be found
among scholars within the discipline. Our goal here is not to provide a definitive
overview of the entire field of metaethics but rather to encourage you to understand that people can view morality, even its very existence, in many different
ways. Ideally, this will also encourage you to devote some thought to morality
from the vantage point of your own experience, thought, and learning.
2 Toor, A. (2013, Feb. 15). Harrowing image of Palestinian funeral named World
Press Photo of the year. *The Verge*. https://www.theverge.com/2013/2/15/3991548/
world-press-photo-of-the-year-2012-paul-hansen
3 Krug, M. & Niggemeier, S. (2013, May 8). Exploring the boundaries of
photo editing. (C. Sultan, Trans.). *Spiegel Online*. https://www.spiegel.de/
international/world/growing-concern-that-news-photos-are-being-excessively-
manipulated-a-898509.html
4 Anthony, S. (2013, May 13). Was the 2013 World Press Photo of the year faked
with Photoshop or merely manipulated? *ExtremeTech*. https://www.extremetech.
com/extreme/155617-how-the-2013-world-press-photo-of-the-year-was-faked-
with-photoshop

[5] As quoted in Chappel, B. (2013, May 14). Experts say prize-winning photo of Gaza funeral is authentic. *National Public Radio*. https://www.npr.org/sections/thetwo-way/2013/05/14/183983184/photographer-defends-prize-winning-photo-of-gaza-funeral

[6] The World Press Foundation commissioned independent experts to review the photo. Those experts concluded that, although the photo was retouched, the editing did not involve excess manipulation or compositing. See, for example, NPPA. (2013, May 14). World Press Photo verifies Paul Hansen's winning picture. https://nppa.org/news/world-press-photo-verifies-paul-hansens-winning-picture. Krawetz continues to maintain that the image is a composite rather than a photograph. Krawetz, N. (2013, May 23). Angry mob. *The Hacker Factor Blog*. http://www.hackerfactor.com/blog/index.php?/archives/550-Angry-Mob.html

[7] Bazon, A. (1960). The ontology of the photographic image. (H. Gray, Trans.). *Film Quarterly*, *13*(4), pp. 4–9.

[8] Avedon, R., & Wilson, L. (1985). *In the American West 1979–1984: Photographs*. Abrams.

[9] Hare, R. (1952). *The language of morals*. Oxford University Press, p. i.

[10] Ayer, A. J. (1952). *Language, truth and logic*. Dover Publications, p. 67.

[11] Dall'Agnol, D. (2002). Quasi-realism in moral philosophy—An interview with Simon Blackburn. *ethic@*, *1*(2), 101–114. https://periodicos.ufsc.br/index.php/ethic/article/view/14588

[12] Ibid., pp. 102–103.

[13] Mackie, J. (1977). *Ethics: Inventing right and wrong*. Penguin Books, p. 15.

[14] Ibid., pp. 48–49.

[15] See, for example, Nichols, S. (2004). After objectivity: an empirical study of moral judgment. *Philosophical Psychology*, 17(1), pp. 5–28.

[16] Firth, R. (1952). Ethical absolutism and the ideal observer. *Philosophy and Phenomenological Research*, *12*(3), 317–345.

[17] Scholarship in metaethics often uses the terms "moral subjectivism" and "ethical subjectivism" interchangeably, and there is debate about which, if any, usage is correct. For the sake of consistency here we will differentiate the two in much the same way we distinguished morality and ethics in chapter 1.

[18] We simplify here to avoid diving into the well of metaethics and to likewise avoid conflating ethical subjectivism with cultural relativism, discussed later in this chapter. Suffice it to say that a decades-long if not centuries-long battle continues to be waged over meaning in the study of meaning.

[19] Firth, (1952), p. 323.

[20] Darwin, C. (1981). *The descent of man, and selection in relation to sex*. Princeton University Press. Photo reproduction of the 1871 edition published by J. Murray, (pp. 71–72). https://teoriaevolutiva.files.wordpress.com/2014/02/darwin-c-the-descent-of-man-and-selection-in-relation-to-sex.pdf

[21] Ibid., p. 93.

[22] Moore, G. (1922). *Principia ethica*. Project Gutenberg, p. 113. https://www.gutenberg.org/files/53430/53430-h/53430-h.htm

[23] We say "loosely" because existence in one semantic school of thought does not mandate existence in a specific ontological category. For example, not all ethical subjectivists could be fairly placed into the area of moral ontology.

[24] Gertz, N. (2020, Jan. 16). What nihilism is not. *The MIT Press Reader*. https://thereader.mitpress.mit.edu/what-nihilism-is-not/

[25] See, for example, the video Optimistic Nihilism on YouTube (https://www.youtube.com/watch?v=MBRqu0YOH14). The video had garnered more than 15.8 million views as of July 26, 2017.

[26] Clyde Manschreck addresses this succinctly, pointing out "The difficulty roots in a seeming paradox or inconsistency in that a complete nihilist would presumably have no basis for existing; yet nihilists (or incomplete nihilists) do exist

and nihilism is expressed." In Manschreck, C. (1976). Nihilism in the twentieth century: A view from here. *Church History, 45*(1), 85–96. doi:10.2307/3164567

27   Darwin, C. (1981), p. 95.

28   Ibid., p. 90.

29   Dalai Lama. (1984). *A human approach to world peace.* Wisdom Publications, p. 13. https://www.corteidh.or.cr/tablas/4876.pdf

30   Shariff, A. F., Piazza, J., & Kramer, S. R. (2014). Morality and the religious mind: Why theists and nontheists differ. *Trends in Cognitive Sciences, 18*(9), 439–441; p. 441.

31   For a layperson's account of the problem with gravity, see Panek, R. (2019, August 2). Everythingyouthoughtyouknewaboutgravityiswrong.*TheWashingtonPost*.https://www.washingtonpost.com/outlook/everything-you-thought-you-knew-about-gravity-is-wrong/2019/08/01/627f3696-a723-11e9-a3a6-ab670962db05_story.html

32   A detailed history of the Church's views on capital punishment can be found in Brugger, E. C. (2014). *Capital punishment and Roman Catholic moral tradition.* University of Notre Dame Press.

33   Bordoni, L. (2018, Aug. 2). Pope Francis: "Death penalty inadmissible." Vatican News. https://www.vaticannews.va/en/pope/news/2018-08/pope-francis-cdf-ccc-death-penalty-revision-ladaria.html

34   Pope Francis. (2020, Oct. 3). Fratelli Tutti [Encyclical letter]. https://www.vatican.va/content/francesco/en/encyclicals/documents/papa-francesco_20201003_enciclica-fratelli-tutti.html

35   Some today maintain the argument that pets are fundamentally "animal slaves." See, for example, Fancione, G. and Charlton, A. (2016, Sept. 8). The case against pets. *Aeon.* https://aeon.co/essays/why-keeping-a-pet-is-fundamentally-unethical

36   Donnelly, J. (2017). Cultural relativism and universal human rights. In M. K. Addo (Ed.), *International Law of Human Rights* (pp. 173–192). Routledge.

37   Snyder, W. (2011). Principles and practices for advertising ethics. *The Institute for Advertising Ethics.* https://static1.squarespace.com/static/5f6238b0df7f2d2f02a7e7a2/t/60884fc047c25635e56dbda7/1619546048632/IAE%2BPrincipals%2Band%2BPractices.pdf

3

Virtue Ethics

In this chapter, you will learn about:
- Three main approaches to normative ethics
- Defining virtue ethics
- Aristotle's virtue ethics and the Golden Mean
- Eastern approaches to virtue ethics

As we saw in the previous chapter, metaethics broadly explores *what* morality/ethics is—what it means to be good or to do good. Now we can begin transitioning to normative ethics, which provides the *how* and the *why* of ethical character, behavior, and action. *Normative ethics* is the branch of ethics that examines the standards or norms of ethical behavior and how we make ethical decisions. Modern scholars generally divide normative ethics into three main approaches: virtue ethics, consequentialism, and deontology.

Deontology holds that the most important factor to consider when making an ethical decision is one's duty. We act because the action itself is good, not because of what good the action might bring. For example, most journalistic codes of ethics assert that a journalist's highest duty is to the truth. A deontologist would argue that journalists should tell the truth for its own sake, because it is the right thing to do, even when that truth could be hurtful or even dangerous. For deontologists, a good end does not justify using improper means, such as shading the truth, to achieve that end. Immoral actions are immoral, regardless of their consequences. We will discuss deontology more explicitly in chapter 5.

Consequentialism maintains that the most important factor when making an ethical decision is the outcome or consequence of that action. A consequentialist might argue that we tell the truth because doing so brings about good, making it easier to deal with others, enhancing the reputation of oneself or one's profession, and generally creating a positive communication environment. However, if the truth were to bring about harm, the consequentialist would weigh that harm against the good of telling the truth and choose to tell the truth or not based on the foreseeable consequences. We will discuss consequentialism more explicitly in chapter 4.

Virtue ethics stands apart in normative ethics by taking a holistic approach that focuses on the character of the individual rather than on individual actions, thus emphasizing *being* at least as much as *doing*. Virtue ethicists examine the nature of virtue and its role in a good life and suggest how the individual might lead a virtuous life. They also assess the role of the community in supporting that life. It is the difference between a rules-based approach (e.g., the Ten Commandments) and a more holistic approach (e.g., "What would Jesus do?"). Both religious and secular virtue ethicists often take such an approach to ethical action, focusing on how the virtuous behave rather than emphasizing duty, rules, or consequences.

Virtues are ideals such as truth, justice, patience, caring, courage, and so forth that are deemed desirable by individuals and society. Virtue ethics explores the virtues, specifically or generally, within a person that measure moral character and the degree to which that person leads a good life. Originally the dominant form of ethical theory in the West, virtue ethics declined over the centuries. In 1958, Elizabeth Anscombe wrote a seminal paper that criticized popular approaches to ethics.[1] Her paper launched a revival of interest in virtue ethics and returned it to a place of prominence in the modern discussion of ethics.

Scholars generally agree that the articulated philosophical concept of virtue ethics originated among the ancient Greeks, most particularly with Aristotle (384–322 BCE).[2] Aristotle's virtue ethics does bear similarities to teachings that had been popular centuries earlier in Eastern traditions, including those of Confucius (551–479 BCE) and the Buddha (circa 563–483 BCE). Most scholars believe that the Western and Eastern traditions developed independently, at least in part because translation difficulties long delayed the spread of the writings of Confucius.[3] Some contend that the Greeks were influenced by Zoroastrian teachings emerging from Persia in the area of modern-day Iran.[4] We will explore Eastern intellectual traditions later in this chapter. For now, let's consider Aristotle.[5]

Aristotle and Virtue Ethics

Aristotle wrote the first truly systematic exposition of ethics more than 2,000 years ago, and it remains required reading for anyone studying philosophy. *Nicomachean Ethics*, believed to be named for Aristotle's son Nicomachus, who also may have edited the text, discusses the good "at which everything aims."[6] Aristotle named this the *summum bonum* (the highest good), which he sought to define and to describe how it might be achieved.

Aristotle believed that every act aims toward some good—real or perceived. These goods, in turn, usually aim at some other good. When asked what they want out of life, some individuals might respond that they desire money. But money is amoral, neither good nor bad. We want money for what it can do, and it can be used toward a variety of ends. Some people seek money because they want to buy things. Others desire what money brings, from basic security for themselves and their family to the ability to exercise power over others. But even these are ultimately not ends in themselves. We want security or power for some other reason. Like money, they have *extrinsic value*, the ability to provide something else we see as worthy. Aristotle concluded that the *summum bonum* must have *intrinsic value*—worthiness in and of itself rather than as a means to something else.

Most of our desires possess extrinsic value. For example, we might want a family, a career, or a purpose in our community because of what those attainments bring to our lives. They are not "good" in and of themselves. Instead of thinking about what we want for ourselves, think of what parents might want for their children. Certainly, they might point to a healthy lifestyle, enough money to be comfortable, a successful career, and so forth. But most parents would say that above all they want their children to be happy in life.[7] And that, says Aristotle, is the *summum bonum*. When we say we want money, security, power, love, or anything else, we want those because we believe they will make us happy. Happiness is an intrinsic value, an end in itself and a fulfillment of human nature.

If we stopped right there, it would seem that Aristotle's philosophy of ethics simply involves finding whatever makes us happy. If sitting in the basement, gorging on salty snacks, and playing video games all day makes one happy, then that would be a "good" life. But that's pleasure, not happiness. Aristotle pointed out that people take pleasure in what they love. One who loves playing video games takes pleasure in video games. While there is nothing wrong with playing video games, it is not by its nature good in the way that noble virtues such as justice are good. As Aristotle said,

> [T]hose who love what is noble take pleasure in that which is naturally pleasant, so they are both pleasant to them and pleasant in themselves.[8]

Loving and taking pleasure in these virtues constitutes a good life. In fact, Aristotle said, one is not good at all unless one takes pleasure in such noble deeds.

For Aristotle, "happiness" transcends pleasure and represents a much deeper sense of fulfilling one's purpose. The word he used for this was *eudaimonia*, a term often translated as "happiness" but also as "flourishing."[9] It represents the kind of true happiness and fulfillment that comes from becoming who you were meant to be. He offers the example of an eye. When we speak of a good eye, we mean one that is in good condition and that performs its natural function well. The purpose and virtue of an eye lies in its ability to see. So, an eye that sees well can be deemed a good eye. So it is for everything. To be called "good," things must perform nature's purpose; and they must perform it well.

We can easily transfer this to occupations. Aristotle used the examples of his time—carpenters, cobblers, and the like—but we can extend that to modern professionals in communication, such those in public relations, marketing, journalism, advertising, and so on. A good public relations specialist is one who is capable of doing the work of public relations and who does it well. If it works the same for everything as it does for professions, then we could expect that a good person would be one who performs the function of a human being well. Of course, that forces us to ask, what is the function of a human being? What makes a human good?

Aristotle noted that the true function of a human must be specific to humans. It cannot be reproduction or living, which we share with plants and animals. Nor could it be the ability to sense things, or even to enjoy pleasure, which we share with many animals. The characteristic unique to humans, he said, lies in our rational nature—our ability to exercise reason and to utilize it in guiding our actions. Other qualities could be said to be peculiar in some degree to humans, such as the ability to appreciate beauty or to communicate across vast distances or even across time. However, Aristotle noted that the excellence of all these things depends in large measure on the exercise of reason. While other animals can be said to possess some reason, none appears to employ reason to the degree humans do. Thus, Aristotle concluded that the proper function of human beings is to exercise reason. However, the use of reason alone does not make us good human beings.

While reason might be the defining human trait, like most traits it can be used for good or ill. Evil geniuses and criminal masterminds figure prominently in our literary tradition because they represent a fact of human existence. Not all possessed of great reason use it for purposes we might deem good. To be good, reason needs to be applied in the right way, to the right object, for the right purpose, and so on.

The Golden Mean

Eudaimonia, true happiness, constitutes "a kind of activity or life" involving the exercise of the intellect (rational excellence) in accordance with virtue (moral excellence). For Aristotle, this represented an excellence of the soul or what some today might conceive of as the mind and conscience. We tend to view this soul or mind/conscience, exercised through reason, as uniquely human. For example, consider that we often excuse actions in animals, such as toying with prey or even killing young within the same species, that we would readily condemn in humans. Animals do not have the same ability to reason as humans. Reason enables the potential for good or evil, right or wrong, truth or falsity. Even in humans, when individuals lack sufficient reasoning capability to judge right from wrong, we might tolerate or pardon behavior that would otherwise be unacceptable. We also excuse people from responsibility for actions they were compelled to commit. If forced to do something against your will, you do not bear responsibility for that action.

Reason provides us with the ability to discern virtue and places on us the responsibility to live in accordance with it. But how do we go about this? How do we know what is right? Aristotle argued that a person's mind and actions have three possible dispositions, two of vice and one of virtue. The two vices consist of excess (too much) and defect (too little), while virtue lies somewhere in between. The *Golden Mean* refers to the precise point, somewhere between the vices of excess and defect, where rightness or virtue lies.

Consider something as simple as drinking water. If we drink too little, we die. But if we drink too much, we could also die.[10] The proper or good amount of water to drink lies somewhere between the two extremes. Aristotle said that the same is true of virtues. For example, imagine you are out walking in the woods, leading a young relative by the hand, and you encounter a threatening bear. You might heedlessly charge at the bear attempting to kill it or drive it off. This would be foolishly reckless, a vice of excess. You might drop the child's hand and run for safety. This would be cowardly, a vice of defect. The virtue of courage—the good and proper action—lies somewhere between the extremes of too much and too little fear.

If virtue is a precise point between two extremes, how can we know where that point lies. In the previous example, an experienced park ranger would undoubtedly handle the situation differently than a person who had never seen a live bear before. Yet, even taking different actions, both could be said to be acting with courage according to their own experience and ability. Indeed, Aristotle recognized that action constituting virtue, the precise mean between the extreme of too much and too little emotion, would be different for every person. For that reason, people sometimes refer to the Golden Mean as a Goldilocks principle or Goldilocks theory.[11] We each seek our own "just right" place between too much and too little.

Aristotle used the example of food to illustrate the point. In his time, people described the number of pounds an individual might eat. Today we speak of food in terms of calories. Consistently eat too many calories and you gain weight, become obese, and risk a variety of health problems that could lead to death. Consistently eat too few and you lose weight, eventually become malnourished, and risk a variety of health problems that could lead to death. So, what is the right number of calories for an individual to consume? The U.S. Food & Drug Administration recommends a daily intake of 2,000 calories, but the agency points out that an individual's needs will vary depending on age, sex, height, weight, and physical activity level.[12] Some people need less. Others need more, sometimes much more. Olympic swimmer Michael Phelps said he ate "[m]aybe eight to ten thousand calories per day," yet he burned it off while training and never put on weight.[13] Each individual must use reasoning to determine the right amount of food to consume.

The Golden Mean can be used by itself or in conjunction with other ethical principles when trying to determine a proper course of ethical action. For example, the American Marketing Association's Statement of Ethics says that marketers must embrace the value of "fairness—to balance justly the needs of the buyer with the interests of the seller."[14] Put in Aristotelean terms, fairness lies at some Golden Mean between unjustly favoring the seller at one extreme and unjustly favoring the buyer at the other. Using the Golden Mean, one would understand that the correct action would be a point of balance that would change as the buyers, sellers, products, and other details of the situation changed, requiring the marketer to assess situations and seek the good on a case-by-case basis.

Aristotle stressed that not every action lends itself to moderation, pointing out that things like murder, theft, and adultery would always be considered wrong. Conversely, virtues themselves could not be said to be wrong in the extreme because they are themselves moderate. One cannot have too much or too little justice because, by definition, this would no longer be justice. Moreover, Aristotle said that one must use caution with decisions that involve pleasure or pain. Pleasure encourages us to overlook moral value in our decision making when we find one decision more pleasurable than the other. Pain prompts us to avoid choosing the proper course of action when doing so would be painful. This is not limited to physical pleasure or pain. When seeking out evidence in a professional communication setting, people tend to prefer that which they find pleasurable and avoid that which they find painful. We know this as *confirmation bias*—the tendency to favor evidence that confirms our preexisting notions (giving us pleasure) and reject that which contradicts those notions (causing us pain). When a decision gives us pleasure or pain, we must make extra effort to ensure that we focus on the virtue (e.g., truth, fairness) rather than our own pleasure or pain.

In an effort to avoid the push and pull of pleasure and pain, some try to reduce or even remove emotion so that it does not hamper reason. For example, the Greek philosophical school known as *Stoicism* emphasized that reason and virtue were sufficient for *eudaimonia*, and one should seek to limit emotion. An example from our modern-day experience might be the race of Vulcans in Star Trek. Vulcans feel emotion, but they attempt to purge their minds of those feelings lest anything interfere with reason. For them, logic is the path to fulfillment. Another rough parallel might be traditional journalists who place high value on objectivity—defined as the removal of emotions and biases from stories. These journalists place the ultimate value on getting the facts so their audience has a sound basis for decision making.

Moderation, Habit, and Virtue

Virtue lies in moderation between extremes. By consistently acting in accordance with virtue, people become virtuous. For example, a person who chooses to be fair for the sake of fairness and does so consistently becomes what we would call a fair person. As Aristotle observed,

> Virtue, then, is a habit or a trained faculty of choice, the characteristic of which lies in moderation or observance of the mean [relative] to the persons concerned, as determined by reason.[15]

These two features, moderation and habit, represent the keys to a virtuous life and consequently to true happiness (*eudaimonia*).

As we have seen, being a virtuous person requires virtuous actions. But is that enough? How many good acts are required before one can be deemed a good person? For Aristotle, being virtuous meant a habit, a life of virtuous actions that could be characterized by three conditions.

1. One must know what one is doing. People cannot be good by chance—without knowledge of what they are doing. Nor can they be bad or unvirtuous by chance, except perhaps through negligent ignorance of what they should know. Journalists who get a fact wrong might be excused if they did all they could to verify the fact before publishing it. However,

journalists who fail to check a highly questionable statement of fact before publishing it must bear the consequences of that action even if they did not knowingly publish a falsehood. And no journalists can be virtuous who do not realize what they are doing. Virtue requires a conscious choice to do good.

2. A virtuous person must *choose* the course of action and choose it for its own sake, because it is the virtuous thing to do. We cannot be held responsible for actions for which we had no choice. When we do choose an action, we must do so for the right reason. Doing the right thing for the wrong reason does not constitute virtue.

3. The action must be "the expression of a formed and stable character."[16] The virtue of an action thus depends in part on the virtue of the actor. Action constitutes an expression of one's character, and so a truly virtuous action requires that it be made by a person who has acquired and lives by virtue. As John Dewey notes, this is a matter of degree rather than an absolute and should be considered a sign of habit formed by character.[17] For Aristotle, character matters, and one forms one's character over a lifetime of virtuous acts.

As we have already mentioned, habit plays a vital role in achieving true happiness. Habit comes from repeated action. By repeating good actions, we build good habits, which leads to a virtuous life. Conversely, repeating bad actions leads to bad habits and away from a virtuous life. The code of ethics for bloggers, social media, and content creators says that online content creators should be accountable, which means they should "admit and correct mistakes immediately."[18] When an error is found, the content creator corrects it promptly. This makes the next correction a bit easier, which makes the correction after that easier still. Before long, it becomes a routine, a habit, to control one's emotions and promptly correct errors. The individual who develops such a habit finds it easy to do what is right and virtuous. Conversely, the individual who fails to correct mistakes immediately develops a bad habit and finds it increasingly difficult to choose the path of virtue.

A good life then consists of moderation in one's choices, always using reason in the pursuit of virtue so that virtue becomes part of one's being and life. In Aristotle's words: "It is not enough to know about virtue, then, but we must endeavor to possess it and to use it, or to take any other steps that may make us good.[19] Those who would be virtuous must make virtue part of their daily lives—thinking about virtue, talking about virtue, exercising virtue, and ultimately putting virtue into action. Only in this way, after many years of practice and devotion, can a person be considered truly virtuous.

Eastern Virtue Ethics

In the movie *Bohemian Rhapsody*, lead singer Freddie Mercury's father repeatedly reminds him, "Good thoughts, good words, good deeds,"[20] which is the threefold path that forms the core of Zoroastrianism, the family's faith. Dating back to sometime before 1000 BCE in Persia (modern-day Iran),[21] Zoroastrianism emerges from the teachings of Zoroaster, considered by many to be the first true philosopher. One of the world's oldest continuously practiced monotheistic religions, Zoroastrianism likely had a profound influence on Islam,[22] as well as Christianity and Judaism.[23]

Zoroastrianism maintains an ethical code founded "upon a systematic theory of morality and . . . on philosophic principles."[24] Chief among these is the concept of free will and the idea that good requires that individuals make a choice. Good thoughts lead to good words, and good words lead to good deeds in a series of dispositions that together constitute the path to becoming "righteous."[25] We can see many parallels between the fundamental principles of Zoroastrianism and Aristotle's *Nicomachean Ethics*. Moreover, the early Greeks were certainly aware of Zoroastrianism. Some scholars argue that Zoroastrian thought influenced Aristotle's own views of ethics and morality and that Aristotle even sought "to demonstrate the dependence of certain aspects of Greek philosophy on the teachings of Zoroaster."[26]

As Zoroastrian teachings impacted the West, they also extended into the civilizations of the East. In India, Zoroastrian ideas influenced early Buddhist thinking, especially in relation to karma[27] and the bodhisattva (a being on the path to awakening and achieving highest wisdom) doctrine.[28] The Buddhist bodhisattva doctrine in turn may have influenced the Confucian notion of the sage[29] and other concepts as Buddhism and Confucianism cross-pollinated over the first few centuries of their development. All this occurred during the period from 800 BCE to 300 BCE, known as the *Axial Age*, during which coincident schools of religious and philosophical thought arose in the world's most dominant civilizations including those of Greece, Persia, India, and China. The Axial Age provided what philosopher Karl Jaspers called a kind of "unity" that "laid the basis for human history."[30] Aristotle, Buddha, and Confucius shared a tradition that might be described as one of virtue ethics, a philosophy centered on becoming a person of virtue. Together, they are sometimes said to form the ABCs of moderation and virtue ethics.

Buddha

Siddhartha Gautama, the man who would become Buddha, grew up in northern India in what is modern-day Nepal.[31] Legend depicts him as having been a member of a wealthy family, where he enjoyed all the trappings of upper-class life completely shielded from all miseries. One day, he escaped his confines and encountered in turn an old man, someone suffering from disease, a decaying corpse, and finally an ascetic—a person seeking wisdom through self-denial of all but those things absolutely necessary to stay alive. Seeing that a life of privilege had not brought him happiness, he sought enlightenment or awakening in its opposite. Becoming an ascetic, he refused help from his wealthy family and friends while living off what he could gather or beg. This provided Siddartha with insight, but it did not fulfill him.

The film *Little Buddha* depicts the moment of Siddhartha's departure from the ascetic life. After six years of privation, an emaciated Siddhartha sits meditating by the side of a river when he hears a musician speaking to his student while passing by in a boat: "If you tighten the string too much, it will snap, and if you leave it too slack, it won't play."[32] For Siddhartha's character, it is an epiphany leading him to realize: "The path to Enlightenment is in the Middle Way. It is the line between all opposite extremes."[33] For Siddhartha, it meant the middle between the extremes of self-indulgence (too many self-pleasures) and self-deprivation (too few self-pleasures). The Buddhist Middle Way is remarkably similar to Aristotle's Golden Mean and vice versa, both valuing a moderate approach that seeks a middle ground between the extremes.

The Buddhist principle of the Noble Eightfold Path to awakening or enlightenment also shares with Aristotle a self-oriented understanding of virtue.[34] The Noble Eightfold Path, like Zoroastrianism's threefold path, consists of developing the right approach to life and living. Its eight factors are often divided into three themes: *wisdom*, consisting of (1) right understanding and (2) right thought; *ethical conduct*, consisting of (3) right speech, (4) right action, and (5) right livelihood; and *mental discipline*, consisting of (6) right effort, (7) right mindfulness, and (8) concentration.[35] This rightness prioritizes compassion for all things. Buddha's teaching, spanning thousands of discourses, effectively comes down to an extended explanation and elucidation of the Noble Eightfold Path.[36]

In the Noble Eightfold Path we see commonality with not only Zoroastrianism but also with Aristotle who said that being affected "at the right times, and on the right occasions, and toward the right persons, and with the right object, and in the right fashion, is the mean course and the best course, and these are the characteristics of virtue."[37] The *summum bonum* of the Noble Eightfold Path, like that of

Aristotle, represents a kind of human perfection. As Damien Keown points out, while there are "inevitable cultural differences" in how we define or translate this highest good, the concept of human beings fulfilling their proper function through the exercise of intellect in pursuit of virtue and a final goal characterized by true happiness can be seen in the teachings of both Buddha and, later, Aristotle.[38] The path to that happiness lies in not just doing good things but also in being good—reflected in everything from thought to speech to action.

Confucius

The emphasis on virtue, together with the need for moderation and discernment in the pursuit of virtue, forms an essential part of the ethics of Confucius as well. The name Confucius is a Latinized version of the Chinese K'ung-fu-tzu, which translates as "Master Kong"—an honorific referring to Kong Qiu, a man who lived from 551 to 479 BCE in northeastern China and who would go on to become the most revered figure in Chinese history. His father had been a member of the "low aristocracy" of his time, but he died when the boy who would become Confucius was only 3 years old. The family fell into poverty, but Confucius was still able to pursue an education, first with his mother and later at one or more of the schools available to commoners. He also worked a series of menial jobs to support the family, but his focus remained on education. Confucius later wrote, "when I was fifteen, I set my heart on learning."[39] He soon distinguished himself as a scholar and later a teacher as a way to help others but also to help himself. He said that one made a life of learning "for the sake of the self," in the pursuit of self-knowledge and self-realization.[40] Yet, learning is not for the sake of the self alone but also for the benefit of others. Confucius taught that self-cultivation of virtue could positively influence both government and society.[41]

The *Analects* is a collection of Confucius' sayings and conversations compiled during the centuries following his death. Though developed separately, the *Analects* and Aristotelean ethics overlap in many ways.[42] For example, both stress the value of moderation, at times in remarkably similar ways. As Confucius said, "The Central Mean in conduct is where virtue reaches its pinnacle."[43] He often seeks the middle ground. When one of his students is too forward, he pulls him back. When another is too reticent, he draws him forward.[44] In this we also see the idea that virtue, the Central Mean, represents acting in the right way to the right person. Aristotle and Confucius both focus on the possession of virtue as essential to ethical decision making. For example, when asked if the *junzi* (the ideal moral actor)[45] prized valor, Confucius replied:

> The *junzi* gives righteousness the topmost place. If a *junzi* had valor but not righteousness, he would create chaos. If a small person has valor and not righteousness, he becomes a bandit.[46]

How one acts depends on one's character, and virtuous individuals will, by their very nature, engage in virtuous actions. Both Confucius and Aristotle emphasize not only being able to know what is virtuous and to do what is virtuous (e.g., noble deeds) but more importantly to find happiness in it. As Confucius said, "Knowing it is not so good as loving it; loving it is not so good as taking joy in it."[47] Virtuous people choose to act virtuously not only because it is right but because they love and take pleasure in virtue. Confucian scholar Ann Pang-White observes that virtue is excellence of character, a cultivated disposition enabling a person to live an excellent life.[48] Virtue practiced becomes virtue possessed and leads one to a life of true happiness.

Both Aristotle and Confucius also spoke of virtue arising from habit. For Aristotle, virtue was a product of intellect (brought about through reason) and morality (brought about through habit). If one develops a habit of integrity, integrity becomes easier and natural. By contrast, Confucius placed greater emphasis on humanity and ritual civility than on reason.[49] He focused on the vital interaction of *ren* and *li*, two terms that thwart precise translation into English.

Ren can be thought of as the comprehensive ethical virtue that encompasses goodness, humanity, compassion, and more.[50] Its definition flows from the many ways that Confucius uses it in the *Analects*. For example, "People who are *ren* are first to shoulder difficulties and last to reap rewards. This may be called *ren*."[51] Or, "Conquer yourself and return to *li*: that is *ren*. . . . Being *ren* proceeds from oneself, how could it come from others?"[52]. Or, "Incorruptibility, steadfastness, simplicity, and reticence are near to *ren*."[53] When one of his disciples asked about *ren*, Confucius responded, "Cherish people."[54] It is vital to the ideal moral actor or *junzi*:

> If one takes *ren* away from a *junzi*, wherein is he worthy of the name? There is no interval so short that the *junzi* deviates from *ren*. Though rushing full tilt, it is there; though head over heels, it is there.[55]

We can see that *ren* represents deep-seated virtue, governing how one thinks, acts, and relates to other people and the world. Some scholars interpret it with an Aristotelean tilt as "human excellence."[56]

The term *li* has no direct parallel in English. Translators often record it as "ritual" or "civility," but again it is much more than that.[57] Given that we do not have many formal rituals in day-to-day American life, it might help to think of *li* as something like *mores*, traditional customs and ways of behaving in a society.[58] For example, imagine you are waiting for an elevator to arrive. The doors open, and you see that it is crowded, but you could squeeze in. What do you do? If you decide there is enough space that a reasonable person wouldn't be upset by you entering, you get on the elevator. How do you get to your floor? Do you reach to press the button yourself? What if it's on the other side of the elevator? Do you ask someone? Once that's resolved, where and how do you stand? Where do you look? The floor? Up at the elevator display? Is it okay to speak to anyone near you? What would be an appropriate or inappropriate topic of conversation?[59] There is a protocol for how a civil person should behave in this situation, as well as how not to behave. Now think of the entire world as the elevator, with customs governing how you should behave at all times and toward all things, even while alone. That gives us some small idea of what Confucius meant by *li*,[60] realizing that such rituals in the time of Confucius were much more highly defined and the result of centuries of refinement.

According to Confucius, *li* requires *ren*, being directed toward others compassionately, assuming the burdens of those around us. He noted that behaving properly with *li* meant nothing unless one did so with *ren*.[61] These concepts require one to behave in accordance with custom, written and unwritten, for the benefit of others. In the example of the elevator, we behave as we do for the other people on the elevator, for the good of all rather than for the good of ourselves. The teachings of Confucius require the proper disposition of both *ren* and *li* for an individual to be a truly fulfilled person.

Summary

Virtue ethics focuses on the character of the individual rather than on that individual's actions, thus emphasizing being rather than doing. Virtue ethics seeks to define what it means to be a virtuous person and to lead a virtuous life. The philosophical concept of virtue ethics originated among the ancient Greeks, most particularly with Aristotle.

Aristotle's major work on ethics, *Nicomachean Ethics*, explores what he called the *summum bonum*, the highest good. Most ethical goods for humans have *extrinsic value*, providing something outside their essential nature. Aristotle argued that the highest good had to possess *intrinsic value*, worthiness in and of itself rather than as a means to something else. Happiness is an intrinsic value and constitutes the *summum bonum* of Aristotle's philosophy.

Eudaimonia means taking pleasure in and loving virtue. How do we know virtue when we see it? Aristotle said we use reason to discern the *Golden Mean*—the precise point between the vices of excess and defect where virtue lies. Too much of anything is a vice. Too little of anything is a defect. Acting virtuously requires: (1) that you know what you are doing; (2) that you choose virtue for its own sake; and (3) that your action be an expression of your moral character. People become virtuous by discerning virtue and making a habit of constantly choosing the virtuous path.

Buddhism's Noble Eightfold Path consists of eight factors: (1) right understanding, (2) right thought, (3) right speech, (4) right action, (5) right livelihood, (6) right effort, (7) right mindfulness, and (8) right concentration. This rightness prioritizes compassion for all things. Buddha's teaching revolves around explaining this as a path to human beings fulfilling their proper function through the exercise of intellect in pursuit of virtue and a final goal characterized by true happiness or Nirvana.

Confucian philosophy likewise emphasizes self-cultivation and taking pleasure in noble deeds. However, Confucius places special emphasis on the cultivation of self for others. The virtuous person lives in accordance with *ren* and *li*, mutually dependent concepts that require one to behave in a manner consistent with the rules of a just society, while focusing on the welfare of others.

Aristotle, Buddha, and Confucius can be said to form the ABCs of virtue ethics. All share the following ideas: (1) virtue requires conscious action; (2) virtuous action requires moderation; (3) moderation constitutes a balance point (e.g., a Golden Mean, a Middle Way, or a Central Mean) between extremes; (4) identifying the balance point is the work of reason together with a moral view; (5) to be virtuous requires not only virtuous acts but also that one love and take pleasure in those acts; and (6) making a habit of virtuous acts in this manner infuses one's character with virtue—making one a paragon not only of virtue but of human excellence.

NOTES

[1] Anscombe, G. E. M. (1958). Modern moral philosophy. *Philosophy*, *33*(124), 1–19.
[2] See, for example, Hursthouse, R. (1999). *On virtue ethics*. Oxford University Press.
[3] For a fascinating explanation of the challenges in translating classical Chinese texts attributed to Confucius, see Hamburger, M. (1956). Aristotle and Confucius: A study in comparative philosophy. *Philosophy*, *31*(119), 324–357.
[4] Chroust, A. H. (1980). The influence of Zoroastrian teachings on Plato, Aristotle, and Greek philosophy in general. *The New Scholasticism*, *54*(3), 342–357.
[5] It must be noted that many of the sources we discuss in virtue ethics overlap with religion. Zoroastrianism is a religion with an ethical foundation. The same can be said of Buddhism, which currently boasts approximately 535 million followers worldwide. Scholars debate whether the teachings and ways of behavior emerging from Confucius' work should be considered a religion, an ethical prescript, or both. Even Aristotle, whom we firmly ground in the realm of philosophy, speaks of the supernatural in *Nicomachean Ethics*—frequently mentioning the gods, wondering whether the dead can become happy or unhappy and so on. Virtue ethics in philosophy typically

focuses on the more natural and societal aspects of ethics, as we do here. However, that should not be taken as dismissive of the religious views that have inspired the following of billions of human beings throughout the past two millennia.

6   Aristotle. (2004). *Nicomachean ethics* (F. Peters, Trans.). Barnes & Noble. (Original work published 1893.), p. 1.

7   See, for example, HSBC Holdings. (2015). *The value of education: Learning for life*. http://online.wsj.com/public/resources/documents/HSBCSurvey.pdf

8   Aristotle. (2004), p. 13.

9   More evidence that Aristotle's definition of *eudaimonia* involved more than our modern notion of happiness can be found in the fact that he argued animals could not experience *eudaimonia*, nor could children because true human happiness required the fullness of life's experience, p. 15.

10   A condition known as "water intoxication." Although we often use "intoxication" with regard to alcohol or drugs, it literally means poisoning.

11   Referring, of course, to the old English fairy tale of Goldilocks who entered the home of three bears in a forest. Sampling their porridge, she observed that one adult bear's porridge was too hot and another's too cold, but the little bear's porridge seemed just right. One of many retellings of the story can be found at https://americanliterature.com/childrens-stories/goldilocks-and-the-three-bears

12   U.S. Food & Drug Administration. (2022, February 25). How to understand and use the nutrition facts label. https://www.fda.gov/food/new-nutrition-facts-label/how-understand-and-use-nutrition-facts-label

13   OlympicTalk. (2020, May 5). How many calories Michael Phelps consumed as a swimmer. *NBC Sports*. https://olympics.nbcsports.com/2020/05/05/michael-phelps-calories-swimming/

14   American Marketing Association. (2021, October 11). *AMA Statement of Ethics*. https://myama.my.site.com/s/article/AMA-Statement-of-Ethics

15   Aristotle. (2004), p. 31.

16   Ibid., p. 28.

17   Dewey, J. (1996). *Theory of the moral life*. Irvington Publishers, p. 9.

18   Rand-Hendriksen, M. (2020). Code of ethics for bloggers, social media and content creators. https://github.com/mor10/CodeOfEthics

19   Aristotle. (2004), p. 222.

20   Singer, B. (Director). (2018). *Bohemian rhapsody* [Film]. Regency Enterprises.

21   Boyce, M. (1996). *A history of Zoroastrianism*. E. J. Brill, p. 3. Some place the religion's origins closer to 6000 BCE.

22   Hajati Shoroki, S. M., & Naqavi, H. (2018). An analysis of the direct influence of Zoroastrianism on Islam eschatological doctrine. *Religious Research, 5*(10), 41–62.

23   Applegate, L. R. (2000). Zoroastrianism and its probable influence on Judaism and Christianity. *Journal of Religion & Psychical Research, 23*(4).

24   Jackson, A. W. (1896). The moral and ethical teachings of the ancient Zoroastrian religion. *The International Journal of Ethics, 7*(1), 55–62, p. 56. https://www.journals.uchicago.edu/doi/pdf/10.1086/intejethi.7.1.2375373

25   Ibid., p. 57.

26   Chroust, A. H. (1980), p. 346.

27   Attwood, J. (2014). Escaping the inescapable: Changes in Buddhist karma. *Journal of Buddhist Ethics, 21*, 493–525.

28   Dayal, H. (1999). *The Bodhisattva doctrine in Buddhist Sanskrit literature*. Motilal Banarsidass, p. 39.

29   Angurarohita, P., & Mair, V. H. (1989). Buddhist influence on the neo-Confucian concept of the sage. In *Sino-Platonic Papers 10*, p. 15. http://sino-platonic.org/complete/spp010_buddhist_confucian_sage.pdf

30   Jaspers, K. (1948). *The axial age of human history*. (R. Manheim, Trans.). Commentary, 6, 430.

31   The youth and adolescence of Buddha and Confucius plays an overt role in their emergent philosophies.

[32] Bertolucci, B. (Director). (1993). *Little Buddha* [Film]. CiBy 2000.

[33] Ibid.

[34] This should not be taken to be about the self for the self's sake. Buddhism emphasizes the concept of anatta or "no-self," which holds that the idea of a self is a myth—an idea shared by some neuroscientists in the West (see, for example, Lancaster, B. L. (1997). The mythology of anatta: Bridging the East–West divide. In J. Pickering (Ed.), *The authority of experience: Essays on Buddhism and psychology* (pp. 170–204). Curzon Press.

[35] Rahula, W. (1974). *What the Buddha taught*. Grove Press. pp. 46–49.

[36] Ibid., p. 76.

[37] Aristotle. (2004), p. 31.

[38] Keown, D. (1992) *The nature of Buddhist ethics*. Palgrave.

[39] Eno, R. (2015). *The Analects of Confucius: An online teaching translation*, p. 5. https://chinatxt.sitehost.iu.edu/Analects_of_Confucius_(Eno-2015).pdf

[40] Tu, W. M. (1998). Confucius and Confucianism. In W. H. Slote & G. A. De Vos (Eds.), *Confucianism and the family*, (pp. 3–36), SUNY Press, p. 9.

[41] Ibid.

[42] Cheng notes that "It is evident that there is more affinity between the Aristotelian view of morality and ethics and the Confucian ethics of virtues than any other Greek and Chinese comparison." Cheng, C. Y. (2002). Editor's introduction: On comparative origins of classical Chinese ethics and Greek ethics. *Journal of Chinese Philosophy*, 29(3), 307–311; p. 311.

[43] Eno, (2015), (6.29), p. 28. Parenthetical references follow standard practice in quoting book and passage from the *Analects*.

[44] Ibid., (11.22), p. 55.

[45] Ibid., p. 1.

[46] Ibid., (17.23), p. 99.

[47] Ibid., (6.20), p. 27. Indicates that Confucius speaks here of the *dao*, often translated as "the way." In this instance, obvious parallels can be seen with Aristotle's admonition that the virtuous person must both love and take pleasure in virtuous acts.

[48] Pang-White, A. (2021). Virtues and the *Book of Rites*. *Journal of Chinese Philosophy*, 48(1), 56–70.

[49] While pointing out that scholars have indicated formal reasoning does not play an overtly specific role in the determination of ethical behavior, David E. Soles counters that Confucius, in addition to placing high value on education, uses both inductive and deductive arguments, and his moral theory itself constitutes a rational argument. Soles, D. E. (1995). Confucius and the role of reason. *Journal of Chinese philosophy*, 22(3), 249–261.

[50] Eno, (2015), p. vi.

[51] Ibid., (6.22), p. 27.

[52] Ibid., (12.1), p. 59.

[53] Ibid., (13.27), p. 72.

[54] Ibid., (12.22), p. 64.

[55] Ibid., (4.5), p. 14.

[56] See, for example, Li, C. (2007). Li as cultural grammar: On the relation between *li* and *ren* in Confucius' *Analects*. *Philosophy East and West*, 57(3), 311–329.

[57] Lai, K. (2006). Li in the *Analects*: Training in moral competence and the question of flexibility. *Philosophy East and West*, 56(1), 69–83. Lai notes that scholars continue to debate *li* in relation to contemporary society, with some engaging it with "a more flexible, morally sensitive approach" (Endnote 1).

[58] Waley, A. (2005). *The Analects of Confucius (Vol. 28)*. Psychology Press. Arthur Waley observes that, "as used in early China *li* would cover everything from the opening of the great doors of St. Peter's down to saying 'Bless you!' when someone sneezes," p. 64.

[59] Consider how those rules changed during the pandemic, for example.

[60] Waley said that one needed to master an estimated 3,300 rules and observances to be considered a civil person in ancient China.

[61] Eno, (2015), p. 9.

4

Consequentialism

In this chapter, you will learn about:
- A definition of consequentialism
- Differences between act and rule consequentialism
- Other-oriented consequentialism in altruism and effective altruism
- Self-oriented consequentialism in egoism and reciprocal altruism
- Group-oriented consequentialism in hedonistic and eudaimonistic utilitarianism

While virtue ethics embraces a more holistic approach to ethics that focuses on the character of the individual as well as what that individual does, the other branches of normative ethics devote attention to evaluating the actions themselves. *Consequentialism* maintains that the rightness or wrongness of an action rests in its consequences. That which produces the best consequences is the best action. After all, what is ethics if it isn't about doing good? However, consequentialism is not as straightforward as it might seem at first glance.

The International Public Relations Association's Code of Conduct advises members to "Neither propose nor undertake any action which would constitute an improper influence on public representatives, the media, or other stakeholders."[1] Suppose you are a public relations executive representing a client who wants to construct a new gymnasium in town. The client has been having difficulty securing a building permit, so you agree to help. You visit the building inspector. After a friendly half-hour chat, the official agrees to help get your client the building permit, but in return you will need to provide the inspector with a free family membership. The cost of the membership would be negligible for your client. In return, you would help secure the permit, move the project along, and make a friend in local government. Doing so would violate not only the IPRA code of ethics but several laws as well. What should you do?

Act and Rule Consequentialism

Act consequentialism looks at each action individually, judging the consequences of that one action based on the total net good it generates. The example above would be a violation of the IPRA code and the law prohibiting bribing a public official, but act consequentialism is about results rather than rules. It would be bad for you and your client if you were caught. On the other hand, the "bribe" is relatively small and very hard to discover. Even if discovered, one small gift like this might be excused rather than prosecuted. It would get your client's building permit approved and expedited—something far more valuable to your client than the cost of the membership. On the other hand, would the official demand additional, increasingly valuable bribes in the future from you or from others? The act consequentialist weighs all these details and more before deciding what would be "right" in this case. Whether the action itself is virtuous doesn't directly affect the decision—only the consequences matter.

Rule consequentialism, while remaining concerned foremost with the consequences, considers what rules should be followed in order to maximize the good. It's not about whether the rules are right or wrong so much as whether or not they produce good consequences. A rule consequentialist would consider whether making small "gifts" to public officials would produce the best consequences in the long run—not just this one time. Individual actions might not generate negative consequences on their own; however, they might be bad in the aggregate. Rule consequentialists don't follow rules for the sake of duty. They do so to produce good consequences.

A number of questions arise with consequentialism.

1. *Ends vs. Means:* If the consequences are all that matter, are there no limits to what I may do to produce good consequences? Critics of consequentialism often point out that if the only thing that matters is the consequence of an action, then "the end justifies the means." In other words, I can use any means necessary—lying, stealing, extortion—as long as the consequences are a net good.

2. *Expected vs. Actual Consequences:* Am I ethical if things just happen to turn out right and unethical if they turn out

wrong? Suppose I am advertising a new vaccine for a specific form of cancer. The vaccine has been rigorously tested
and approved for use by federal and state governments. But
a year into release, scientists discover that the vaccine dramatically increases the chance of other forms of cancer, and
they recommend removing it from the market. I helped to
sell that vaccine. I tried to do good, but it turns out the vaccine is harmful. Is my action now unethical? Consequentialism concerns itself with results. Does intent matter? If I try
to produce good consequences, and I am not negligent in my
research or reason, is that enough? Or must I be judged by
the consequences alone rather than my intent? Consequentialists differ on the answer.

3. *Long-term vs. Short-term Consequences:* Now suppose that
the vaccine instead works perfectly. One of the people who
saw my advertising campaign decided to get the vaccine.
Without it he would have died from cancer within two years.
Instead, he remains healthy, rises to the presidency, and
transforms the United States into a totalitarian dictatorship
that pushes the world into nuclear conflict. The net good effect of my efforts to advertise the vaccine has become a net
bad effect. Was I unethical in advertising the vaccine? Consequentialism can have difficulty separating the rightness of
short-term and long-term consequences.

Defining Good Consequences

Neither act consequentialism nor rule consequentialism tried to
define what they meant by good consequences. Most consequentialist theories approach good like a mathematical formula. An action
generates x amount of good and y amount of bad. Subtract bad from
the good and you can determine whether an action has a "net good"
consequence or a "net bad" consequence. If an action results in
more good than bad, then it's a good consequence.

"Good" itself can be said to have many possible definitions, but
most consequentialist formulas can be described in one of three
ways: hedonistic, eudaimonistic, or pluralistic. *Hedonism* refers to
the pursuit of pleasure and the avoidance of pain. A hedonistic consequentialist would judge the goodness of an action by how much
pleasure it generated relative to the pain it would cost. *Eudaimonia*,
as we discussed in the previous chapter, describes a kind of happiness that might better be understood as flourishing or perhaps
true happiness. A eudaimonistic consequentialist would judge the

goodness of an action by the degree to which it furthers true happiness as opposed to mere pleasure. *Pluralism* is a kind of moral relativist approach suggesting that the good of a given action depends on the individual making the assessment. I might judge the consequence of an action to be good because it benefits something or someone I value. You might judge that same consequence to be bad because it harms something or someone you value. Pluralism thus serves as a kind of catchall for judging goodness by some mechanism other than pleasure/pain or happiness.

Consequences for Whom

All the above leaves out an important aspect of our judgment regarding the consequences of an action—good for whom? As we noted, good for me might not be good for you and vice versa. What should I do in such a situation? Should I work for your good or mine? Or should I try to generate the most good possible, regardless of who benefits? These questions form the trunk from which different theoretical branches of consequentialism emerge.

Altruism

Ethics focuses on interpersonal morality—how we should act with other people. Individuals from Darwin to the Dalai Lama share a belief that what we call "good" is that which benefits others. In consequentialism, the philosophy of *altruism* suggests that one's ethical decisions should be based on producing good consequences for others, even at a cost to oneself. Altruism—an unselfish regard for the welfare of others—has roots in Latin (*alter*, meaning "other") and French (*autre*, also meaning "other").[2] Compte's philosophy of *positivism* emphasizes subordinating self-love to "social love" and ultimately to universal love. An atheist, Comte believed that positivism, the science of society, could serve as a religion of humanity. He envisioned a world where universal love served as a kind of *summum bonum*, both above and beyond reason. It acts as a formative principle, which he summed up as "Placing our highest happiness in universal Love, we live, as far as it is possible, for others."[3]

Most societies value altruistic actions, such as charity, sharing, helping a stranger, and so on. The greater the self-sacrifice, the greater society's praise for the action and the greater moral value it places on the action. Even more value is placed on actions for which one receives no reward. We view the anonymous donation as superior to the one that appears with a press release. Holding virtue to be other-oriented and self-sacrificing, altruism maintains that any self-reward diminishes the moral value of an action. Altruism would place the highest value on a selfless act, performed for the benefit of others by someone who realized that no other person would ever discover the sacrifice.

Some might conclude that the philosophy of altruism requires adherents to give away all their belongings and work solely for the benefit of others. After all, how can we eat well when others are starving or worry about how we dress when others lack clothing? But a life of privation does not necessarily equate to a reasoned life of service. Aristotle and Confucius both thought that the prudent philosopher should pursue a life of politics to spread virtue to as many as possible. The modern philosopher Peter Singer argues that altruists living in a well-developed country like the United States could generate far more good by using their fortuitous place in life to maximize their wealth so they might provide even more to their fellow human beings.

Singer recalls a promising graduate student who, after being accepted for postgraduate study at Oxford University, chose instead to work for a Wall Street trading firm. The student, Matt Wage, donates 50 percent of his income to charity.[4] He decided the most effective use of his work life would be to take the high-paying job so he could donate a larger sum to charities that fought malaria and other diseases in the developing world.[5] Singer and others call this "effective altruism." *Effective altruism* maintains people should not only sacrifice for the benefit of others but also use reason to determine how to maximize the effectiveness of that self-sacrifice.

Effective altruists in the field of professional communication might work to become the best at their profession and to generate as much income as they ethically can, enabling them to donate greater amounts to the right charities. Some critique this as "consumer-hero hubris" designed to sell altruism, while at the same time ignoring political and other options.[6] Removing the focus on donating money, those in advertising or public relations might choose to devote themselves to promoting causes that they believe deliver the most good to others. Journalists could take positions that enable them to focus public attention on problems that society overlooks but that could be improved if more people understood the issues. All this requires research, seeking out evidence, and ensuring that one maximize one's efforts at working for the benefit of others.

Egoism

Ask people why they want to do good in the world, and they will likely give a wide range of responses, including some of the following. They want to live in a world where people treat each other well.

They will be rewarded in the afterlife. Putting good in the world eventually brings good back to them. They want others to think well of them. It just makes them feel good. Notice that in all these examples people do good because it benefits them in some way. The ethical philosophy of *egoism* suggests that one's ethical decisions should be based on producing good consequences for oneself. We do good because doing so benefits us materially, emotionally, spiritually, or socially.[7] Justification for egoistic behavior can be viewed from three perspectives: psychological, rational, and ethical.

Psychological egoism suggests that our actions naturally derive from and seek to advance our self-interest. As noted above, when people explain why they perform a good act, their explanation often points to some self-benefit. Even sacrificing one's own life could yield a benefit in the afterlife, leave a positive memory in those one saved, or be advantageous in the theological Court of Conscience where one's honor and ultimate self-image stand trial.

Rational egoism argues that not only is it natural to pursue our own self-interest but also that reason dictates that we should do so. As in the short story "The Gift of the Magi," sacrificing for the sake of others guarantees the sacrifice but not necessarily the benefit.[8] Only when we act for our own interests do we rationally control both the cost and the benefit sought. To be considered rational, egoistic actions must emphasize the use of reason to maximize one's own interest not only in the short-term but also over time. One might envision egoists as people who trample over others while focused solely on themselves. However, such actions would no doubt generate more harm than good for the egoist. It would not be rational to pursue a short-term benefit that does not maximize one's long-term good.

Ethical egoism takes everything a step further, maintaining that it is both rational to act in our own interest and is the morally right thing to do. Ethics, by definition, involves interpersonal morality, how we should act with other people. As a result, philosophers tend to reject so-called "personal" egoism—egoism that completely disregards the good of others. To be considered ethical, egoism must accept that others have an equal right to maximize good consequences for themselves. A corollary is that egoism, like all ethical philosophies, must respect other human beings as ends and not merely as means to desired ends.[9]

One of the foremost ethical egoists, Ayn Rand developed the philosophy of *Objectivism*, which she described as "the concept of man as a heroic being, with his own happiness as the moral purpose of his life, with productive achievement as his noblest activity, and reason as his only absolute."[10] Like Aristotle, she viewed the purpose of human life as the reasoned pursuit of happiness. However, she argued that happiness should be the result of one's own work and practical achievement for the benefit of oneself. She tied to this the value of self-esteem, which she said one earns through pride in one's own effort rather than from the praise of others.

Objectivism calls for an unbiased view of reality, especially regarding truth. All that people owe each other is to communicate openly, using reason and citing objective facts, so that all self-interested parties can make informed choices of their own free will.[11] Rand believed that professional communicators had the same duty to deal in facts about the objective world, but she also believed that they were doing a poor job of it. As a result, people often lacked the information necessary to make free choices and to pursue their own rational self-interest.

Like Comte, Rand was an atheist—a fact important to her philosophy. Objectivism grounds itself in the natural world and rejects any notion of the supernatural. In particular, Rand denied the idea that one should lead a life of self-sacrifice with the promise of reward after death, which she believed amounted to no reward at all. In her magnum opus, *Atlas Shrugged*, Rand wrote that philosophies demanding altruistic effort turn one into "a sacrificial animal who exists for the pleasure of others."[12] One should instead exist for one's own pleasure, derived from a life of rational creation and production.

That does not mean that one should refuse to act kindly toward fellow human beings. Rand contrasted benevolence (kindness or generosity) with altruism. Altruism calls for self-sacrifice and placing others above oneself. One person's genuine need therefore creates in others an obligation to meet that need. Fulfilling that need becomes a moral requirement rather than a moral choice. Instead, Rand advocated voluntary benevolence, which she regarded as a higher moral good because it derived from choice rather than compulsion. Even so, she opposed self-sacrifice in the name of benevolence. She defined sacrifice as "the surrender of that which you value in favor of that which you don't."[13] For example, she said, we do not "sacrifice" for our children, because we value them more than the material goods or wealth we surrender for their benefit. Individuals could certainly contribute to charity as they wished, but Rand denied that they had a moral *duty* to do so.[14]

One important issue with such an approach is that it leaves out those who, because of illness, advanced age or other impediment, are not able to take care of themselves. Certainly, some members of society, including family and friends, might voluntarily agree to help such individuals. However, because no entity, including the government, has an obligation to do so, it remains entirely possible that such individuals would suffer because of bad luck or bad choices. Egoism does not entail a moral obligation to alleviate suffering in others.

Is that truly rational and self-interested? Imagine you work at a public relations firm with two team leaders. Both appear to be efficient and effective on the job. However, one of the managers shows a genuine interest in others, remembering birthdays, always offering a hand where needed, and so on. The other does the job well but only seems to help when some kind of reward is involved. For which team leader would you want to work? For which leader would you work harder? And for whom would you be more likely to make yourself available if help were needed?

Sociobiologist Robert Trivers found that evolution favors altruistic behavior in some species, including humans, because the altruism favored survival. He called such behavior "reciprocal altruism."[15] People who engaged in activities that offered a substantial benefit to others, usually at a small cost to themselves, helped the species survive and produce offspring. Reciprocal altruism could involve helping others who were in danger, sharing food, helping the sick, and so on.[16] Trivers noted that species become so fine-tuned to these benefits that they become effective at identifying and punishing "cheaters" who appear to reciprocate but actually fall short of reciprocation.[17] As a result, people who display truly altruistic tendencies would be more likely to survive and pass on their genes. To the degree that altruism is genetic, it would be passed down as well.

In evolutionary biology, reciprocal altruism does not need to be a conscious choice. An animal's "altruistic" behavior, if it leads to reciprocal altruism, presents an evolutionary advantage regardless of intent. However, ethics deals not merely with how one acts but with how one ought to act. Reciprocal altruism encourages acting for others *because it benefits us*. Regardless of the name, it is a form of egoism aimed at producing good consequences for ourselves. But it represents a kind of soft egoism, requiring that one temper actions in the name of self-interest. Moreover, it is not enough to try to "fake" interest in the good of others. One must exhibit a genuine interest in the good of others and be truly altruistic, if one is to derive the benefits of reciprocal altruism.

Utilitarianism

Altruists maximize the good for others. Egoists maximize the good for themselves. Utilitarians try to maximize the good for everyone involved. The philosophy of *utilitarianism* suggests that one's ethical decisions should be based on producing good consequences for the greatest number of people possible.

Utilitarianism as an organized philosophy emerges from the work of Jeremy Bentham, whose initial efforts involved changes to the legal system. In *An Introduction to the Principles of Morals and Legislation,* Bentham argued that nature provides pleasure and pain to govern human behavior.[18] Reason dictates that any system that attempts to produce happiness should therefore be grounded in what Bentham called the *principle of utility,* maximizing pleasure while at the same time minimizing pain. Because of its focus on pleasure, we sometimes refer to Bentham's philosophy as *hedonistic utilitarianism.* But how does that form a rule for a community? After all, communities do not feel pleasure or pain.

Bentham noted that any community consists of individual members. The community's happiness could be said to represent the sum total of the happiness of its members. Add together the happiness of each individual member of a community, subtract the pain of those individual members, and you have a sum representing the community's happiness. Thus, Bentham said, any action taken within a community should be judged good if it increases the sum total of that community's happiness.

Bentham measured seven qualities of pleasure: (1) intensity, (2) duration, (3) certainty, (4) propinquity (nearness in time), (5) fecundity (the degree to which pleasure is reproduced), (6) purity (how much pain a pleasure contains); and (7) extent (the number of other people affected by the pleasure).[19] He even developed an algorithm, known as the *felicific* or *hedonistic calculus,* which represents a method for calculating the relative goodness of any action.[20]

A few problems arise with Bentham's hedonistic utilitarianism. First, for Bentham all pleasures were equal. It didn't matter if you got pleasure from teaching yourself to play a musical instrument or quietly making fun of overweight people at Walmart. Pleasure is pleasure. Second, and more importantly, Bentham rated good simply by the sum total of pleasure generated. A strong utilitarian might therefore argue that inflicting pain on others is morally acceptable, even good, as long as it generates more overall pleasure than pain.

Suppose someone from your marketing firm has used a company computer to post an anonymous, racially offensive rant online. Your investigation reveals that your top salesperson posted the rant. Firing that person will mean a large loss of revenue for you and the firm. Jobs will be lost. But activists are calling for someone's head. Now suppose that you can instead alter the evidence to blame the post on another salesperson who has had trouble meeting sales goals recently because of family problems. Fire that person and you can avert the public relations disaster while keeping your top salesperson on staff. Of course, you will need to speak to the top salesperson about the improper use of corporate computers to ensure it does not happen again. You might even use the opportunity to discourage any posting of future racist rants. So, what should you do? From a strong utilitarian perspective, the likely answer is to fire the scapegoat because it saves revenue and jobs, producing the greatest good for the greatest number of people.

The philosopher John Stuart Mill, a follower of Bentham's, set out to address these perceived flaws in utilitarianism.[21] First, Mill argued against what he called *expediency*, actions that promote the greater good in a practical way but through actions that one might otherwise deem to be improper or immoral.[22] Today we use the term *act utilitarianism* to refer to the theory that one should act to produce the best consequences for the greatest number of people regardless of what actions one takes to produce those consequences. Act utilitarians would weigh the consequences of their actions rather than the actions themselves. Thus, the end could indeed justify the means.

Mill defined utilitarianism in line with what we would today call *rule utilitarianism*, which proposes that we should act to produce the best consequences for the greatest number of people but, at the same time, ensure that our actions adhere to standard moral values. For example, one might certainly find it expedient to produce a greater good by telling a lie. However, such an action weakens our respect for truth, as well as the trust of others, and so damages the good of all. Of course, Mill noted, we make exceptions for lies told in certain circumstances. If someone trying to rob you asks if you have anything else worth taking, rule utilitarians would not condemn you for lying about the money in your shoe. But, in general, one should uphold moral values in attempting to produce good consequences.

Mill also said that utilitarianism should be grounded in equality and justice, which meant that one could not violate agreements, show personal bias, or deprive others of their rightful possessions or freedoms.[23] He argued that being part of a community or society entails that we do not violate the rights of others.[24] Individuals should be free to pursue their own good as they see fit, provided that they do not interfere with the rights of others to do the same.[25] Society should not interfere with these rights of individuals, except to prevent harm to other members of the society. Even in cases where individuals might be seen as acting against their own best interests, society should protect their freedom to act as they please.[26] Mill's utilitarianism was not interested in producing good at the expense of individuals but rather, as Deni Elliott says, "the greatest good for *all* of the people who can be identified as being affected by a particular action."[27]

Mill also took issue with Bentham's hedonistic utilitarianism, with all pleasures being equal. Instead, Mill argued that "some kinds of pleasure are more desirable and more valuable than others."[28]

Like Aristotle, he said that pleasures grounded in reason and intellect were superior to physical pleasures. Given the opportunity to be known as a person of intelligence, who would instead choose to be a fool? A life of pleasure derived from the mind is better than one derived from physical pleasures. For this reason, we often refer to Mill's philosophy as *eudaimonistic utilitarianism*, a form of utilitarianism that places greater value on the so-called higher pleasures than on lower pleasures.

Summary

Consequentialism maintains that the rightness or wrongness of an action rests in its consequences. That which produces the best consequences is by definition the best action. We can judge actions in isolation based on their short-term consequences (act consequentialism) or whether they conform to rules aimed at generating good consequences over the long term (rule consequentialism).

Altruism suggests that one's ethical decisions should be based on producing good consequences for others, even at a cost to oneself. August Comte developed the philosophy of positivism, which emphasizes subordinating self-love to universal love. The less we receive in return for our actions, the more other-oriented and altruistic the actions are. Peter Singer's effective altruism maintains that people should not only sacrifice for the benefit of others but also use reason to determine how to maximize the effectiveness of their self-sacrifice.

Egoism suggests that one's ethical decisions should be based on producing good consequences for oneself. Psychological egoism maintains that all of our actions naturally seek to advance our own interests. Rational egoism argues that reason dictates it is natural to pursue self-interest. Ethical egoism takes things a step further, maintaining that it is not only rational to act in our own interest but also the morally right thing to do.

Philosopher Ayn Rand's theory of Objectivism holds that people should pursue their own happiness, using reason devoted to productive work for one's own benefit. Our goal should be self-esteem from justified pride in our own achievements rather than from the praise of others. Reciprocal altruism represents a kind of soft egoism suggesting that we should treat others well because it benefits us to do so—either because other people will treat us well in the future or because it strengthens our community.

Utilitarianism as an organized philosophy emerged from the work of Jeremy Bentham, who argued that nature provides pleasure and pain to govern human behavior. Bentham's principle of utility called for maximizing pleasure while at the same time minimizing pain. Because of its focus on pleasure, we sometimes refer to Bentham's philosophy as hedonistic utilitarianism.

John Stuart Mill set out to address perceived flaws in Bentham's utilitarianism. He argued against what he called expediency, actions that promote the greater good in a practical way but through actions that one might otherwise deem to be improper or immoral. Instead, he defined utilitarianism according to what we would today call rule utilitarianism, which proposes that we should act to produce the best consequences for the greatest number of people but at the same time ensure that our actions adhere to standard moral values. He believed utilitarianism should be grounded in equality and justice, which meant that one could not violate agreements, show personal bias, or deprive others of their rightful possessions or freedoms. Finally, he took issue with Bentham's hedonistic utilitarianism, with all pleasures being equal. Instead, he proposed what we know today as eudaimonistic utilitarianism, a form of utilitarianism that places greater value on the pleasures of the mind than on physical pleasures.

NOTES

1   International Public Relations Association (IPRA). (2020). *IPRA code of conduct*. https://www.ipra.org/member-services/code-of-conduct/
2   Merriam-Webster. (n.d.). Altruism. In *Merriam-Webster.com dictionary*. https://www.merriam-webster.com/dictionary/altruism
3   Comte, A. (1865). *A general view of positivism*. (J. H. Bridges, Trans.; digitally reprinted 2009) Cambridge University Press, p. 426.
4   Kristof, N. (2016, April 4). The trader who donates half his pay. *New York Times*. https://www.nytimes.com/2015/04/05/opinion/sunday/nicholas-kristof-the-trader-who-donates-half-his-pay.html
5   Singer, P. (2015). *The most good you can do: How effective altruism is changing ideas about living ethically.* Yale University Press.
6   Wells, T. (2021, April 20). Why effective altruism is not effective. *Australian Broadcasting Corporation*. https://www.abc.net.au/religion/why-effective-altruism-is-not-effective/13310708
7   Even Comte (1865) admitted that people have "an insufficiency of natural goodness," and so public praise becomes necessary to motivate altruistic action because "there is no reward for doing right so satisfactory as the approval of our fellow-beings," p. 147.
8   Henry, O. (1992). *The gift of the magi and other short stories.* Dover Publications. (Original work published in 1905). In the short story, Jim and Della have no money for purchasing Christmas presents for each other. Each have something they personally cherish—Jim a gold watch given to him by his father and Della her long, beautiful hair. Willing to sacrifice what they love for the sake of their spouse, Della sells her hair in order to buy Jim a platinum chain for his watch, and Jim sells his watch in order to buy Della a set of beautiful tortoise-shell combs for her hair. As Henry says, they "most unwisely sacrificed for each other the greatest treasures" (p. 5).
9   Regis Jr., E. (1980). What is ethical egoism? *Ethics, 91*(1), 50–62. Regis argues for a definition of ethical egoism that favors universal rational self-interest, noting

that this "pre-supposition of universal rights therefore establishes a general constraint against conduct harmful to others, of which self-interested conduct harmful to others is but a special case" (p. 62).

[10] Rand, A. (1996). *Atlas shrugged*. Signet. (Original work published 1957), p. 1070.

[11] The admonition to treat other people always as ends and deal with them openly and truthfully helps to mediate concerns that ethical egoism serves as a kind of "anything goes" philosophy that allows all manner of destructive behavior when others are not looking or when one knows one will not get caught.

[12] Rand, A. (1996), p. 979.

[13] Ibid., p. 941.

[14] Rand rejected the idea of mandatory taxes, advocating government services such as the police, courts, and military be paid for with voluntary taxes from those who use or benefit from the services. Even care of the aged, the sick, and those incapable of taking care of themselves should be done on a voluntary basis. Any mandatory taxes, even to support desirable ends, she considered theft. See, for example, Rand, A. (1964). *The virtue of selfishness*. Penguin.

[15] Trivers, R. L. (1971). The evolution of reciprocal altruism. *The Quarterly Review of Biology*, *46*(1), 35–57.

[16] Ibid., p. 45.

[17] Ibid., p. 47.

[18] Bentham, J. (2000). *An introduction to the principles of morals and legislation*. Batoche Books. (Original work published 1781). https://historyofeconomicthought.mcmaster.ca/bentham/morals.pdf

[19] Ibid., p. 32.

[20] Think by Numbers provides a mathematical formula for the calculus along with Bentham's instructions at https://thinkbynumbers.org/empiricism-2/felicific-calculus/

[21] Mill developed his ideas in collaboration with his friend, and later his wife, Harriet Hardy Taylor. As Mill wrote in his autobiography, "What I owe, even intellectually, to her, is in its detail, almost infinite." Mill, J. S. (2022). *The classic autobiography of John Stuart Mill*. Compass Circle, p. 73. (Original work published 1924).

[22] Mill. J.S. (2001a). *Utilitarianism*. Batoche Books, p. 24. (Original work published 1863). https://socialsciences.mcmaster.ca/econ/ugcm/3ll3/mill/utilitarianism.pdf

[23] Ibid., pp. 42–45.

[24] Mill. J.S. (2001b). *On Liberty*. Batoche Books, p. 69. (Original work published 1859). https://socialsciences.mcmaster.ca/econ/ugcm/3ll3/mill/liberty.pdf

[25] Ibid., p. 16.

[26] Ibid., p. 13.

[27] Elliott, D. (2007). Getting Mill right. *Journal of Mass Media Ethics, 22*(2–3), 100–112.

[28] Mill, (2001a), pp. 11.

5

Deontological or Duty-based Ethics

In this chapter, you will learn about:
- A definition of deontology
- Divine command theory
- Aquinas' natural law theory
- Kant's categorical imperative
- W. D. Ross and pluralistic rule deontology

As we saw in the last chapter, the consequences of our actions can be difficult to predict even in the short term, and they can ripple far into the future. Judging our actions solely by their consequences means that we will likely never know if what we did was ultimately good or not. Act consequentialism might permit us to use otherwise immoral/unethical means to achieve good consequences. And rule consequentialism can take the focus off immediate, intended consequences to such a degree that some scholars argue it should not even be considered consequentialism.[1] Instead of looking at consequences, *deontology* maintains that the rightness or wrongness of an action rests in the quality of the action itself and the intent of the actor to adhere to duty and the rules of morality/ethics—to perform an act because it is good in and of itself.

When the United States government launched a vaccine program during the COVID-19 pandemic, some Americans were skeptical about its safety. Despite assurances from scientists, who said that the vaccines represented an important step toward ending the pandemic, roughly 1 in 5 Americans said they would refuse to get vaccinated.[2] Suppose you are a journalist and you learn that two people in your area recently died from vaccine-related complications.³ A few of your coworkers suggest that your organization should just sit on the story. Reporting the story could convince more people not to be vaccinated, which could be dangerous for them as well as for others. What should you do?

For a traditional journalist who is also a deontologist, the answer is simple—you report the story. As noted in chapter 1, the first principle of the code of ethics for the Society of Professional Journalists directs journalists to seek truth and report it. You realize that reporting the truth about the two deaths could be used as evidence that people should not get the vaccine. From a deontologist's perspective, the potential consequences of reporting that truth cannot override one's duty as a journalist.

Divine Command Theory

Perhaps the oldest form of deontology is *divine command theory*, which stipulates that the rightness or wrongness of an action rests in whether it obeys God's commands.⁴ This theory depends on several understandings: (1) God exists; (2) God knows what is good; (3) God wants us to know what is good; (4) God has communicated and/or is communicating to us what is good; (5) God commands us to do what is good; and, most importantly, (6) goodness depends on following God's commands. Let us assume for the sake of argument that God exists. How does God know what is good? Socrates confronts this issue in Plato's dialogue *Euthyphro.*⁵

The Euthyphro Dilemma, as it has come to be known, asks whether a moral value is good because God commands it or whether God commands it because it is good. In other words, does goodness emanate from God's command, or does God's command simply identify what is good? That might appear simple, but it has far-reaching implications. Suppose that God perceives what is good and then commands us to do that which is good. In that case, God is not omnipotent. Goodness lies outside of God, who simply recognizes and communicates what is good. God appears to be bound by moral good rather than the other way around.

On the other hand, if goodness emanates from God's commands, what if God says murder is good? Suppose God commands that you kill your own child, as with Abraham in the religious texts of Judaism, Christianity, and Islam. Is this command now inherently "good" in a moral sense? If God determines goodness, then goodness is not eternal or universal but rather potentially subject to change depending on God's choice. It's arbitrary in a way that reduces its value as a guide to human behavior.

Aquinas and Natural Law

How do we know what God commands? Most religions maintain established sets of rules, with the three major monotheistic religions each having a text laying out God's commands within that religious tradition. But what about people of other faiths, as well as agnostics and atheists? Thomas Aquinas indirectly had an answer for this and for the Euthyphro Dilemma in his *natural law theory*, which holds that God created the natural world and created humans with reason so that they could discern good and evil. It is a rejection of the principles of divine command theory in that it suggests that following God's commands is not, by itself, the source of good.

Like Aristotle, Aquinas held that all things have a purpose or function; for humans, that purpose lies in the use of reason. Natural law consists of general principles, such as good is to be pursued, and evil is to be avoided.[6] Aquinas argued that God does not force humans to obey those laws, because one is neither truly free nor truly good if one is compelled by God to act a certain way.[7] Instead, natural law theory suggests that morality is hardwired into the system and therefore into human beings as well. We possess a conscience, an inner guide to moral value and action. God's commands serve as rules to help guide us as we use reason to discern what's good. Nontheist scholars often adopt some features of natural law (e.g., what we call good emanates from human nature and reason) while removing God from the equation entirely.[8]

The rise of Christianity gave power to divine command theory and natural law, transforming the Aristotelean view of ethics into what Elizabeth Anscombe referred to as a "*law* conception of ethics."[9] As a result, she said, ethics took on the language of divine command theory to the extent that Greek words that had referred to a poor ethical choice as a "mistake" now exhibit a legalistic connotation of "guilt" or a theological one of "sin." As we will see, this view carried on to other deontological theories and, to some degree, the study of ethics as a whole.

Kant's Categorical Imperative

Most of the time when we refer to deontology in discussing professional communication ethics, we focus on the work of eighteenth century philosopher Immanuel Kant. He sought to establish the supreme principle of morality—a moral/ethical law that we follow not to please God, nor to produce good consequences of any kind, but simply because it embodies goodness.

For Kant, the rightness or wrongness of an action rests in the good will of the actor, which he describes as the reasoned intent to act solely from a sense of duty to moral/ethical law. Kant emphasizes this duty as the source of goodness. Imagine that you are a public relations executive. You love your work because you're good at it, it pays well, and you like helping people. When you represent a client's interest, it gives you a feeling of fulfillment. Meanwhile, some of your coworkers hate the job and don't like the people with whom they work. They serve the interests of clients well but only because they have an ethical duty to do so. For Kant, *why* you do a thing is as important as *what* you do. You must act because the action itself is good. Your coworkers' service of the clients is good because it emerges from a sense of professional duty. Your service is *not* inherently good because it emerges instead from your own desires, inclinations, character, happiness and so forth. Intent matters, and only actions taken for the sake of duty truly qualify as good actions. That does not mean you are acting badly or that you have to dislike your work or perform your action grudgingly in order to be morally/ethically good.[10] It simply means that duty should be at the forefront of your decisions, especially when it comes to ethics, if your decisions are to be considered good.

Freedom, reason, respect for humanity and unconditional, universal duty form the foundation of Kantian ethics. One needs the freedom to choose, the reason to discern the proper decision, respect for all humans, and the recognition that duties are unconditional and universal, binding all people equally. Kant called his supreme law of morality *the categorial imperative*, which commands that our actions should have the form of moral conduct—they should be derived from moral principles.[11]

Suppose you are on a creative team working to develop an advertising campaign for the next iPhone. In creating the campaign, you might have access to valuable, confidential information. If someone approaches you to buy that information, should you sell it? If you say yes then Kant might argue that the maxim of your action, the rule you operate by, is "When I want money, I shall sell confidential information." If that becomes a universal law, then anyone who wants money would be morally/ethically permitted to sell confidential information. In that case, no promise of confidentiality could be trusted, and "confidentiality" has no value. Kant would say that as a universal law, this contradicts itself.

Kant offered three formulations of the single, universal categorical imperative, serving as principles designed to help us comprehend the law of morality:[12]

Formulation 1 (The Principle of Nature): "[A]ct as if the maxim of your action were to become by your will a universal law of nature."[13]

The rules that you follow become the universal rules created by your actions. As we have seen, some rules, when universalized, would contradict themselves and so could not logically become laws of nature. This principle emphasizes the "natural purpose" of certain actions.[14]

Formulation 2 (The Principle of Humanity): "So act that you use humanity, whether in your own person or in the person of any other, always at the same time as an end, never merely as a means."[15] Kant's principle of humanity can be recognized as a defining feature of modern ethical theory. All rational beings exist as ends in themselves. As we are ends, so are other people ends in themselves. Their status as rational beings prohibits us from using our fellow humans merely as tools for our own purposes without regard for their humanity. In a sense, this represents the covenant of human society.

Formulation 3 (The Principle of Autonomy): "[E]very rational being must act as if he were by his maxims at all times a lawgiving member of the universal kingdom of ends."[16] By "kingdom of ends," Kant meant an autonomous (self-governing) community of rational beings united through laws created by those beings. Being a *member* of such a kingdom means that you are also subject to the universal laws you create. Because the laws we create through our actions govern the entire community, those laws must be rationally acceptable to all members of the community. Only rationally acceptable laws would suffice to unite a community of rational beings. Thus, when we act, we should act as though we are creating a law that would and *could* be accepted by and govern an autonomous community of rational beings.

When we employ Kant's deontology within professional communication ethics, we often adapt it to emphasize the role of duty. For example, we might seek to define the ethical duties of a journalist, a social media marketer, a public relations practitioner and so on. We might further ask whether those duties are "good." Can they be generalized to all people in that career field without self-contradiction? Do they respect all rational beings as ends and not merely as means? Do they work as rules for the profession within a society of rational beings? These questions can lead to some interesting—and at times uncomfortable—ethical discussions. We can also adapt Kantian deontology to individual decisions. For example, am I okay if everyone in my situation acts this way all the time? If I treat Person A (whom I like) this way, am I willing to treat Person B (whom I dislike) the same way? Remember, decisions should be based on reason, not emotion or personal bias.

So far so good. Kant says we should act in a way that we would want everyone else to act, as though we were making a universal law that respects all people and that would be rationally accepted by all. However, problems arise when we try to put a strong Kantian deontology into actual practice. Scholars have debated for more than two centuries how we should apply Kantian deontology to decide situations where ethical values or duties conflict, which is the essence of most problems in applied ethics. Kant partially addressed this issue by arguing that we can never have an actual conflict of duty. When we have a dilemma, we have only one duty—to act in accordance with the categorical imperative. A conflict of duty is thus, for Kant, "not even conceivable."[17] Instead, we have a conflict between what he called "grounds of obligation,"[18] only one of which can truly become a duty under the categorical imperative. Grounds of obligation are not universal and binding, only duty is. So, the stronger ground of obligation wins out. But having a "conflict of the grounds of obligation" still leaves us with the problem of choosing between them. Some scholars point out that Kant's explanation is less than helpful, leaving us without clear criteria for sorting out ethical dilemmas.[19]

One of the more troublesome examples of the categorical imperative in action is the famous "murderer at the door" scenario.[20] Suppose a person comes to your house seeking refuge from a murderer chasing them. You agree to help and let the potential victim in. A few minutes later, the blood-covered murderer comes to your door asking if you know where the potential victim went. Should you lie?

You might be tempted to argue that the murderer has no right to the truth. But Kant says that's meaningless. It's not about the murderer's right to the truth. For Kant, rights are about what we possess independent of others (e.g., liberty) or what *we* can actively do rather than what we require that others do. Therefore, it's not about whether the murderer has the right to the truth but rather about whether you have the right to lie. When it comes to that, Kant argues that everyone has a "formal duty" to tell the truth to everyone else as part of the contract with society.

Remember that Kant proclaims himself to be anti-consequentialist. Lying to save someone is essentially lying to produce good consequences, which we cannot predict. As Kant observes, perhaps your truth causes the murderer to try to enter the building, waking up your neighbors who come to defend you and the victim. On the other hand, perhaps your lie causes the murderer to turn around and then, by chance, catch the victim sneaking out another door. In that case, *you* share responsibility for what happens because it resulted from your lie. It cannot be proper to do something we know is bad in order to achieve a consequence that we merely hope will be good. Ultimately, Kant says, if you cannot avoid answering, the only right thing to do is to tell the truth to the murderer.

Kant's argument is perfectly consistent within his ethical framework. For him, moral/ethical rules are universal and binding without exception. But as you might imagine, his critics argue that it does not ultimately seem just that we should tell the truth to a murderer when the odds convincingly suggest that a lie could save a human life. Strong Kantian deontology, though internally consistent, seems to lose at least some of its popular value when deciding practical ethical situations—especially in extreme cases like the murderer at the door.

Ross and Pluralistic Rule Deontology

Kant's ethical deontology is *monistic*; it maintains one strict definition of what is ethically good. As we observed earlier, Kant asserts that goodness lies in acting in accordance with the categorical imperative. The one categorical imperative is the only ethical measure. Bentham's utilitarianism is also monistic, asserting that goodness lies in maximizing pleasure and minimizing pain (hedonism). The principle of utility is the only ethical measure. Kant and Bentham each effectively propose one definition of goodness, but they propose different definitions.[21] If we judge ethics to be monistic, Kant and Bentham cannot both be right. But what if they are both wrong, at least when it comes to the monistic nature of ethics? If the two strongest arguments for monism can be refuted, that suggests monism itself can be refuted. Scottish philosopher W. D. Ross suggested just that.

Ross argued against a monistic view of ethics.[22] To illustrate his point, he first imagined two worlds, both of which have equal amounts of pleasure. All the people in one world are highly virtuous, and all the people in the other are mean-spirited and cruel. Can we say that the virtuous world is superior to the vicious one? If so, then pleasure cannot be the only measure of goodness, and Bentham is wrong. Conversely, Ross imagined two worlds that have equal amounts of virtue. One world consists of good people living in pleasure, and the other of good people living in pain. Is the pleasurable world superior to the painful one? If so, then virtue cannot be the only measure of goodness, and Kant is wrong.

While rejecting the monism of the categorical imperative, Ross agreed with Kant that acting ethically meant acting in accordance with duty—that is, intending to act because the action itself is good. When a person makes good on a promise, that person does not think about the total consequences of keeping that promise. Instead of looking forward to the consequences, one looks backward to the fact that the promise has been made. A promise should be kept because one made the promise not because of the consequences.[23] In fact, promises as we know them would have little value if everyone understood that the promise held no force in itself but rather at all times depended on a continual analysis of the consequences of breaking or fulfilling the promise.

Ethical duties or rules, such as promise keeping are thus good in and of themselves rather than dependent on the consequences they produce. However, Ross objected to Kant's idea that ethical rules bind everyone at all times, *without exception.* If this were true, we could never overcome the inevitable conflict of ethical rules. For example, we have a responsibility to tell the truth and a responsibility not to cause harm to others. But the truth can hurt—not only feelings but potentially someone's livelihood or even the life of an innocent (e.g., the murderer at the door). When two ethical rules conflict, they cannot both be binding. Indeed, Ross said that it's difficult to believe that *any* ethical rule is universally true and binding. Instead, he says, we must recognize that while ethical rules or values are by their nature good, they can nonetheless be wrong when they conflict with stronger ethical rules or values.[24]

Ross proposed instead a theory now referred to as *pluralistic rule deontology*, a rule-based view of ethics recognizing that we have many duties and that those duties can and do conflict. Ross called such duties *prima facie* (literally "first face" but understood as "taken as fact until proven otherwise") Here we will use his alternate term for *prima facie* duty—conditional duty. Let's return to the question of whether we have a duty to tell the truth. If that were an absolute duty, we would need to conclude, as Kant does, that we must tell the truth at all times to all people. Instead, Ross argues that telling the truth is a conditional duty. We need weigh it against other conditional duties with which it might conflict before we decide what the actual duty would be in particular circumstances. Ross thus argues that instead of being absolute and universal, *all moral/ethical duties are conditional until applied to a specific situation.* Only when applying conditional duties to a specific set of circumstances can we determine the proper duty.

Ross suggested seven specific examples representing broader categories of *prima facie* duties:[25]

1. *Fidelity*—the duty to keep promises that you have made.

2. *Reparation*—the duty to make amends for wrongs that you have done.

3. *Gratitude*—the duty to repay what others have done for you.

4. *Justice*—the duty to ensure others are treated as they deserve, according to their merit.

5. *Beneficence*—the duty to make better the lives of other people.

6. *Self-improvement*—the duty to improve ourselves.[26]

7. *Non-maleficence*—the duty not to harm others.

These duties should not be taken simply as life advice or consequentialism (e.g., pay back what you owe because bad things might happen if you don't). Rather, prima facie duties possess inherent moral/ethical significance (e.g., one should keep promises because promise keeping is good).

Ross recognized the potential shortcomings of his prima facie list, noting that it represents "a list of authentic conditional duties, correct as far as it goes though not necessarily complete."[27] For example, the duty of truth-telling is conspicuously absent from this list. Ross suggests that the duty to tell the truth might fall under one or more of the categories. For example, even if no promises have been made to tell the truth, there is "a duty not to tell lies, since to tell lies is *prima facie* to do a positive injury to another person" and so would constitute a duty of non-maleficence.[28]

Ross also suggests that the duty to tell the truth arises from the reasoned expectation of truth from others. Deceit is more forgivable if "no implicit undertaking to tell the truth has been established."[29] Deception may be forgiven if an offender "has no reason to suppose that the other is not deceiving."[30] Here we can see Ross' potential solution to Kant's dilemma of the murderer at the door. The murderer has no reason to expect the truth when asking the whereabouts of the intended victim, so you might be pardoned for not telling the truth in that circumstance. Truth retains its moral/ethical standing as a *prima facie* duty, but the conditions suggest that truth does not constitute a proper or actual duty (i.e., the "right" thing to do) in this situation.

This leads to consideration of how one should decide among *prima facie* duties when they conflict. Ross does not provide a truly systematic answer to that problem. He offers no general rules. Instead, he suggests that the decision should be "preceded and informed by the fullest reflection we can bestow on the act in all its bearings."[31] We have to carefully weigh the *prima facie* duties against one another in an effort to determine which is the stronger duty (i.e., the proper or actual duty in this situation). Then we render a decision. Often, once the evidence has been presented and analyzed, we will arrive at an obvious conclusion. However, despite our best efforts, good people might sometimes disagree as to what constitutes the proper duty in a given situation. Ross admits that this method for handling ethical conflict "is highly fallible, but it is the only guide we have to our duty."[32]

Summary

Deontology maintains that the rightness or the wrongness of an action rests in the quality of the action itself and the intent of the actor to adhere to duty and the rules of morality/ethics—to perform an act because it is good in and of itself.

Divine command theory, which stipulates that the rightness or wrongness of an action rests in whether it obeys God's commands, is one of the oldest forms of deontology. The Euthyphro Dilemma asks whether a moral value is good because God commands it or whether God commands it because it is good. If God commands something *because* it is good, then something outside of God determines what is good. If something is good *because* God commands it, then morality becomes arbitrary and changeable rather than universal and eternal. Thomas Aquinas, while a firm believer in Christianity, disagreed with the idea that goodness depends solely on following God's commands. Instead, his *natural law theory* holds that God created the natural world and created humans with reason so that they could discern good and evil.

Immanuel Kant argued that the rightness or wrongness of an action rests in the reasoned intent to act solely from a sense of duty to moral/ethical law. He set out to define a law of morality that could govern human action in all ethical matters—a *categorical imperative*. Three principles undergird the categorical imperative. *The Principle of Nature* indicates that actions cannot be self-contradictory; they should be capable of becoming universal laws of nature. *The Principle of Humanity* requires treating others as independent rational beings and not as the means to some end. *The Principle of Autonomy* holds that the universal laws we create through our acts must be acceptable to everyone in governing a community of rational beings.

The Scottish philosopher W. D. Ross took issue with Kant on two points. First, he argued against Kant's *monism*, the idea that only one categorical imperative strictly defines of what is ethically good. Second, he rejected Kant's idea that ethical rules were absolute and universally binding. Instead, Ross proposed a *pluralistic rule deontology*, a rule-based view of ethics recognizing that we have many duties and that those duties can and do conflict. When deciding among conflicting ethical duties, Ross suggested a process that involved careful reflection on the facts of the situation and the ethical duties involved. We then use reason to discern the stronger of the ethical duties.

Notes

1   Howard-Snyder, F. (1993). Rule consequentialism is a rubber duck. *American Philosophical Quarterly, 30*(3), 271–278.
2   Such deaths do occur, but they are incredibly rare—less than 0.002% of all people who receive the vaccine. Monmouth University. (2021). "National: One in five still shun vaccine." April 8 to 12, 2021, [Survey Report]. Retrieved from https://www.monmouth.edu/polling-institute/documents/monmouthpoll_us_041421.pdf/
3   Centers for Disease Control. (2021, July 21). Selected adverse events reported after COVID-19 vaccination. Retrieved from https://www.cdc.gov/coronavirus/2019-ncov/vaccines/safety/adverse-events.html.
4   Or "the gods" in polytheistic religious traditions, which predate the major monotheistic religions known today.
5   The *Euthyphro* begins with a discussion of piety but expands to other moral/ethical goods, such as justice. It is not uncommon to substitute "good" for "piety" when discussing "The Euthyphro Dilemma."
6   Koritansky, P. (n.d.) Thomas Aquinas: Political philosophy. Internet Encyclopedia of Philosophy. https://tinyurl.com/bdezhw6n.
7   To be good or bad requires a choice. When you are compelled to perform a specific act, responsibility for your action rests on the individual who actually wills the act into being (i.e., the one who is compelling you to act, not you). This assumes that punishment for nonaction constitutes a greater evil than the action itself.
8   For example, Charles Darwin, as we discussed in chapter 2.
9   Anscombe, G. E. (1958). Modern moral philosophy. *Philosophy, 33*(124), 1–19, p. 5. https://tinyurl.com/mrxywhvv
10   See, for example, Korsgaard, C.M. (2012). Introduction. In M. Gregor & J. Timmermann (Eds.), *Kant: Groundwork of the metaphysics of morals* (M. Gregor, Trans., rev. ed., pp. ix–xxxvi). Cambridge University Press.
11   Ibid., p. xiii.
12   Nuyen, A. T. (1993). Counting the formulas of the categorical imperative: One plus three makes four. *History of Philosophy Quarterly, 10*(1), 37–48. Scholars differ on how the categorical imperative and its various formulations or principles should be expressed. Nuyen offers a cogent argument that Kant's categorical imperative should be understood as one "basic formula," together with three principles. We use that system here.
13   Gregor, M., & Timmermann, J. (Eds.). (1998). *Kant: Groundwork of the metaphysics of morals* (M. Gregor, Trans; original work published 1797). Cambridge University Press, p. 31.
14   Korsgaard (2012), p. xix.
15   Gregor & Timmermann (1998), p. 38.
16   Ibid., p. 45.
17   Ibid., 9–26)
18   Ibid., 9–26)
19   See, for example, Timmermann, J. (2013). Kantian dilemmas? Moral conflict in Kant's ethical theory. *Archiv für Geschichte der Philosophie, 95*(1), 36–64, most notably pp. 51–52.
20   Kant, I. (1889). On the supposed right to lie from philanthropy. In *Critique of practical reason and other works on the theory of ethics* (T. K. Abbott, Trans.). Kongmans, Green and Co. Reprinted essay retrieved from http://www.sophia-project.org/uploads/1/3/9/5/13955288/kant_lying.pdf. This is sometimes translated instead as "On the supposed right to lie from benevolent intent."
21   Here we try not to stray too far down the path of theoretical ethics. However, it's worth noting that Kant holds that an action is right (correct) because it is morally/ethically good. We do what's good, which makes our action right. Bentham asserts the opposite, that an action is morally/ethically good because it is right. We do what's right, which makes our action good. Limitations of time and space force

us to put that discussion aside for now, though Ross addresses it at length in *The Right and the Good.*

[22] Ross, W. D. (2002). *The right and the good.* (P. Stratton-Lake, Ed.; original work published 1930). Clarendon Press. The full name of Ross is Sir William David Ross.

[23] Ibid., pp. 17–18.

[24] We should note again that Ross distinguished "right" from "good." Saying an action is "not right" is *not* the same as saying it is "not good." For example, in a given situation we might conclude that it is not right to tell the truth, but that does not mean that telling the truth is not inherently good.

[25] Ross (2002), p. 21. Ross discusses fidelity and reparation as separate issues under the broader category of duties resting on things the actor has done in the past (e.g., made a promise or wronged someone).

[26] It is interesting to note that while Ross talks about making better the lives of others "in respect of virtue, or of intelligence, or of pleasure," he conspicuously omits "pleasure" when speaking about the duty to improve one's own "condition" (p. 21). The reason for this is that we rarely act for our own pleasure simply out of the duty to do so. As Ross (2002) says "[O]ne's own pleasure is a good and there is a duty to produce it. [I]t is only if we think of our own pleasure not as simply our own pleasure, but as an objective good, something that an impartial spectator would approve, that we can think of the getting it as a duty; and we do not habitually think of it in this way" (p. 26). So, one might act out of duty when one says *and literally means,* "I owe it to myself." It is then a *duty* to oneself and nothing more.

[27] Ibid., p. 23.

[28] Ibid., p. 55.

[29] Ibid.

[30] Ibid.

[31] Ibid., p. 42.

[32] Ibid.

6

Codes of Ethics

In this chapter, you will learn about:
- The role of ethical codes in communication professions
- The difference between moralizing and moral philosophy
- Problems with professional ethical codes
- Benefits of professional ethical codes
- Values common to most professional ethical codes

Every major field in mass communication has at least one professional code of ethics. Most have more than one.[1] Codes can vary from nation to nation or state to state. In addition, most corporations and small businesses have separate, individual codes of ethics—sometimes written and sometimes unwritten. Codes can and often do conflict among fields, nations, professional organizations, businesses and sometimes even within a code itself. They can also conflict with an individual's moral sense of right and wrong. It can be very confusing, especially for someone just entering a career in mass communication.

In the United States and many other countries, codes of ethics in mass communication are not enforceable—at least not by the government or the professional organizations that create them. Violate a code of ethics and you will not go to jail unless you also violate the law. On the other hand, acting unethically in the eyes of your boss can get you fired in almost any industry. This can be problematic, especially when you are unfamiliar with existing codes of ethics or when your idea of ethics does not match your employer's position.

Imagine you are a photographer for a small community newspaper. You have just taken a photo of a local softball team holding up their new trophy. A few minutes after you get back to the office, a member of the team shows up with her coach. She explains that she missed the photo and asks you to take her picture now so you can digitally add it to the team photo before publication. What should you do?

The National Press Photographers Association is very specific about such scenarios. It says; "Editing should maintain the integrity of the photographic images' content and context. Do not manipulate images or add or alter sound in any way that can mislead viewers or misrepresent subjects."[2] The Society of Professional Journalists agrees: "Never deliberately distort facts or context, including visual information."[3] The softball player was not present for the photo. You cannot make it appear that she was. Using image editing software to add the player could get you fired at many news organizations, even if you were unfamiliar with the professional codes of ethics and even if your organization did not have its own written code of ethics.

Now suppose your editor tells you that he wants you to go ahead and add the player to the photo. Perhaps he says that it is not a real "news" photo, that the team's coach agrees, that the softball player would appreciate the newspaper's cooperation ,and that he cannot imagine any reader being upset by the decision. What should you do? You will hear a lot of different responses to that question. Some would counsel strict adherence to the professional code of ethics. Others would advise that you should do what your editor commands if you intend to keep your job. Still others would suggest an ethical discussion and perhaps a compromise with your editor.[4] Consequences abound, but the decision is yours to make.

Problems with Professional Codes of Ethics

Professional codes of ethics in mass communication have some troublesome aspects. First, they don't really help professionals make ethical decision. Second, they don't usually encourage independent ethical thinking. Third, they usually cannot be broadly enforced.

When it comes to making ethical decisions, professionals would do better not to rely on written codes of ethics. As ethicist Philip Meyer observes:

> The values they list are obvious values, the behaviors enjoined are clearly bad behaviors. Ethics is more complicated than that. . . . Having a list of unethical behaviors to pull out of a desk drawer and look at when a decision has to be made is not of much help if the decision involves a choice in which at least one of the caveats on the list will be violated no matter what you do.[5]

Here Meyer echoes the complaints of researchers such as Jay Black and Ralph Barney who argued that codes of ethics ultimately evolve to the point that they focus more on the interest of the business than on doing the right thing: "That is, they tend to protect the industry, or elements of the industry, at the expense of individuals and other institutions, even of the full society."[6] In short, they shield the industry while simultaneously serving as public relations documents designed to reassure society that professional communicators care about ethics.

To the extent that codes do offer ethical direction, it is in the form of advice or telling people what to do rather than advancing the ability to think critically about conflicting choices.[7] Codes represent a narrower, more dogmatic way of thinking that provides a checklist of dos and don'ts when confronting an ethical problem rather than a logical process for resolving a dilemma. High-minded exhortations and admonitions within a code of ethics can inhibit ethical discussion by presenting the professional with a false sense of security when thoughtful deliberation would prove more valuable in resolving an ethical problem.

In the movie *Absence of Malice*, reporter Megan Carter (Sally Field) interviews Teresa Perone (Melinda Dillon), a reluctant source who is the alibi witness in a murder case. Carter conducts that interview in accordance with the codes of journalistic ethics: identifying her source, testing the accuracy of her information, clearly identifying herself as a reporter, and so on. She tells Perone that if information is revealed it will "probably" have to be in the newspaper and that she can't promise anonymity. Carter even reminds Perrone: "I'm a reporter. You're talking to a newspaper right now. Do you understand?" When Perone reveals the information, Carter runs the story with disastrous results. Later the subject of the story, Michael Gallagher (Paul Newman) asks the reporter, "Don't you see what it was to her? Couldn't you just stop scribbling for a second, put down your god-damned ballpoint pen and just see her?"[8] Codes encourage the reporter to check boxes (e.g., "Identified self," "Refused to promise anonymity," and so on) rather than to engage in an ethical decision-making process (e.g., "Should I publish the source's name in these circumstances?"). Looking at the code may preclude analyzing the situation and the individuals involved.

Even when an action clearly violates core precepts of ethical code, there's not much that anyone other than your employer can do about it. Mass communication codes of ethics have no teeth—no regular, broadly enforceable punishment. For example, while laws prohibit some specific types of deception such as libel and fraud, it is generally not a crime to lie.[9] When progressive blogger Tom McMaster, a 40-year-old American man living in Scotland, deceived readers by pretending to be a young, homosexual girl living in Syria he may have acted unethically, but he didn't break any laws.[10] While he was roundly criticized for his actions, no one could stop him from continuing to write on the internet.[11] The same is true in so-called "mainstream media." For instance, journalist Mike Barnicle was accused of fabricating all or part of several stories while at the *Boston Globe*. He resigned amid controversy in 1998 but reemerged to write for the *New York Daily News* and the *Boston Herald*. He subsequently became a broadcast journalist.

Benefits of Professional Codes of Ethics

Professional codes may not be the best tools for rendering ethical decisions, but they do have two major benefits beyond their use in reassuring the public: (1) codes of ethics help clarify minimum ethical standards for those new to a profession; and (2) codes of ethics articulate the ideal ethical values of a profession.[12]

Even critics of ethical codes in mass communication agree that such codes have some value when it comes to educating those entering a career in the field.[13] For these beginners, codes point out the minimum expected ethical standards of a profession. These are often the *don'ts* of an ethical code. For example, the PRSA Code of Ethics states that its members shall "Safeguard the confidences and privacy rights of present, former, and prospective clients and employees."[14] This does not mean that members should actively guard the information but rather that they should *not* be careless with or actively disclose that information. The code cites an example of a member who deliberately leaks confidential information that damages another party.

As ethicist Deni Elliott notes, "one is held morally (and often legally) blameworthy for failing to uphold this type of standard but is not perceived as morally praiseworthy for doing so."[15] Rarely would one compliment a public relations executive for *not* revealing a client's proprietary information. On the other hand, revealing such information would be cause for rebuke and, most likely, punishment.

The second benefit of professional ethical codes lies in their tendency to promote ethical ideals within the profession. These tend to be the *dos* of the profession. Individuals who approach or attain such ideals often win the praise of their colleagues. Those who fail to do so suffer no blame. The ideals merely represent those things for which members of the profession should strive. For example, the Institute for Advertising Ethics states: "Advertising, public relations, and all marketing communications professionals have an obligation to exercise the highest personal ethics in the creation and dissemination of commercial information to consumers."[16] The specifics of "the highest personal ethics" are not defined. The principle simply articulates an ideal.

Professional Codes and Ethical Values

If professional codes of ethics aim to describe the values of a given field, then what are those values? Looking at some of the most widely used codes of ethics in mass communication, we can find a number of values cited across the professions.[17]

The Public Good

Every major code of mass communication ethics recognizes an obligation to the public. Individuals working in various mass communication fields accept that they have a role to play in society, and they work to define that role for the public and for themselves. Advertising/marketing professionals have a desire to win and maintain public confidence, to act as stewards facilitating the economy, to connect buyers with sellers, and to otherwise serve the public interest. Those in public relations and business communication likewise proclaim themselves advocates for their clients who contribute factual information and thus aid public debate. They further assert that they promote the free flow of information, especially in times of crisis. Meanwhile, those in journalism and visual communication often see themselves as guardians of the public interest who actively pursue information in the name of the public's right to know. Some see their role as transcending the ages, declaring a responsibility "to document society and to preserve its history through images."[18]

Truth, Accuracy and Honesty

Professional associations in mass communication also assert loyalty to truth. However, "truth" can take on different meanings in different fields. Those in persuasive communication fields tend to see truth as largely subjective. Thus, advertising and marketing professionals might prize truth and reject false statements, misleading price claims, poorly supported claims and questionable testimonials—but at the same time recognize that some areas are "subject to honestly different interpretations and judgement."[19] Public relations professionals recognize this as well, asserting the need for dedicated advocates supporting all of those interpretations in a free and open debate so that individuals can decide truth for themselves.

Journalists and other informative communicators tend toward a more neutral stance toward truth. While they may advocate for one side or another in clearly labeled opinion pieces, the bulk of their work focuses on treating all sides without bias. The concepts of impartiality and objectivity permeate codes of ethics in these fields.

Independence and Conflicts of Interest

Codes of ethics uniformly recommend that professionals in all areas of mass communication eschew any interests that would conflict with their professional obligations. In public relations this specifically includes conflicts that endanger the professional's responsibility to the client or to the public. In journalism and visual communication, duty lies with the public alone. "Independence from influences that conflict with public interest remains an ideal of journalism."[20]

Nearly all codes of ethics and statements of professional conduct specifically bar giving or receiving gifts—cash or otherwise—that might influence the communication process. Various codes in journalism and visual communication warn that journalists should refuse gifts, secondary employment, and even membership in organizations that might compromise their independence. Public relations and advertising obviously involve payment for their communication services, but professionals are warned that they should "not accept any form of payment in connection with those services from anyone other than the principal."[21]

Privacy

The increasingly intrusive nature of communication technology, from social media to behavioral marketing, has prompted correspondingly greater promises of respect for individual privacy. Advertising organizations support allowing customers to opt in or out of online *behavioral tracking*, the use of cookies, databases, or other technological means to follow the behavior of consumers, often without their knowledge or consent. The American Marketing Association extends privacy protection to employees and partners, as well as customers.

Concerns in journalism and visual communication lie primarily with members of the public who become the subject of news. In general, professional organizations recognize that individuals have the right to control information about themselves. However, individuals can and often do surrender their right to privacy through their actions. The public's need to know can also supersede an individual's right to privacy.

Professional organizations also recognize that some particularly vulnerable individuals deserve special respect with regard to their privacy, including children, crime victims, inexperienced news sources, and individuals dealing with grief or tragedy. The use of hidden cameras or microphones, as well as other newsgathering techniques that potentially impinge on an individual's privacy, give additional cause for concern.

Confidentiality

Confidentiality refers to the obligation not to reveal information with which one has been entrusted. Like privacy, confidentiality deals with information that professionals should *not* communicate. In business communication, including public relations, marketing and advertising, this primarily involves information about one's clients—past or present. So, for example, a professional who accepts a job with a new firm should feel bound to continue safeguarding information obtained from his or her previous clients.

Journalistic confidentiality usually focuses on the practice of entering into "off the record" agreements with a source. While professional organizations advise journalists to be circumspect about promising anonymity to sources, they should also be steadfast in keeping any such promises. Other confidentiality concerns involve information that might cause harm. For example, journalists should "balance a suspect's right to a fair trial with the public's right to know."[22]

Fair Competition

Dealing with one's competition generates a number of ethical concerns in professional mass communication. These tend to be more prevalent in advertising, marketing, and public relations where agencies sometimes battle fiercely over clients. In these cases, some professionals merely evoke the Golden Rule—treat others as you would like to be treated. Others go into substantially more detail, discouraging everything from the poaching of clients to unfair competitive practices such as rumormongering.

Fair competition does not present quite the same ethical problem in journalism and visual communication that it does in the persuasive communication fields. Indeed, the Associated Press Managing Editors group cautions about being too concerned with competition, advising in its section on independence that "stories should not be written or edited primarily for the purpose of winning awards and prizes."[23] Again, the needs of the public should come first.

Journalists rarely stand accused of poaching stories from one another. However, in the sometimes rough and tumble world of photojournalism, individuals are instructed to avoid sabotaging their peers. Codes of ethics also warn against *plagiarism*, copying someone else's words and attempting to pass them off as your own.

Diversity and Respect

In many mass communication codes of ethics, the concepts of diversity and respect appear intertwined. The American Marketing Association's section on ethical values includes "Respect—to acknowledge the basic human dignity of all stakeholders" as well as "to value individual differences and avoid stereotyping."[24] A variety of professional communication associations recommend that members should avoid using their own cultural values to judge others. Instead, members should work to promote understanding between groups, combat prejudice, and generally support a broad diversity of viewpoints in the public sphere.

Transparency and Accountability

When all else fails, mass communication professionals should at least be transparent in their actions and accountable for the decisions that they make. To this end, most professional organizations place a high value on transparency—being open and honest with regard to the ethical decisions you make, as well as the values and logic that went into making those decisions.

The Institute for Advertising Ethics grants the highest priority to transparency, placing it first among values discussed in the preamble to its Principles and Practices: "The one constant is transparency, and the need to conduct ourselves, our businesses, and our relationships with consumers in a fair, honest and forthright manner."[25] It goes on to say that advertisers need to make full disclosure to consumers, especially with regard to endorsements and testimonials, as well as decisions regarding personal privacy.

In public relations, transparency means letting the public know who sponsors and pays for the agency's public relations efforts. Agencies should also disclose when they have a financial interest, such as stock ownership, in a client's business. It means being forthright with clients as well, openly discussing prices, financing, special deals, and so on.

In journalism as well as business communication, being transparent includes *accountability*, standing behind one's work, explaining internal processes to the public, inviting criticism, and encouraging ethical dialog within the organization, as well as admitting mistakes and making corrections.

Summary

Numerous professional codes of ethics exist within the various fields of mass communication. Unfortunately, these guides for ethical behavior don't help professionals make ethical decisions or encourage independent ethical thinking; they usually cannot be broadly enforced.

Despite these problems, there are benefits with professional ethical codes. First, they help clarify minimum ethical standards for new members of professions. The second benefit of codes of ethics is that they articulate the ethical ideals of a profession—those values to which practitioners should aspire.

Codes in various mass communication professions emphasize a number of common ethical values, including:

- Interest in the public good
- Truth, honesty and accuracy
- Independence and avoiding conflicts of interest
- Privacy
- Confidentiality
- Fair competition
- Diversity and respect for others
- Transparency and accountability

These values represent the core of "good behavior" to which mass communication professionals aspire.

NOTES

[1] For example, separate codes for the Society of Professional Journalists, the American Society of News Editors, and the Radio Television Digital News Association among others.

[2] National Press Photographers Association. (n.d.). *NPPA code of ethics.* http://nppa.org/code-ethics

[3] Society of Professional Journalists. (2014, September 6). SPJ code of ethics. http://spj.org/ethicscode.asp

[4] One compromise might be to take the player's photo then add it as an inset. In this way, you might make her happy while still preserving the integrity of the original image.

[5] Meyer, P. (1987). *Ethical journalism: A guide for students, practitioners, and consumers.* Longman, 17–18.

[6] Black, J. and Barney, R.D. (1985). The case against media codes of ethics. *Journal of Mass Media Ethics, 1*(1), 27–36; p. 29.

[7] Ibid., 30.

[8] Pollack, S. (Producer and Director). (1981). *Absence of malice* [Motion Picture]. United States: Columbia Pictures.

[9] In fact, the Supreme Court reaffirmed the individual's First Amendment right to lie as recently as June 2012 when it struck down legislation that would have made it a crime to lie about possessing military honors, medals or awards.

10 Addley, E. (2011, June 12). Syrian lesbian blogger is revealed conclusively to be a married man. *The Guardian.* http://www.guardian.co.uk/world/2011/jun/13/syrian-lesbian-blogger-tom-macmaster

11 The University of Edinburgh, whose equipment McMaster used to make his blog posts while a student, did mandate that he write a letter promising he would not "engage in any further actions of this kind." Like an employer, the most the university could do was threaten removal from that institution.

12 Elliott-Boyle, D. (1985). A conceptual analysis of ethics codes. *Journal of Mass Media Ethics, 1*(1), 22–26. Elliott-Boyle talks about two ethical "standards," which are adapted somewhat for use here.

13 See, for example, Black and Barney (1985), 28, and Meyer (1985), 20.

14 Public Relations Society of America. (n.d.). *PRSA code of ethics.* https://www.prsa.org/about/ethics/prsa-code-of-ethics

15 Elliott-Boyle (1985), 23.

16 Institute for Advertising Ethics. (2020). Principles and practices for advertising Ethics. https://www.iaethics.org/principles-and-practices

17 Specifically the values described derive from ethical codes or statements of the American Association of Advertising Agencies, the American Advertising Federation, the Institute for Advertising Ethics, the American Marketing Association, the Canadian Public Relations Society, the Public Relations Society of America, the International Public Relations Association, the International Association of Business Communicators, the Associated Press Media Editors, the American Society of News Editors, the Society of Professional Journalists, the National Press Photographers Association, the Society for News Design, the Radio Television Digital News Association, and various codes aimed at bloggers.

18 National Press Photographers Association. (n.d.).

19 American Association of Advertising Agencies. (2016, October 14). 4A's standards of practice. https://www.aaaa.org/4as-standards-practice/

20 Radio Television Digital News Association. (2015, June 11). *Code of ethics and professional conduct.* https://www.rtdna.org/ethics

21 International Public Relations Association. (2020). *IPRA code of conduct.* https://www.ipra.org/member-services/code-of-conduct/

22 Society of Professional Journalists. (2014).

23 Associated Press Managing Editors. (1994). *Statement of news values and principles.* http://www.columbia.edu/itc/journalism/j6075/edit/ethiccodes/APME.html

24 American Marketing Association. (2021, October 11). AMA statement of ethics. https://myama.my.site.com/s/article/AMA-Statement-of-Ethics

25 Institute for Advertising Ethics. (2020).

7

Rendering
Ethical Judgments

In this chapter, you will learn about:
- Models of applied decision making in professional communication
- The three levels of justification in Bok's ethical decision-making framework
- Benefits and limitations of the Bok model
- The origin and structure of the Potter Box
- The Potter Box and ethical decision making
- Using the Potter Box in case study analysis

Up to this point we have been dealing with the "big picture" questions of ethics—what it means to be or to do good. Now the time has come to utilize what we have learned so that we may address specific ethical problems in the field of mass communication. This is the realm of *applied ethics*, the branch of ethical study dealing with the examination of right and wrong behavior (civic morality) in what might be called "real world" situations. Over time, various professions have adapted the study of applied ethics to their individual fields. For example, medical ethics deals with the kinds of problems faced by the health professions, such as stem cell research, cloning, reproductive issues, and how to communicate with the dying. Business ethics focuses on corporate responsibility, management concerns, fair trade practices, and the like. Mass communication ethics addresses issues of privacy, intellectual property, conflicts of interest, the public's right to know, and other matters of concern to communication professionals.

The study of applied ethics typically involves the examination of *case studies*, single incidents or a series of related incidents that require the reader to identify, analyze, and offer a solution to one or more ethical problems. In this chapter, we will explore models for evaluating ethical case studies. Because case studies require readers to make a reasoned argument for their ethical decisions, we will also explore a few techniques that aid in formulating and refuting ethical arguments.

Bok's Model of Ethical Justification

We began this book by pointing out that ethics rarely involves a clear choice between right and wrong. Instead, it typically forces one to resolve a *dilemma*—a difficult choice between alternatives. Imagine that you are working for an advertising company that adheres to the American Advertising Federation's code of ethics, which advocates a commitment to truth. Your client wants to film a television commercial at an ice cream parlor, but the ice cream keeps melting under the hot lights. Would it be ethically permissible to use a substitute, say mashed potatoes,[1] if it accurately conveys an image of how the ice cream would appear absent the special lighting?

In *Lying: Moral Choice in Public and Private Life*, Sissela Bok discusses such decisions.[2] She argues that choosing to lie, or by extension making any ethical choice, requires several levels of justification to pass what she calls the "test of publicity." Two fundamentals underlie her model: we must have empathy for the people involved in ethical decisions, and maintaining social trust is a fundamental goal.[3] Her three levels move from private to public, and all three levels must be addressed.

First Level of Justification. When deciding whether an ethical choice is the correct one, the first recourse should be one's own conscience.[4] Determining how one feels about the rightness of an action is the first step in weighing a decision.

Second Level of Justification. Seek advice from others. Consult friends, colleagues, and experts. Research similar cases to determine precedents. Are there alternatives that do not raise ethical questions?

Third Level of Justification. There should be an opportunity for public discussion. Invite participation and be open about the ethical decisions being rendered. Public deliberation by reasonable people is necessary for an ethical choice to meet the test of publicity.

Bok notes several benefits to her approach, such as cautioning those considering a career in professions that routinely face dilemmas regarding ethical choices. She does, however, point out some limitations in the justification model:

> While the test is a useful check on bias and rationalization, and thus helps us go beyond our immediate intuitive judgments, it is no more than a check. It is obviously of no avail in situations where the opportunity to reflect and to discuss is absent, as where immediate action is required. Nor does the test work well in moral quandaries which have no good answer, given our limited information, powers of reasoning and foreknowledge.[5]

During times of crisis when ethical decisions in mass communication must be made within minutes or hours, the publicity test has more theoretical than practical value as a decision-making aid. That is not to dismiss its value but rather to acknowledge that reality sometimes means the third level of justification will occur hypothetically.

Although time constraints might prohibit full implementation of Bok's levels of justification on a deadline, the model does an excellent job reminding the ethical decision maker of the need to reflect on the rightness of an action, the necessity of considering options, and the obligation to remain transparent throughout the decision-making process. The strength of Bok's model lies in the fact that it invites ethical discourse—from your conscience, your friends, your coworkers, those affected by the decision and, eventually, from anyone who might disagree with your choices.

The Potter Box

Harvard divinity student, Ralph Potter, Jr., wrote his dissertation on the relationship of Christian conscience to questions of nuclear arms policy in the United States. He developed a four-part analysis for analyzing the structure of ethical arguments that could be applied to a broad range of topics: (1) analyze the structure of ethical arguments presented, (2) trace ethical terms back to their philosophical roots, (3) determine the locus of primary loyalty, and (4) examine the derivation of a definition of the situation. "The four elements interpenetrate one another. They are analytically distinguishable but never separable."[6] His approach was based on a general theory of action by sociologist Talcott Parsons. "One cannot predict the content of any one category from knowledge of the others. For example, two commentators may stand firmly within the same theological tradition, employ the same ethical apparatus, agree upon the locus of ultimate commitment, but come to diverse policy views because of variations in the definition of the situation."[7]

Potter's work remained largely unknown outside of Harvard until the 1970s, when theological ethicist Glen Stassen adapted the analysis for his social theory model of ethical decision making. Stassen transformed Potter's four dimensions into four steps with directional arrows indicating how the elements worked together, how a judgment formed, and adding feedback to the process.[8] Since then, various forms of what has been labeled the Potter Box have been used to tackle ethical issues in everything from audiology[9] to business[10] to school lunches.[11] The Potter box facilitates "the careful consideration of multiple perspectives. It can be particularly useful in real-world professional dilemmas, because it helps the user consider the views and needs of all affected parties.[12] Nowhere has Potter's work seen more widespread use than in the field of mass communication and, more specifically, journalism.

Building on Stassen's work, media scholar Clifford Christians and his colleagues made significant changes to the Potter Box, adapting it for use in journalism ethics.[13] The resulting decision-making model (see figure 7.1) described four steps in rendering an ethical decision.[14] The user moves from one step to another and back again as needed until a defensible ethical decision emerges.

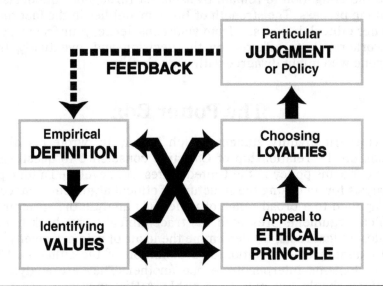

Figure 7.1   The Potter Box.

The Potter Box provides a framework for linking facts, values, principles, and loyalties to reach a justified decision. The two quadrants on the left side explain what actually happens. The two on the right side are concerned with what ought to happen. The left half of the box is descriptive, and the right half is normative. The model is cyclical, with the potential for continual expansion and feedback.

This version of the Potter Box has become the most commonly used ethical decision-making model in the field of mass communication ethics. However, scholars vary considerably in how they interpret steps in the process. For example, some define values as "the beliefs that you and your organization stand for."[15] Others see them as "societal values."[16] Still others say that the decision maker should identify "*his or her* most important values" [emphasis added].[17] A similar lack of consistency exists with regard to the "appeal to ethical principle" and "choosing loyalties." Should one consider multiple principles or select and apply a single principle? Are loyalties owed to values such as telling the truth[18] or to people?[19] Are loyalties owed to all or should you grant loyalty primarily or solely to "your most important stakeholder"[20] or to a single entity to whom or to which you are "ultimately loyal?"[21]

> A significant discovery is that reasonable and intellectually honest people who use the box may reach different ethical decisions, based on their individual input in each or all of the four quadrants. It is a linked system that asks you to think about an ethical decision in a logical order. The goal is not to force a choice, but to help you understand and ethically justify a decision.[22]

The Modified Potter Box

In an effort to guide professional communicators through the decision-making process, this text introduces a modified version of the Potter Box (see figure 7.2). First, the steps are reordered. Loyalties had been the fourth step; principle has replaced it as the final motivator of one's decision. Identifying loyalties is now an important early step of analysis—informing the decision but with principle driving the actual decision.

Second, the modified Potter Box includes details that might vary from earlier interpretations. Facts are objective and nonjudgmental. Loyalties are to specific people or groups, not to ethical values. Values are ethical and are ascertained from one's loyalties as well as the events that give rise to an ethical decision. Principle constitutes the reasoning for one's position, providing the argument that ultimately leads to a decision.

The modified Potter Box restructures the original steps into three fundamental dimensions: background, analysis, and argument.[23] The situation/facts step of previous versions constitutes the *background dimension*—an objective account of the events and individuals involved in the ethical dilemma. The loyalties and values steps combine to form the *analysis dimension*—inferences about who will be affected by the decision and what ethical values stand in competition with one another. The principle quadrant represents the *argument dimension*—the single principle chosen to provide logical reasoning for the decisions made regarding the loyalties and values

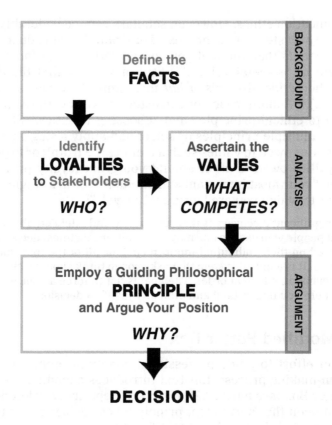

Figure 7.2 The Modified Potter Box.

previously identified. These three dimensions provide a progressive process for reaching a reasoned, defensible ethical decision. The process remains a series of four interactive steps:

Step One: Define the Facts of the Situation

Any ethical analysis of a decision-making situation must begin with an objective description of the facts that define that situation. The details of a specific case can range from quite simple to amazingly complex. The ethical decision maker must pare down all the details to the empirical facts most relevant to the case.

In practice, the facts step in the modified Potter Box analysis constitutes a brief narrative of the situation. It should include all pertinent details in a clear, concise form—just enough information to focus attention on the important concerns while avoiding extraneous elements that could clutter the discussion.

Step Two: Identify Loyalties to Stakeholders

Ethical decisions typically affect individuals other than our-selves.[24] This is the "who" of ethical decision making in the modi-fied Potter Box. We often use the term stakeholders to refer to any individuals or organizations potentially affected by an ethical deci-sion, especially those who stand to gain or lose from that decision. These stakeholders include people with whom the communications professional has some type of relationship in the ethical situation, such as advertiser/audience, marketer/client, journalist/source, and so on.

As the philosopher W. D. Ross noted, relationships often serve as a foundation for duties.[25] Duties morally obligate the professional communicator, depending on loyalties to the stakeholders involved. Imagine two podcasters preparing to interview a whistleblower who plans to leak information about a secret government project. The podcasters would have a loyalty to themselves, their audience, the source, the government and, ultimately, to the public. One could argue that they should also have a loyalty to other podcasters because their actions could be seen as reflecting on the industry as a whole.

We must also realize that different individuals will have differ-ent loyalties based on their personal relationships as well as their professional roles. In a situation where a journalist interviews a public relations representative about an executive's recent indis-cretion, the two communication professionals both have a loyalty to the executive, but those loyalties differ. The public relations rep-resentative has a loyalty to the executive as a client, which might involve trying to ensure that the executive appears in the most favorable light possible. The journalist has a loyalty to the execu-tive as a news subject, which might involve ensuring that the exec-utive has an opportunity to speak without regard to whether that portrays the executive favorably or unfavorably. Both are loyal to the executive according to their professional relationship with that individual, but the nature of the relationships affects both loyalty and potentially the outcome of any ethical decisions made.

Loyalty can be quite a powerful motivator in ethical decision making. As Potter noted, individuals "may invest meaning and give themselves over to a great variety of groups and causes. The identity of that which gives them their own identity and purpose is a most important determinant of moral reasoning."[26] Psychologist Geoffrey Cohen found that loyalty to a group can result in some members siding with their group on moral matters even when the objective content of the material contradicted the individual's ideological belief system. Moreover, Cohen said, individuals can make factual assumptions and moral conclusions without realizing that it was group influence, rather than their personal beliefs, that guided their decisions.[27] When making an ethical decision, we must be transparent about our loyalties and forthright about the reasoning behind our decision.

Step Three: Ascertain the Ethical Values

Values are desirable ethical goods. For example, "truth" is a value recognized by most professional communication organizations. An ethical situation involves a choice among values, some of which will conflict when making a decision. This conflict of values constitutes the core dilemma of the ethical problem being discussed. We may have an ethical reason for acting one way and an ethical reason for acting in one or more alternative ways. Thus, at least two ethical values are present; any conflict between those values necessitates an ethical choice. In a sense, ethical values are the "what" of ethical decision making in the modified Potter Box. What goods are we deciding between? The ethical decision maker must thus ascertain all the ethical values that pertain to the case in order to render a fully informed decision.

One benefit of identifying loyalties in the previous step is that, once identified, loyalties often help us ascertain many of the ethical values at stake. In the example we explored earlier, the podcasters' loyalty to their audience might include ensuring that the information provided by the whistleblower represents the truth (an ethical value). Their loyalty to the public might include ensuring that the information does not cause public harm (also an ethical value). They would also have values brought about by loyalties to their source, to themselves, to the government, and perhaps to others as well. Every stakeholder is owed some loyalty, and every loyalty has the potential for engendering one or more ethical values.

Step Four: Employ a Guiding Philosophical Principle

In the modified Potter Box, the term *principle* refers to a specific philosophy that provides justification for an ethical decision. The principle is the "why" of ethical decision making in the modified Potter Box.

Ethical principles provide the justification for your decision and explain how to resolve conflicts between values. A consequentialist might seek to resolve the conflict by attempting to maximize the good consequences. A deontologist might try to determine duty to a certain value or values. A virtue ethicist might seek a middle ground between competing values. Indeed, we could discuss many variations of these and countless other philosophical principles. Ultimately, we must identify and employ a single guiding philosophical principle to decide the case—the reason you have decided to choose one action over all others. While your decision might benefit the greatest number of people (utilitarianism) and also yourself (egoism), one of those is a secondary reason. Ultimately only one principle serves as the guiding principle behind the decision.

Once one has progressed through all the steps of the modified Potter Box, a decision should logically emerge from the deliberation. But is it *the* "right" decision? No—at least not in the sense that it is the one, true decision that somehow proves all other decisions wrong. Instead, if facts, loyalties, and values are complete and the principle well reasoned, we can say the result constitutes *a* right decision. By that we mean that it is an *ethically defensible decision*—a decision that recognizes one's loyalties and employs values that are logically connected by ethical reasoning to a well-justified conclusion. The goal of ethical analysis is to render such ethically defensible decisions.

Pinpointing Disagreement Using the Potter Box

In a 1972 follow up to his dissertation, Potter identified four potential sources of ethical disagreement roughly corresponding to the four dimensions of the Potter Box.[28] First, people can disagree about the facts of a situation. In describing a situation, ethical decision makers should stick to *empirical facts*, data that can be verified through investigation. Often the decision maker can move unconsciously into the area of *inferences*, conclusions based upon facts. If a piece of evidence is missing from a police investigation, we may cite that as a fact (something we can verify as true or false). To state that the police officer in charge lost the evidence constitutes an inference and should be avoided without ample direct evidence to support that claim. The same could be said of *judgments*, opinions drawn from facts and inferences. For example, one might conclude that the police officer in question had been "careless," thus making an evaluative statement, which would be difficult to verify. When examining an ethical case, one should stick to empirical facts. If disputes arise regarding the empirical facts of a case, Potter indicates that the parties involved might try to agree upon procedures for verifying those facts.

Loyalties are yet another source of disagreement among individuals, according to Potter. Consider the case (discussed in chapter 1) of Peter Jennings and Mike Wallace deciding what to do when witnessing a fictional North Kosanese ambush set up to kill American soldiers. Jennings initially felt his strongest loyalty should be with his adopted country and its soldiers. Wallace disagreed, preferring to offer his first loyalty to the profession of journalism. In each case, the journalist's ethical decision came down to a question of where his loyalty fell, which led to ascertaining different ethical values at stake in the case. Individual disagreements regarding loyalties sometimes can be difficult to resolve.

Ascertaining values can also lead to disagreement, which could be much more difficult to resolve. Take, for example, the value of "truth" to which most major communication organizations aspire. As we will see later in this text, not everyone agrees on the definition of the word "truth." If a photograph of a battlefield does not appear as smoke filled as the scene did in person, should it be published anyway? Should the photographer use image editing software to add more smoke so that the photograph better represents the battlefield as it appeared to observers at the time? Individuals might disagree as to which of those actions represents "truth," and they will have difficulty resolving their dispute.

Professional codes of ethics help to inform many disputes involving values and loyalties, but they are much less effective regarding the fourth source of possible disagreement. Potter refers to the mode of ethical reasoning, which he notes is "concerned with the procedures for defining relevant considerations and allotting them appropriate weight . . . the subject of the ethicist's expertise."[29] This mode of ethical reasoning corresponds to what we have referred to as principles. Disagreements based on differing principles are usually the most difficult to overcome.

Using the Potter Box in Case Study Analysis

Potter Box approaches can present some difficulty for those new to the study of ethics. To make analyzing case studies easier, we will break down some of the more common concerns in each step of the process.

Facts

1. *Be concise.* When listing the important facts of an ethical case study, it can be easy to go overboard in describing the situation. If a 32-year-old female editor of a suburban weekly newspaper with a circulation of approximately 53,000 faces an ethical dilemma, do you really need to describe her as such? Is it important to your analysis that she is 32, or a woman, or that the newspaper is suburban, or that it's a weekly, or that it has a circulation of approximately 53,000? If you can just say that a newspaper editor faces a dilemma, you will save a lot of time, space, and effort, focusing more attention on the facts that truly matter.

2. *Be complete.* Don't leave out important details. If the fact that the newspaper comes out only once a week plays a role

in your decision—for example, allowing a bit more time to verify details before publication—you must make sure to mention it. If you use a fact in your decision, be certain it appears in the facts section of your analysis. If not, go back, add it and go through the process again.

3. *Be objective.* Note that the modified Potter Box begins with an *objective* description of the situation. That means you should not offer a premature decision. You may have run through all four steps, but your reader has not. Offering a decision before proper analysis can be viewed as unreasoned prejudice. You should work to avoid all judgment, and therefore all judgmental language, at this stage of the analysis. Imagine that you are a newspaper reporter who must leave opinions out of an article. That's your task here.

Loyalties

4. *Remember yourself.* As Thomas à Kempis said, "wherever you go you take yourself with you."[30] Unless guided purely by altruism, you must recognize some loyalty to yourself. And even then, you should acknowledge your lack of such loyalty.

5. *Remember your professional duty.* A reporter, an editor, and a publisher might share many journalistic loyalties, but they also each have loyalties unique to their position within the organization. While I might possess loyalty to you as a fellow reporter and a friend, my loyalties as an editor might be different.

6. *Remember others.* Ethics is civic morality. It exists in large part to recognize our obligation and loyalty to others. Even many egoists would argue that a decision made entirely for your own benefit, without any regard to others whatsoever, can be difficult to defend ethically. Indeed, Nietzsche, who called egoism "the essence of a noble soul,"[31] conceded that others do have rights over us. Thus, we must be certain to examine our loyalty to others.

Values

7. *Identify more than one value.* If only one value is at stake, there's not much of a decision to make. Should I tell the truth? The answer will always be "yes," unless there is some justification not to tell the truth—some other ethical value at stake. If you worry about properly and thoroughly identifying values, consider reviewing an appropriate code of ethics that lists values endemic to the profession involved in the case.

8. *Identify a conflict of values.* Ethics involves a difficult choice between alternatives. If there is no conflict regarding values, no decision needs to be made. For example, public relations values advocating for one's client. Public relations also values acting in the public interest. If advocating for one's client serves the public interest—or at least does not affect the public interest—no conflict of values exists and therefore no ethical decision needs to be made. However, if a client demands that you act contrary to the public interest, you might face an ethical dilemma arising from a conflict of values.

9. *Observe the standards of necessity and sufficiency.* Every value you identify must be *necessary* to your analysis—either to justify your decision or as a potentially valid contradiction of your decision (i.e., the values of the hypothetical "other side" in your argument). You should not include unnecessary values in your analysis. Furthermore, all of the values discussed must, when taken together, be *sufficient* to justify your decision.

Principles

10. *Use principles that reflect your personal beliefs.* Do not choose a principle just because it conveniently fits the case in question. Instead choose the principle that best reflects your sense of moral goodness. Applying principles you believe in enables you to learn something about yourself. Your decision, in addition to being well reasoned, must align with your conscience.

11. *Be certain your principle leads logically to your conclusion.* It can be frustrating to work your way through a long ethical argument only to arrive at a conclusion that goes against your "gut reaction" to a case. When such dissonance occurs, the cause usually lies in the principle—the ethical reasoning—you used to reach your conclusion. If you employed the principle well, then you might need to reflect on your conscience. Does your "gut feeling" align with your core beliefs? Remember though that an ethical argument relies on logic, which is why decisions must be based on principle and not conscience alone.

12. *Stick to ethical principles.* Principles provide the reasoning for your argument—the "why" of your decision. "It makes good business sense" by itself doesn't cut it when rendering an ethical decision. Neither does "If I didn't do it someone else would." To render an ethical decision, you must use ethical principles.

Summary

Applied ethics involves the study of right and wrong behavior in real-world situations. Various professions adapt ethics for application to specific problems within their field. In mass communication, this covers privacy, intellectual property, conflicts of interest, the public's right to know, and a wide array of similar concerns. We examine these concerns by analyzing *case studies* that require the reader to offer a solution to one or more ethical problems.

Ethicist Sissela Bok argues that making ethical choices requires first an examination of one's own conscience, then discussion with friends/colleagues/experts, and finally deliberation with everyone potentially affected by the ethical decision. Given limitations of time, money, and other considerations, Bok's model must often be employed hypothetically. Its value lies in stressing the importance of discourse during the ethical decision-making process and transparency once a decision has been made.

The widely used Potter Box, created by Harvard theologian Ralph Potter Jr., proposes four steps in the process of ethical decision making. We have modified it for use here so that we can: (1) define the facts; (2) identify loyalties to people, institutions, and ideas; (3) ascertain the ethical values at stake; and (4) employ a philosophical principle to act as the mode of ethical reasoning. The modified Potter Box not only clarifies the decision-making process but also helps us recognize individual sources of ethical disagreement. When using the modified Potter Box in analyzing an ethical case, one develops a complete and concise description of facts, recognizes all pertinent loyalties, defines a conflict in values, and employs an ethical principle before offering a decision. In this way, one can hope to render a decision that—while it might not be universally accepted— will be recognized as well reasoned and ethically defensible.

NOTES

[1] Alan Pearcy notes that mashed potatoes are often substituted for ice cream in food photography. Indeed, the topping may be motor oil, which looks better on film than chocolate sauce. Pearcy, A. (2011). 8 tricks of the food photography trade. Ragan's PR Daily. http://www.prdaily.com/Main/Articles/8_tricks_of_the_food_photography_trade_7542.aspx.

[2] Bok, S. (1999). *Lying: Moral choice in public and private life.* New York: Pantheon Books, 90–106. Bok specifically mentions the mashed potato trick on page 85.

[3] Wilkins, L., Painter, C., & Patterson, P. (2022). *Media ethics: Issues and cases* (10th ed.) Rowman & Littlefield.

[4] Ibid., 94.

[5] Ibid., 100–101.

[6] Potter, R. B. (1965). *The structure of certain American Christian responses to the nuclear dilemma, 1958–1963.* (Doctoral dissertation.) Harvard University, 26. https://dash.harvard.edu/handle/1/32749952

7 Ibid., 267.

8 Stassen, G. H. (1977). A social theory model for religious social ethics. *The Journal of Religious Ethics, 5*(1), 9–37.

9 Hosford-Dunn, H., Roeser, R. J. and Valenta, M. (2000). *Audiology: Practice management*. Thieme, 212.

10 Smith, B. (1998). Ethics of Du Pont's CFC strategy 1975–1995. *Journal of Business Ethics, 17*(5), 557–568.

11 Miura, M. R., Smith, J. A., and Alderman, J. (2007). Mapping school food: A policy guide. http://www.phaionline.org/wp-content/uploads/2007/11/mappingschoolfood.pdf

12 Ibid., 35.

13 Peck, L.A. (2001). Beyond war stories: Clifford Christians' influence on the training of future journalists, 1976–1984. Paper presented to the Association for Education in Journalism and Mass Communication.

14 Christians, C. G., Fackler, M., Richardson, K. B., & Kreshel, P. (2020). *Media ethics: Cases and moral reasoning* (11th ed.). Routledge, 5.

15 Swain, K. (1994). Beyond the Potter Box: A decision model based on moral development theory. Paper presented to the Media Ethics Division of the Association for Education in Journalism and Mass Communication, 4. http://www.academia.edu/download/30734007/beyond_the_potter_box.doc

16 Fink, C. (1995). *Media ethics*. Allyn & Bacon, 9.

17 Peck, L.A. and Reel, G. (2016). *Media ethics at work: True stories from young professionals* (2nd ed.). CQ Press, 38.

18 Wilkins et al. (2022), 106.

19 Roberts, C., & Black, J. (2022). *Doing ethics in media: Theories and practical applications* (2nd ed.). Routledge, 65.

20 Kirtley, J. & Ison, C. (2016). *Media ethics today: Issues, analysis, solutions*. Cognella, 11.

21 Gordon, D., Kittross, J. M., Merrill, J. C., Babcock, W., & Dorsher, M. (2011). *Controversies in media ethics* (3rd ed.). Routledge.

22 Roberts & Black (2022), p. 65.

23 At the most basic level this bears some resemblance to Louis Day's SAD Formula (Situation-Analysis-Decision). Day, L. A. (2006). *Ethics in media communications: Cases and controversies* (5th ed.). Cengage Learning.

24 Many ethicists would include animals as well. See, for example, Regan, T. and Singer, P. (Eds.). (1989). *Animal rights and human obligations* (2nd ed.). Prentice-Hall. However, professional communication only rarely involves such dilemmas.

25 Ross, D. (2002). *The right and the good*. (P. Stratton-Lake, Ed.). Clarendon Press. (Original work published 1930).

26 Potter, R. B. (1972). The logic of moral argument. In P. Deats (Ed.), *Toward a discipline of social ethics: Essays in honor of Walter George Muelder* (pp. 93–114). Boston University Press, 109.

27 Cohen, G. L. (2003). Party over policy: The dominating impact of group influence on political beliefs. *Journal of Personality and Social Psychology. 85*(5), 808–822.

28 Potter. (1972), 109–110.

29 Potter. (1972), 109.

30 à Kempis, T. (1940). *The imitation of Christ*. (A. Croft and H. Bolton, Trans.). The Bruce Publishing Company, 38. (Original work published ca. 1400). http://www.copticplace.com/files/imitation_of_Christ.pdf

31 Nietzsche, F. (1886). *Beyond good and evil* (H. Zimmern, Trans.) Project Gutenberg, 265. https://www.gutenberg.org/files/4363/4363-h/4363-h.htm

8

Freedom, Responsibility, and the Public Interest

In this chapter, you will learn about:
- Limitations on the First Amendment
- Potential implied duties of the First Amendment
- Differing interpretations of freedom and responsibility
- Demands of and for a "socially responsible" press
- Ethical ideals of traditional, civic, citizen, and advocacy journalism
- Public relations, advocacy, and the marketplace of ideas
- Advertising, the economy, and the interests of consumers and the public
- The role of "intent" in serving the public interest

In democracies and representative republics, the people rule. They ultimately make or at least consent to the decisions that govern society. While citizens of the United States might not individually vote on a bill in Congress, their representatives do. If representatives consistently or dramatically thwart the will of the citizenry, those citizens can vote to remove them from office.

To govern themselves, citizens must possess the information necessary to make effective decisions about their own welfare and that of others in their society. Mass communication plays a vital role. As the French historian Alexis de Tocqueville observed in his classic *Democracy in America*:

> When the right of every citizen to a share in the government of society is acknowledged, everyone must be presumed to be able to choose between the various opinions of his contemporaries and to appreciate the different facts from which inferences may be drawn. The sovereignty of the people and the liberty of the press may therefore be regarded as correlative, just as the censorship of the press and universal suffrage are two things which are irreconcilably opposed, and which cannot long be retained among the institutions of the same people.[1]

With more than 330 million people, the United States is the third most populous country in the world. Enabling so many people to govern themselves requires not only that they have access to information but also that they be able to communicate with one another as well as with their elected representatives. It requires mass communication.

The First Amendment

The First Amendment to the United States Constitution offers specific protections to both communication (freedom of speech) and mass communication (freedom of the press). These protections are not absolute. For example, they exclude libel, child pornography, incitement, and other forms of speech deemed contrary to the public good. However, the Constitution upholds the basic position that freedom of speech and of the press are broad rights. Freedom is the rule, and censorship is the rare exception.

Until the mid-1970s *commercial speech*—economic speech on behalf of an individual or corporation aimed at turning a profit—did not receive substantial protection under the First Amendment.[2] Because the government had a right to regulate commerce, legislators believed it made sense that commercial speech could be similarly regulated. A series of Supreme Court decisions beginning in 1973 gradually expanded First Amendment protection for commercial speech. However, certain limitations remain, giving the government much more latitude to regulate advertising and commercial speech than other forms of communication such as political and religious speech.[3]

While there is broad agreement that advertising clearly lies within the realm of commercial speech, the same cannot be said of public relations. Because it usually does not propose a commercial transaction—often a defining feature of commercial speech—public relations falls into something of a grey area. Consumer activist Marc Kasky decided to challenge the limits of that grey area when he filed a lawsuit against the Nike corporation alleging that the company engaged in "false advertising" through a public relations campaign in which it defended itself against allegations of unfair labor practices.

Nike had been the subject of allegations of unsafe factories and underpaid workers in Southeast Asia.[4] The company commissioned an independent review of its operations, which concluded the charges against Nike were largely unwarranted. Nike publicized the results through press releases, letters to newspapers, letters to university presidents and athletic directors, and full-page advertisements. In 1998, Kasky sued Nike under California's unfair competition and false advertising laws alleging Nike made false statements about working conditions in Southeast Asian factories.

Nike held that its press releases, letters to the editor. and image-oriented advertisements were protected under the First Amendment. Kasky argued that the campaign constituted commercial speech because Nike had been attempting to influence consumer decision making. The California Supreme Court in 2002 sided with Kasky.[5] Nike appealed to the U.S. Supreme Court. The justices there agreed to review the case, but then sent it back to a lower court without ruling on the issue. Kasky and Nike subsequently settled out of court, leaving the California Supreme Court ruling in place. As a result, constitutional protection for public relations speech remains a subject of debate at the national level.

A Free or Responsible Press?

While advertising and, perhaps, public relations possess less freedom of speech, this is not true of journalism. However, the fact that news media receive special protection under the First Amendment's "freedom of the press" clause has caused some to argue that they also bear a unique ethical responsibility to society. The American Society of News Editors reflects this view in its preamble.

> The First Amendment, protecting freedom of expression from abridgment by any law, guarantees to the people through their press a constitutional right, and thereby places on newspaper people a *particular responsibility*. Thus, journalism demands of its practitioners not only industry and knowledge but also the pursuit of a standard of integrity proportionate to the journalist's *singular obligation* [emphases added].[6]

Christians et al. echo that sentiment in their media ethics text, pointing out that enlightened news leaders recognize that they have a special obligation because the First Amendment uniquely protects the press.[7] To paraphrase Uncle Ben in the movie *Spider-Man*, with great freedom comes great responsibility.

The idea of rules for a socially responsible press flows from the work of the Commission on the Freedom of the Press, chaired by Robert Hutchins, who was then president of the University of Chicago. After four years of consideration, the commission in 1947 determined that the press has an ethical duty to operate in a socially responsible manner and to strive to produce the greatest good for the public. The commission conceded ethical limitations on the media's First Amendment rights, noting for example that lying—either deliberately or carelessly—should not merit constitutional protection. The commission issued five standards that the press should provide.

1. A truthful, comprehensive, and intelligent account of the day's events in a context which gives them meaning.

2. A forum for the exchange of comment and criticism.

3. The projection of a representative picture of the constituent groups of society.

4. The presentation and clarification of the goals and values of the society.

5. Full access to the day's intelligence.[8]

Worried that the people might decide to strip the press of its freedom, the commission concluded that media should regulate themselves and accept an ethical responsibility to act in the public interest.

Others disagree, perhaps none so assiduously as media ethicist John Merrill who wrote in *The Imperative of Freedom* that the First Amendment places no overt responsibility on the press. Those who imply such a responsibility mistakenly conflate two separate and distinct concepts. Yes, Merrill says, citizens in any democratic society depend on truthful information to govern themselves. And, yes, the First Amendment guarantees freedom of the press. But the press freedom does not imply press responsibility. Indeed, placing a responsibility on the press to provide information to the citizenry implies that failure to do so could or even should result in a loss of press freedom. Merrill believes nothing could be further from the truth.

> For quite simply, the press is free and autonomous or it is not; and, of course, if it is regulated, controlled or directed from without (even in the name of "democratic utilitarianism"), it has ceased being free and autonomous.[9]

Given that the First Amendment mentions only freedom, Merrill concludes that the news media have no obligation to be socially responsible. Moreover, those who seek to impose such a responsibility would place limitations on the freedom of the press.

Libertarian thinkers such as Merrill decry many of the tenets of professional journalism organizations as mere platitudes that rob individuals of their right to self-determination.[10] The people do not have a "right to know." If they did, someone would be *required* to provide such information. That simply is not the case. The people don't have a right of free access to the press. Instead, as American journalist A.J. Liebling famously said, "freedom of the press is guaranteed only to those who own one."[11] The press is not a fourth branch of government; neither is it a watchdog on government. In fact, it has nothing to do with the government unless it so chooses. Merrill calls such ideas myths intended to inculcate would-be journalists into a kind of hive mentality to which they should offer resistance rather than surrender.

Many journalists *choose* to act for the public good. Many encourage their colleagues to do the same. But to demand that news media operate for the public good—to suggest that journalists have an obligation that arises merely from engaging in mass communication—robs the press of its freedom. Merrill encourages journalists to realize that freedom is in and of itself an ethical good. Accepting a responsibility to act for the public good, like most responsibilities, requires one to surrender a piece of one's freedom. Many professional organizations and many employers ask this of journalists, but it should not be considered an obligation inherent to freedom of the press.

Journalism and Social Responsibility

If a journalist chooses to accept responsibility to act in the public's interest, as many do, the question then arises—just what is in the public's interest? Duty to society "is an increasingly important dimension of applied ethics and has been highlighted for the media under the term *social responsibility*. Questions of privacy and confidentiality, for example, nearly always encounter claims about society's welfare over that of a particular person."[12]

What should a journalist do to serve the public? How should a journalist behave to be socially responsible? While this is a matter of personal decision, and indeed many journalists differ on the answers, various codes of ethics help point to some of the values one should consider.

Support and defend free speech. One can have neither democracy nor a free press without freedom of speech. It is the prime value in journalism and must be defended.

Support and defend freedom of the press. The benefit of free speech remains limited if it cannot be communicated through a mass medium. Journalists should guard against all threats to press freedom, both governmental and private. People do not have a First Amendment right to post something on your door, in your newspaper, or on your website. But they do have a right to post it on their own. Freedom of the press—the freedom to utilize one's own resources to engage in mass communication—is guaranteed to the people and not limited to members of the media. Today that extends to people running their own web page as much as it does to the *New York Times*.

Provide information to the public. To make decisions, the public requires information. Many journalists assume responsibility for providing this information. Many journalistic codes of ethics have asserted in some way that "news" must be impartial and free from bias. Subjective judgments, they argue, should be reserved for editorial or opinion columns and clearly distinguished from "straight news" and even features. Journalists welcome a responsibility not just to the citizenry but also to future generations for whom they attempt to document history as it happens.

Serve as the people's watchdog. Many journalists accept a responsibility to serve as a watchdog on government, as well as on other powerful forces in society. To this end, professional organizations encourage journalists to uphold transparency in government by supporting *sunshine laws*, laws that compel the government to make decisions in the public eye and allow the public access to most governmental records.

Advocate for the people. Beyond ensuring the flow of information to the public, some journalists maintain a responsibility to serve as critics of the government and of the private sector, as well as to advocate for "needed reform and innovation in the public interest."[13]

Traditional and Civic Journalism

A journalist who chooses to serve the public interest must decide how to achieve that goal. Traditionally, journalists have prided themselves on being objective chroniclers with a duty to provide impartial information. This idea of journalistic objectivity dates back to at least 1833 when the *New York Sun* became the first "penny newspaper"—not only representing a significant discount in the cost of newspapers but also a change in editorial policies.[14] Where before the press had largely consisted of highly partisan newspapers that focused on commercial and political news, the *Sun* launched a trend toward independent news organizations that began to write more about crime and other sometimes sensational news stories in an effort to draw a broader audience.

Though born at least in part to increase readership (and therefore advertising rates), objectivity retains a hallowed place in many journalistic codes. Often it appears under the guise of calls for impartiality, independence, and dispassion as well as a lack of bias, political involvement, or other interests that might conflict with a devotion to objectivity. Not all agree with the idea that the press should revere the value of objectivity. A survey by Pew Research Center found that over half (55%) of U.S. journalists say that every side does not always deserve equal coverage, compared to 76% of U.S. adults who said journalists should always strive to give each side equal coverage.[15]

Some criticize objectivity as an impossible goal, given that human beings are subjective creatures who each see the world from a unique viewpoint. A tall person experiences the world differently from a short person. Significant identity factors such as race, gender, age, religion, nationality, and other characteristics influence one's worldview. Is it possible to separate these influences, as well as the totality of life experience, from one's reporting? Others worry that the objectivity norm leads journalists to merely accept what they are told and report it rather than push for a fuller version of the truth. Still others complain that objectivity inherently favors a more conservative or capitalistic view and serves as little more than a smokescreen that "creates a sense of impartial coverage while hiding alternative, especially labor, critiques, maintaining racist hierarchies, and promoting White interests."[16] With these and other concerns in mind, some journalists have sought an alternative to objectivity as a guide to serving the public interest.

Beginning in the mid-1990s and peaking in the early 2000s, a movement emerged encouraging journalists to become dynamic participants in their communities. *Civic journalism* (or public journalism) involves going beyond traditional objective journalism in an effort to play a significantly more active role in the community. Civic journalism places additional responsibilities on journalists to connect with the community, work to strengthen civic culture, and encourage citizens to take charge of their political future. Rather than act as neutral observers, journalists should take steps to make democracy work and to rebuild public life.

Like objectivity, civic journalism emerged from a desire to increase the economic standing of newspapers. In the words of Davis "Buzz" Merritt, one of the leading proponents of civic journalism:

> The economic bases, primarily advertising, of the business structures that support journalism are struggling against rapidly expanding competition. It is no coincidence that the decline in journalism and the decline in public life have happened at the same time. In modern society, they are codependent: Public life needs the information and perspective that journalism can provide, and journalism needs a viable public life because without one, there is no need for journalism.[17]

People who vote and are otherwise active in politics tend to be more likely to subscribe to a newspaper. Increasing political interest and participation should result in an increase in newspaper readership.

Civic journalism enjoyed a fair amount of popularity through the turn of the twenty-first century due to the efforts of Merritt and journalists at other midsized newspapers, as well as more than a few academics. However, newspaper readership continued to decline, limiting the resources that could be devoted to experimental projects such as civic journalism. As a result, the movement has gradually dwindled.

Citizen Journalism and Advocacy Journalism

As the idea of civic journalism faded, proponents redirected their attention to a trend emerging because of increased Web use—*citizen journalism*, which some referenced as "public journalism 2.0."[18] Also called participatory journalism, citizen journalism encourages citizens to play an active role, going beyond occasionally serving as subjects or sources and instead taking part in reporting, analyzing, and disseminating the news.

Citizen journalism outlets largely fell short of offering a true alternative to newspapers, television stations, radio, and online counterparts. For example, a 2009 study concluded that the top 60 citizen websites and bloggers were not filling the information shortfall that resulted from cutbacks in traditional media. While there were some interesting and positive results, citizen journalists lacked the financial resources and business experience to make their websites viable over time.[19] Much of what was called citizen journalism took the form of social media posts and occasional video shot by participants or chance eyewitnesses to news events. However, "Journalism processes can be reimagined, even in the face of daunting circumstances, and the needs and agency of communities may be centered to open pathways for journalism to be a means to larger ends of connection and problem solving."[20] *Solutions journalism* refers to a journalist not only reporting on social problems but also rigorously reporting on responses to them. *Engaged journalism* refers to the practices that build relationships between the public and journalists and involves citizens in the cocreation of journalism.

News organizations were slow to realize the potential of involving citizens early in the reporting process. Typically, citizens became engaged after a story was published, which then prompted comments on social media platforms.[21] Journalist Jennifer Brandel started a program called Curious City for Chicago's WBEZ radio station, which shifted the traditional journalism model by asking listeners what they wanted to know and leveraged the power of a newsroom to supply answers. The public submits questions and votes on which questions the station should answer. Citizens become the driving force behind the stories produced, which makes them feel more invested and more likely to share stories. "With public-powered journalism, professionals continue to do the good work they've always done—reporting, verifying, and synthesizing complex information—but audiences are regarded not only as recipients but as resources to inspire and inform the work they do."[22] Brandel founded Hearken, a company that provides technology and consulting services for public-powered journalism.[23]

ProPublica has a history of involving the public in its reporting. Callouts on the website invite users to submit experiences that inform investigations.[24] Reporters at the *Guardian* became curious about the number of police killings in the United States. There was no reliable database for that information until the *Guardian* launched The Counted in 2015. The public contributes by helping journalists scour local news sources for death reports that don't make national headlines. Newsrooms now recognize that engaging citizens is the key to survival. Involving the public in the reporting process can generate leads, test the potential of a story, enhance reporting, and lead to growth."

A special issue of *Journalism Practice* looked at participatory journalism in newsrooms, classrooms, and beyond.[25] The focus was on understanding citizens as potential producers of news in terms of their interactions with mainstream and other forms of news media, their attitudes and motivations, and effective training for the most marginalized to develop their voices. One issue raised was the ethics of putting citizen reporters in danger as they attempt to cover hard-to-access news.

> Citizen participation in the production of news, whatever it is labeled (citizen journalism, participatory journalism, engagement, etc.), has created new approaches in newsrooms, journalism training projects, and journalism research. . . . Whether pessimists are correct that corporations have already normalized and tamed the threat to their authority or the optimists who present evidence of ever-more sophisticated professional-amateur collaboration does not matter so much as our acceptance that the relationships are, and will permanently remain, fluid and contingent for the foreseeable future.[26]

Some critics complain that civic journalism and, for the most part, citizen journalism are really examples of *advocacy journalism*, a form of journalism that endeavors to be fact based but does not necessarily separate editorial opinion from news coverage. In contrast to journalism that is studiously neutral, advocacy journalism explicitly takes a point of view. "The dominance of objectivity as a journalistic norm means that insufficient attention has been given to the contribution of advocacy journalism (and opinion-driven journalism more generally) to democracy and public life."[27] Advocacy journalists distinguish the "good guys" from the "bad guys" and express opinions about an issue rather than observing and recording events.[28] They often position themselves against what they see as "the moral failings of Western governments."[29] They cite community members and critique or ignore dominant discourses from government and academic experts.[30] Indeed, progressive or liberal agendas are often thought to characterize advocacy journalism.[31] This should not come as a surprise given arguments that objective journalism favors a more conservative viewpoint.[32]

Advocacy is a particularly sensitive issue in environmental journalism. The Society of Environmental Journalists (SEJ) states that its mission is to strengthen the quality, reach, and viability of journalism that advances public understanding of environmental issues. Many mainstream environmental writers view concepts such as impartiality and balance as barriers to truth rather than keys to it. Teya Ryan, a founding member of SEJ, has argued against balanced reporting of environmental issues such as climate change.

> The net result has been confusion among the American people. Who is right? With a "balanced" report the audience is left with more questions than answers. There are some in the environmental community [who believe] we are wasting precious time creating this kind of confusion.[33]

Climate reporter Julia Drapkin launched iSeeChange to involve ordinary people at every stage of the climate reporting process.

> It's a departure from citizen journalism, which leaves reporting in the hands of well-intentioned amateurs, and user-generated content, which casts journalists as curators over material of widely varying quality and reliability. This approach treats audiences as collaborators in a professional managed reporting process, deepening audience involvement and even improving the quality of stories reporters produce.[34]

Some specialized news organizations have had no concerns about engaging in advocacy journalism. For example, the former *Coast & Valley Drum News* prided itself on what it calls Russwurmian advocacy journalism, which is African centered and compels the newspaper to focus its attention on "positive news stories that showcase African American leaders, communities, and organizations throughout the Central Valley."[35] True advocacy journalism like this upholds the virtues of accuracy and transparency, but it does not attempt to be objective in either the kind of news it chooses to cover or the way it covers that news.

Public Relations, Business Communication, and the Public Interest

While the idea of advocacy continues to provoke much hand-wringing in journalism, no such conflict exists in public relations, where practitioners almost universally view themselves first and foremost as advocates for their clients. Like journalists, public relations professionals rely heavily on freedom of speech guarantees. But unlike most journalists, they do not embrace a "special responsibility" to provide objective information, serve as a watchdog on government, or actively promote the public's interest. Instead, organizations such as the Public Relations Society of America (PRSA) assert that merely exercising their rights of free speech on behalf of their clients serves the public interest.

Business traditionally places great importance on the power of the free market to determine the value of products. Good products—products that solve a problem or fulfill a need—become successful. Bad products fail and disappear. In such an environment, the more products that exist, the greater the amount of choice for the public and the greater the chance that good products will emerge.

Now imagine instead a *marketplace of ideas*, a rhetorical bazaar where interested parties can openly present facts and arguments, allowing ideas to compete with one another in the belief that truth will eventually emerge victorious. In such an environment, the public theoretically benefits from encouraging everyone to come forth and have their say. More facts and opinions mean that we have more information and a greater opportunity to discover the truth. This concept dates to the English poet John Milton who argued that truth would always win out against falsehood in a free and open debate.[36] Rather than censor ideas with which we disagree, Milton suggested, we should encourage discussion and trust that truth will win out in the end.

Public relations embraces this view. PRSA argues that by serving as advocates for their clients, public relations professionals "provide a voice in the marketplace of ideas, facts, and viewpoints to aid informed public debate."[37] Accurate information allows the public to make better decisions not only about their government but also about everything from charitable causes to consumer products. Public relations professionals who advocate for their clients thus serve not only the interest of their clients but also the public.

While public relations organizations remain steadfast in their defense of free speech and the free flow of information in the marketplace of ideas, their values become a bit less clear when facing an ethical dilemma in which the client's desires are at odds with the public interest. For example, PRSA notes that "We are faithful to those we represent, while honoring our obligation to serve the public interest."[38] Journalism claims only one loyalty—the public. The ethical struggle of journalism lies in how best to serve the public's interest. By contrast, public relations maintains two loyalties— the client and the public. But what does one do when the client's interests appear to conflict with those of the public?

Public relations organizations would answer that question by asserting that even when a client's interests appear to conflict with the public's interests, advocating on behalf of that client would still serve the public provided that the communication is ethical— accurate, fair, honest, and transparent. Consider a case in which a client wants to situate a new natural gas extraction business on land currently occupied by a public park. While extremely lucrative for the client, the business is not expected to generate many benefits, economic or otherwise, for the local community. Clearly, it would not be in the public's interest. Yet even in a case such as this, professional organizations would say that public relations serves the public. Much like an attorney who represents a client he or she knows to be guilty, public relations practitioners who advocate on behalf of their clients ethically serve the process—free and open communication—and thus serve the public.

A PRSA Board of Ethics and Practice Standards (BEPS) handbook recommends that practitioners reflect on eight questions before acting: (1) Am I going to violate any laws?; (2) Am I going to violate any core ethical values such as honesty, fairness, and civility?; (3) Do I have all the facts I need?; (4) Could I live in a world where everybody did what I am about to do?; (5) How would I feel if what I am about to do was featured on the first page of tomorrow's paper?; (6) How would I feel if someone did to me what I am about to do to others?; (7) What would my mother say or think?; (8) Am I already thinking about a justification or an excuse for what I am about to do?[39]

Communication professor Kathy Fitzpatrick advises: "The bottom line for PR professionals operating in a democratic marketplace of ideas in which truth and transparency are imperative for effective governance is to be sure that our work contributes to— rather than interferes with—informed decision making.[40] Fitzpatrick offers a six-step guide for ethical decision making: (1) define the specific ethical issue; (2) identity factors that may influence the decision; (3) identify key values; (4) identify the parties affected by the decision and the obligation to each; (5) select ethical principles to guide the decision-making process; (6) make a decision.[41] Compare her guide to the Potter box discussed in chapter 7.

Advertising, Marketing, and the Public Interest

Where public relations professionals value their role as advocates in the marketplace of ideas, advertising and marketing organizations stress their importance in the traditional marketplace of goods and services. Indeed, the first line of the standards of practice of the American Association of Advertising Agencies states: "We hold that a responsibility of advertising agencies is to be a constructive force in business."[42] The American Marketing Association holds a similar position, noting in its statement of ethics that "we not only serve our organizations but also act as stewards of society in creating, facilitating, and executing the transactions that are part of the greater economy."[43] In the eyes of their professional organizations, advertising and marketing serve the public by helping to connect businesses and consumers, by promoting commerce, and by contributing to the economic health of society.

The World Federation of Advertisers notes the benefits of advertising in three key areas.[44] *Economic benefits* result from advertising that promotes competition, which provides consumers with options for goods and services and also increases quality and lowers prices as businesses vie to attract consumers. There are *employment benefits* as advertising provides millions of jobs—whether in the advertising industry itself or in media and online businesses funded by advertising. *Social benefits* result from advertising funding or partially funding media services from news to entertainment; supporting media plurality is fundamental to democratic freedoms.

Public service announcements (PSAs) are free messages that advertise services or programs offered by governmental or nonprofit organizations or communicate other messages intended to serve the public interest. Many are developed with the help of the Ad Council, a private, nonprofit organization that coordinates pro bono services from many of the nation's top advertising agencies to generate public service announcements. Beneficiaries of PSAs include the American Heart Association, the American Cancer Association, the Peace Corps, and the U.S. Army.

Some of the ethical questions in advertising arise over perpetuation of gender, racial, and sexual stereotypes; deception in messages; the susceptibility of children; and the promotion of tobacco, alcohol, and pharmaceuticals, Ethical advertising is important to consumers and to a marketplace economy. Ethical advertising should be honest, accurate, fair, and strive for human dignity in its messages and the consumer experience.[45]

Intentions of the Actor

Journalism, public relations, and advertising doubtless serve a variety of public interests. But does that make them ethical? Do people enter the field of public relations to serve the public interest? When a public relations professional advocates on behalf of a client, does he or she truly do so out of a desire to serve as a source of information in the marketplace of ideas? Do students enter the advertising field because of a desire to promote the economy and the public good? When creating an ad campaign, do advertising professionals focus on the benefits to the consumer or solely on the benefits to themselves and their clients? For that matter, do journalists enter their profession and perform their daily functions out of a desire to serve the public, either as partisan advocates or objective truth seekers?

One cannot be ethical by accident. Neither can ethics occur merely as a side effect of one's professional actions. We may not agree completely with Kant that good will alone is sufficient to render an action ethical, but it is certainly necessary. Whether one seeks to do one's duty, to maximize positive consequences, or to achieve a proper state of being, intent matters. While it is certainly possible for journalism, public relations, advertising, and most other professions to serve the public interest, being ethical requires a specific *intention* to do the right thing. Ethics must be the prime motivation behind actions. This ideal lies at the core of the ethical justifications offered by most professional organizations in the field of mass communication.

Summary

Democracies and representative republics rely on an informed citizenry to operate properly. Some journalists and press critics contend that this constitutes the reason that the First Amendment specifically protects freedom of the press—and places specific responsibility on the press to operate in the public's interest. Others argue that the Constitution protects freedom of the press as a public good in and of itself. Journalists can choose to use that freedom for the public good, for pure entertainment, or simply as a profit-seeking enterprise. The existence of a free press represents a public good, regardless of how the press uses that freedom.

Those who believe that journalists have an obligation to act in the public interest differ on how best to do so. Traditional journalism suggests that journalists be objective observers and impartial reporters of information. Civic journalism takes a different tack, arguing that journalists have a responsibility to serve as more than spectators and should instead play an active role in helping the community solve its problems. Citizen journalism takes this one step further, encouraging members of the community to join in the process by gathering, analyzing, and reporting the news in conjunction with or independent of professional journalistic institutions. Traditional journalists complain that civic journalism and, for the most part, citizen journalism are really examples of advocacy journalism, which endeavors to be fact based but does not separate editorial opinion from news coverage.

While the issue of advocacy is a subject of debate in journalistic circles, public relations professionals embrace the concept. They see themselves as serving the public interest by acting as advocates for their clients and providing information in the marketplace of ideas. Like public relations, advertising relies on advocacy on behalf of clients. However, advertising professionals see themselves as providing a valuable service to the public through the marketplace of goods and services—improving the economy, creating jobs, and funding the media as well as promoting government and nonprofit endeavors.

Regardless of the public benefits that each of these industries can generate, practitioners must remember that ethics does not occur by accident. Ethics requires the intent to behave ethically. Ethical practitioners should be motivated to serve the public in the performance of their professional duties.

NOTES

[1] de Tocqueville, A. (1899). *Democracy in America*. (H. Reeve, Trans; original work published 1835). http://xroads.virginia.edu/~hyper/detoc/1_ch11.htm

[2] Mazur, M. (2005). Commercial speech and the First Amendment in the 21st century: Does the Nike test help to keep corporations honest? *Business Law Journal*, 5(9). http://blj.ucdavis.edu/archives/vol-5-no-2/Commercial-Speech-and-the-First-Amendment.html

[3] Bhagwat, A. (2011). A brief history of the commercial speech doctrine (with some implications for tobacco regulation). *Hastings Science and Law Journal*, 2(1), 105–106. http://hstlj.org/wp-content/uploads/2011/08/v2i1bhaghwat.pdf

[4] Stevens, J. (2003, June 26). Nike, Inc., et al., Petitioners v. Marc Kasky, Supreme Court of the United States, on writ of certiorari to the Supreme Court of California, No. 02—575. https://www.law.cornell.edu/supct/html/02-575.ZC.html

[5] *Kasky v. Nike Inc.* Supreme Court of California, No. S087859, decided May 2, 2002. https://caselaw.findlaw.com/ca-supreme-court/1245242.html

[6] American Society of News Editors. (2002. *Statement of principles*. http://www.unm.edu/~pubboard/ASNE%20Statement%20of%20Principles.pdf

[7] Christians, C. G., Fackler, M., Richardson, K. B., & Kreshel, P. (2020). *Media ethics: Cases and moral reasoning* (11th ed.). Routledge.

[8] The Commission on Freedom of the Press. (1947). *A free and responsible press: A general report on mass communication: Newspapers, radio, motion pictures, magazines, and books* (R. D. Leigh, Ed.). University of Chicago Press, 21–28.

[9] Merrill, J.C. (1974). *The imperative of freedom*. Hastings House, 31.

[10] Merrill himself argues that to even consider journalism a "profession" encourages groupthink and conformity at the expense of individuality and freedom.

[11] Liebling, A. J. (1960, May 14). The wayward press: Do you belong in journalism? *The New Yorker*, 109.

[12] Christians et al. (2020), p. 30.

[13] Associated Press Managing Editors. (1994). Statement of ethical principles. http://www.columbia.edu/itc/journalism/j6075/edit/ethiccodes/APME191.html

[14] Mindich, D. T. Z. (1998). *Just the facts: How objectivity came to define American journalism*. New York University Press, 16–18.

[15] Forman-Katz, N., & Jurkowitz, M. (2022, July 13). U.S. journalists differ from the public in their views of "bothsidesism" in journalism. Pew Research Center.

[16] Oh, D. C. (2010). Complementary objectivity and ideology: Reifying white capitalist hierarchies in *Time* magazine's construction of Michelle Rhee. *Journal of Communication Inquiry, 34*(2), 151–157.

[17] Merritt, D. B. (1998). *Public journalism and public life: Why telling the news is not enough* (2nd ed.) Routledge, 6.

[18] Rosenberry, J. and St. John III, B. (Eds.) (2010). *Public Journalism 2.0: The promise of and reality of a citizen-engaged press*. Routledge.

[19] Hurst, N. (2010, July 8). Citizen journalism vs. legacy news: The battle for news supremacy. https://journalism.missouri.edu/2010/07/citizen-journalism-vs-legacy-news-the-battle-for-news-supremacy/

[20] Wenzel, A. (2020). *Community-centered journalism: Engaging people, exploring solutions, and building trust*. University of Illinois Press, viii.

[21] Kosky, O. (2015, November 17. How participatory journalism turns news consumers into collaborators. Nieman Reports. https://niemanreports.org/articles/how-participatory-journalism-turns-news-consumers-into-collaborators/

[22] Ibid., par. 11.

[23] Cardona-Maguigad, A., DeCeault, J., Nagasawa, K., Sivit, M. (2022, December 8). Curious city turns 10! WBEZ Chicago. https://www.wbez.org/stories/curious-city-wbez-chicago-history/e37bc64b-fae3-4d5a-8fdd-9091e120cfcf

[24] Kosky (2015).

[25] Wall, M. (2017). Mapping citizen and participatory journalism. *Journalism Practice, 11*(2–3), 134–141.

[26] Ibid., 140.

[27] Thomas, R. (2022, October). Advocacy journalism. Oxford Bibliographies Online. https://www.oxfordbibliographies.com/display/document/obo-9780199756841/obo-9780199756841-0281.xml

[28] Ruigrok, N. (2010). From journalism of activism to journalism of accountability. *International Communication Gazette, 72*(1), 85–90.

[29] Hammond, P. (2002). Moral combat: Advocacy journalism and the new humanitarianism. In Chandler, D. (Ed.), *Rethinking human rights: Critical approaches to international politics* (pp. 176–195). Palgrave McMillan, 178.

[30] Heitner, D. (2009). Performing black power in the "Cradle of Liberty": *Say Brother* envisions new principles of blackness in Boston. *Television & New Media, 10*(5), 392–415.

[31] Craig, R. L. (2004). Business, advertising and social control of the news. *Journal of Communication Inquiry, 28*(3): 233–252.

[32] The position against objectivity is summed up nicely in Glasser, T. (1984). Objectivity precludes responsibility. *The Quill, 72*(1): 13–16. http://www.columbia.edu/itc/journalism/j6075/edit/readings/glasser.html

[33] Ryan, T. (1994) Network earth: Advocacy, journalism and the environment. C. L. LaMay, & E. E. Dennis. (Eds.), *Media and the environment* (pp. 81–90). Island Press, 86.

[34] Koski (2015), par. 8.

35 Russwurmian advocacy journalism is named after John Brown Russwurm, a Jamaican American abolitionist and coeditor of *Freedom's Journal*, the first black owned and operated newspaper in the United States. CV Drum News (n.d.) What is journalism? http://cvdrumnews.weebly.com/what-is-journalism.html

36 It is an idea echoed by Supreme Court Justice Oliver Wendell Holmes in opposing limitations on free speech during World War I, and later by Justice William J. Brennan who coined "marketplace of ideas" in his 1965 opinion *Lamont v. Postmaster General*.

37 Public Relations Society of America. (n.d.). PRSA Code of Ethics. https://www.prsa.org/about/ethics/prsa-code-of-ethics

38 Ibid.

39 Whitman, B. J., & Guthrie, J. (2018). BEPS history, timeline participants, research & evolving standards in public relations: A historical examination of PRSA's codes of ethics. https://www.prsa.org/docs/default-source/about/ethics/beps_handbook_2018.pdf?sfvrsn=6ceff074_0

40 Fitzpatrick, K. R. (2018). Saying "no" to the boss: Building your ethics portfolio. https://prsay.prsa.org/2018/09/12/saying-no-to-the-boss-building-your-ethics-portfolio/

41 Fitzpatrick, K. R. (n.d.) Ethical decision-making guide helps resolve ethical dilemmas. https://www.prsa.org/docs/default-source/about/ethics/ethics-case-studies/ethics-case-study-ethical-desision-making-guide.pdf?sfvrsn=8a55268f_4

42 American Association of Advertising Agencies. (2016, October 14). 4A's standards of practice. https://www.aaaa.org/4as-standards-practice/

43 American Marketing Association. (2021, October 11). *AMA statement of ethics*. https://myama.my.site.com/s/article/AMA-Statement-of-Ethics

44 World Federation of Advertising. (2017). Value of advertising report. https://valueofadvertising.org/value-of-advertising/value-of-advertising-report/

45 DePalma, J. J. (2021, January 22). 9 steps to build trust: Ethical advertising principles. Microsoft Advertising Blog. https://about.ads.microsoft.com/en-in/blog/post/january-2021/9-steps-to-build-trust-ethical-advertising-principles

8

Case Study

Truth and Public Interest

You are the editor of *The Greenville Citizen*, a small, daily newspaper serving Greenville and surrounding communities. Your paper has been covering a heated story involving the Greenville School District, which is considering whether to replace its 40-year-old elementary school with a new $27 million state-of-the-art facility. With the community extremely divided on the issue, the district's board of directors has agreed to put the matter up for a public vote. Election Day is tomorrow.

Alexander Ramecker, president of the Greenville Taxpayers Association, has rallied opposition to the proposed elementary school. The group argues that the existing school remains safe and usable. Past school buildings, which the district sold to private companies after replacing them with newer facilities, are still being used as office space, elderly housing, and even private schools.

"The elementary school doesn't represent any hazard to the children," said Ramecker. "In this bad economy, why raise our taxes and spend tens of millions of dollars to replace a building that's perfectly usable as it is?"

Teachers in the district disagree. Led by the elementary school's popular principal, Stephen Paquet, they contend that the building is outdated and inadequate to the needs of contemporary education. The principal explains that state mandates have changed over the years, requiring schools to provide specialized reading instruction, physical education, counseling, and other services that have placed a tremendous burden on the school.

"We've tried to make do, but it hasn't been easy," Paquet told the newspaper in a recent article. "We had to turn the band room into a classroom, so now students practice in the stairwells. We've taught some special needs classes down in the boiler room. It's that bad."

The *Citizen's* education reporter, Tina Elwin, has been following the issue closely for months. During a meeting about the next day's newspaper, she notes that Paquet's efforts to persuade the community have been paying off. With the crucial public vote scheduled for tomorrow, she feels that the taxpayer group will fall short of stopping the construction project. Privately, she says she believes this is a good thing for the community and the students.

"The school's positively prehistoric," she says. "The students and the teachers are excited about getting a new school. Sure, the taxes will go up a bit, but it's going to be worth it for the kids. I'm glad the people of the community finally see that."

As Elwin goes off to work on an article previewing tomorrow's vote, the newspaper's police reporter, Jamie Sakata, stops her outside your office. After a quick word, they both return to your office with concerned looks on their faces.

"Hey, you know that elementary school principal who's been in the news so much lately?" asks Sakata. "I just heard he got arrested over in Hudson last night." The police reporter goes on to explain that Stephen Paquet was pulled over for running a red light late last night. The arresting officer smelled alcohol in the vehicle, and a breathalyzer test revealed that Paquet had a blood alcohol content of 0.21—more than twice the legal limit for driving. "It gets worse," Sakata says. "He had a prostitute in the car with him."

"This is awful!" Elwin exclaims. "I don't know what Steve was doing, but this is going to totally sink the new elementary school project. Those poor kids are going to be stuck in that old school now." She goes on to explain that Paquet had been the public face of the fight for a new elementary school. With the vote so close, news of Paquet's arrest could be enough to shift the election. "Do we have to run the story?" asks Elwin. "I mean, why do we even have it. We never run any police reports from Hudson."

Sakata confirms that the newspaper normally doesn't cover the Hudson Police Department. However, she received an anonymous tip about the principal around noon. Because it involved a prominent local person involved in the biggest public issue facing the community, she called over to Hudson to confirm the details. Police confirmed that Paquet, a married man with two young children, was accompanied by a local prostitute at the time of his arrest. However, because of a lack of evidence, police were not charging either the young woman or Paquet with any crimes related to prostitution. Instead, the principal faces only charges related to running the red light and driving under the influence.

"Ramecker's behind this . . . either him or someone else in the tax-payer's group," says Elwin. "They knew they were going to lose the vote tomorrow, so they dropped this story in our lap in an effort to sabotage things. We can't run the story. It's not fair that the students lose a new school that they need just because their principal made a mistake in his personal life."

Sakata disagrees. While she admits that someone from the taxpayer's group could very well have provided her with the anonymous tip, she argues that the story remains true. "I agree that a new school would benefit the students and the community," Sakata says. "But we can't kill the story just because of that. Facts are facts, and we have to report them. Besides, how will it look if members of the taxpayer's group know we have the story but that we refused to run it?"

Elwin decides to try a different angle. "How about if we just delay it for a day then?" she asks. "That way we can still get the story out, but it won't adversely affect the election. We can publish the news, but not be played by Ramecker and his group."

Sakata shakes her head. "Whether it affects the election or not isn't our concern," she said. "We have a news story. The facts have been verified. Sitting on the story, even for a day, is just playing politics. That's not our business."

Elwin turns to you as the editor of the newspaper and says, "I thought our business was doing what's right for the public."

You have a few hours until the deadline for publication. The paper will be out on doorsteps and newsstands before the polls open tomorrow. What will you decide to do?

9

Truth, Accuracy, and Honesty

In this chapter, you will learn about:
- The three major theories of truth
- Facts, inferences, and judgments as representations of truth
- Deception and its two major components, fabrication and manipulation
- Limits implied by a reasonable expectation of truth
- How the struggle with truth creates potential ethical problems in advertising, public relations, and print or visual journalism.

Almost all professional organizations in the field of mass communication claim to value truth. The Society of Professional Journalists tells its members to "seek truth and report it."[1] The Radio Television Digital News Association says "truth and accuracy above all . . . journalism's obligation is to pursue truth and report, not withhold it."[2] The International Association of Business Communicators agrees: "I communicate accurate information and promptly correct any errors[3] The Institute for Advertising Ethics advises: "Advertising, public relations, marketing communications, news, and editorial all share a common objective of truth and high ethical standards in serving the public."[4] Everyone, it seems, places a high value on truth.

But does "truth" have the same meaning for everyone? A newspaper article began: "Evanston sent out its first Guaranteed Income Pilot Program payments earlier this month that will provide 150 randomly selected Evanstonians with $500 a month for 12 months.[5] An advertisement on the facing page said "You could start your new life without knee pain today. We've already delivered knee pain relief successfully more than 250,000 times." Are both items equally true? Do readers expect each to adhere to the same standard of truth knowing that one was written by a reporter and the other is labeled "advertisement?"

Correspondence Theory of Truth

For most people, truth is a fairly easy concept to understand. Something is "true" if it matches reality. In philosophy, this is known as the *correspondence theory of truth*—truth is that which corresponds to reality. The more a statement corresponds with reality, the more it can be said to be true. Simple enough. So simple, in fact, that philosophers sometimes refer to this concept of truth as *pretheoretical truth*, our innate concept of truth before philosophical theories get involved and start calling everything into question.

In general, mass communicators strive for a high level of *accuracy*, a measurement of the degree to which one's statements correspond with reality. One reason is that accuracy can be easier to achieve and to verify than truth. Let's take a simple statement about temperature. If I write "The high temperature today in Philadelphia was 38 degrees," is that accurate? Where did I obtain my information? Perhaps I just looked at the thermometer outside my window. Is it working properly? To make a statement that can be verified, I could write "The high temperature today in Philadelphia was 38 degrees, according to the National Weather Service." Because the National Weather Service is a respected source for measuring the temperature, my statement will be regarded as accurate. But is it "true?"

Real, honest-to-goodness truth can at times be impossible to ascertain. Usually, professional communicators must settle for accurate reporting. They try to avoid constructions such as "Bob Smith thinks he would be a good candidate for the job." Good journalists realize that they do not know what Bob Smith really thinks; they only know what Mr. Smith says. Thus, the preferred construction would be: "Bob Smith *said* that he thinks he would be a good candidate for the job." Attribution makes it a fact (that he said it), whether or not it is actually true (that he thinks it).

This reliance on accuracy can create its own set of problems. For example, I once covered a school board meeting during which one of the board members held up a piece of paper and said: "I have a list here of more than 50 bills that the business manager has refused to pay." The other reporter at the meeting included the board member's statement in his article for a competing newspaper. That account was accurate, at least in the sense that it corresponded to the reality of what happened at the meeting. However, when I went up to the board member after the meeting and asked to see the list, he confessed that the piece of paper was a prop. No such list existed, although he said he believed that many bills were going unpaid. While it would have been accurate to report the board member held up a paper that he said contained a list of unpaid bills, that reporting would have left readers with the false impression that such a list actually existed.

Coherence Theory of Truth

The correspondence theory of truth is based on the idea that there is some kind of objective reality to which statements can be compared. By contrast, the *coherence theory of truth* holds that truth is not a measure of how much a statement corresponds to the "real world" but rather a measure of coherence with other beliefs about the world. For example, when we say "The high temperature today in Philadelphia was 38 degrees, according to the National Weather Service," we are making a statement that fits a number of our beliefs—that there is such a thing as temperature, that it can be objectively measured, that the National Weather Service does so in a way that can be trusted.

Consider something as basic as color. Think about asking students the color of the walls of a classroom. One student might look at them and say they are "yellow"; another student might say "goldenrod." Are they both seeing the same color? How would you explain the color to someone who has been blind from birth? Turn the lights off in the room. What color are the walls now? Has the color changed? Did the color go away, or are the walls still yellow but not visible in the dark?

You might be surprised to learn that the reality of the situation is that the walls do not actually "have" a color. What we call color is nothing more than reflected light. The color we see is the color of the spectrum of light reflected by the object. All the other colors are absorbed by that object. So, in a sense, those yellow walls are actually every color *except* the yellow that is reflected away. We call the walls yellow not because that statement conforms to reality but because it integrates precisely with our existing beliefs about color. That is coherence theory.[6]

Where correspondence theory views truth as a statement that matches facts in an objective reality, coherence theory tends to look at truth as an *inference*, a logical conclusion that we draw from observations. For example, a proposition is true in mathematics if it coheres with other axioms and is logically deducible from them. Inferences are logical and deducible from a common ground of logic and human experience. Inferences can be proven "true" if we agree on the degree of their coherence with other statements and the logic used to establish the coherence.

Mass communication professionals make use of inference in many ways. For example, advertisers know that consumers will make loose inferences based on the words and images to which they are exposed.[7] Watch a commercial for a popular breath mint. What happens when the attractive young person uses the mint? Suddenly, another attractive young person appears willing to get closer. The commercial overtly states that the mint will give the user fresh breath. The consumer infers that the mint will lead to more romantic opportunity. Research indicates that encouraging consumers to make spontaneous inferences about products in turn influences them to develop more favorable attitudes toward the brand.[8] In short, inferences sell.

Journalism, which professes a reliance on fact and accuracy, often views inference as a problem to be overcome or at least to be closely monitored. Research indicates that deceptive news articles—those where the author deliberately deceived his or her editors and readers—tend to feature a higher proportion of inferences than facts.[9] Inference can have significant impact on audiences as well, with even a slight perceived slant in the news affecting viewers and readers. For example, studies show that individuals make inferences about what their fellow citizens think based on the apparent slant of news articles.[10] If an individual perceives a news article as favoring a certain political candidate, the inference is that public opinion is positive toward the candidate. Conversely, if the individual perceives the article to be unfavorable, the inference is that public opinion is negative toward the candidate.

Social Construction Theory of Truth

Correspondence theory postulates an objective reality that can be described as fact. Coherence theory suggests that the truth of a statement depends on its degree of coherence with other knowledge. *Social construction theory* goes one step further and rejects the idea that reality can be known. It argues instead that what we call "truth" is what people in societies have constructed as their reality. We define, interpret, and shape what we perceive and attach meanings to those perceptions; knowledge is created in a social context of shared assumptions. There is no outside, neutral, objective reality; reality is a social construction.

In social construction theory, truth is nothing more than a *judgment*. When it comes to judgments, individuals might agree on the "facts," yet draw entirely different conclusions from those facts. Even the facts themselves can be seen as merely judgments. "Truth" is constructed rather than existing outside of us and immutable.

Consider the example of a statement made by Republican Majority Leader Mike Turzai of the Pennsylvania House of Representatives. In March 2012, just eight months before the presidential election between Mitt Romney and Barack Obama, Pennsylvania's governor signed a controversial voter identification law that would have required all citizens in the state to present photo ID when attempting to vote.[11] Three months later, at a meeting of the Republican State Committee, Turzai was listing the legislature's accomplishments when he said that the Voter ID Law was "going to allow Governor Romney to win the state of Pennsylvania."[12]

Democrats and many journalists instantly seized upon Turzai's comment as an admission that he and Republicans in the state were out to suppress Obama voters, especially minorities in Pennsylvania.[13] Not surprisingly, Republicans saw it differently. To them, Turzai was implying that tighter controls on voter fraud would put Pennsylvania on "a more even keel" for the presidential election.[14] The timing of the legislation, just months before a presidential election, certainly bolstered charges that the move was politically motivated. On the other hand, Turzai's comments made no specific mention of why he thought the legislation would allow Romney to win the state. Whether because of socially constructed political leanings or journalistic skepticism, the listeners' own belief systems often shaped "truth" beyond the factual statement made by the representative. The meaning of the words spoken was a matter of judgment. "Truth" was in the eye of the beholder.

Deception and Lying

While philosophers and others might disagree as to what constitutes "truth," nearly everyone agrees that truth is usually a virtue. By contrast *deception*, attempting to deliberately encourage or allow another to believe as true that which we ourselves do not believe to be true, is broadly viewed as a vice. So, what constitutes deception? First, deception—like all actions involving ethics—must be deliberate. One cannot be ethical or unethical by accident. Second, deception does not need to be successful to be unethical. The intent to deceive matters more than the degree to which the deception works. Third, deception does not require that we actively participate in misleading the other individual. By passively allowing another to believe that which we do not believe, we permit deception to occur and thus must share responsibility for it. Finally, deception depends on what we ourselves believe regardless of whether it is true or not. From an ethical standpoint, what matters is the *intent* to mislead.

There are many kinds of deception, but for our purposes we will break deception into two broad categories: manipulation and fabrication.[15] *Manipulation* involves communication in which intentions are camouflaged to mislead someone into believing something known to be false. Imagine that your supervisor has told you that the firm's regular 3 PM meeting has been moved up an hour today. Later a colleague comes by and asks, "Are we meeting today at 3?" You respond with "Don't we always meet at 3?" You manipulated your response to avoid lying about the time of the meeting, but you encouraged your colleague to believe something that you yourself do not. Manipulation can be passive as well as active. For example, imagine that same colleague came by and said, "See you at the 3 o'clock meeting!" to which you responded by smiling and waving. You did not actively create a deception, but you passively allowed or encouraged a statement that you knew to be false.

The second form of deception, *fabrication*, involves communication to convince someone to believe something the communicator knows to be false. We commonly refer to this as "lying." Notice that fabrication or lying is not simply saying something that is untrue. There are many times that something "untrue" would not be considered a lie—fiction, an error, or a miscommunication for example.[16] Lying necessarily includes an effort to get another to believe the lie.

A Reasonable Expectation of Truth

For a falsehood to constitute an ethical wrong, some ethicists believe the other person must have "a reasonable expectation of the truth."[17] Whether the individual has a reasonable expectation of the truth depends on: (1) the place where the communication occurs, (2) the roles of the communicators, and (3) the nature of the truth involved.[18]

The setting or place of communication can have an impact upon the receiver's expectation of truth primarily in terms of the public/private nature of the context. In general, asking for private, intimate information to be communicated in a public setting lowers any reasonable expectation of truth—especially if the truth could cause harm in such a setting. A broadcast journalist interviewing a politician on camera about an extramarital affair might not have a reasonable expectation of truth, whereas that same journalist might expect a more honest answer in a private, off-the-record setting.

The relationship of the communicators affects the expectation of truth as well. In general, the closer a relationship, the greater the expectation of truth. Friends and family members might have a greater expectation of truth than strangers. At the same time, the expectation of truth might also be affected by the nature of the relationship itself. For example, those whom we perceive as having our best interests at heart might have a more reasonable expectation of truth than those whom we perceive as potentially using us as means to their own ends. The more antagonistic the relationship between the sender and the receiver, the lower the expectation of truth. Imagine a man attempting to rob you. After you turn over your wallet and cell phone, he asks if you have anything else. Does a robber have a reasonable expectation of the truth from his victim in this case?

One can argue that certain mass communication relationships can raise or lower the receiver's reasonable expectation of truth: practitioner/client, advertiser/consumer, broadcaster/viewer, journalist/source. All communication relationships, personal and professional, have an impact on the receiver's expectation of truth. Do we have a reasonable expectation of the truth from a Burger King ad that tells us "it just tastes better"? Do we believe the advertisers are conveying a truth that they themselves believe? In general, individuals have a lower expectation of truth when dealing with advertising and similar commercial communication as opposed to more informative-oriented communication such as journalism. Advertising that masquerades as journalistic editorial copy often seeks to take advantage of the consumer's greater expectation of truth relative to the latter.

The nature of truth itself can also affect receiver expectations. In general, we tend to have a greater expectation of truth when dealing with facts rather than opinions or judgments. We expect the truth in important matters, such as statements that affect public safety, but we have a lower expectation when it comes to less consequential concerns.

The doctrine of "reasonable expectation of the truth" should not be viewed as a license to lie. Rather, it should be considered as an explanation for why individuals feel deceived in some instances but not in others. An advertising team who tells a customer that Burger King "just tastes better" probably does not feel that the action was unethical, even if some of them prefer a burger from Wendy's. And the consumer who views the ad usually does not feel deceived. On the other hand, if an advertisement boasts that you can get a double cheeseburger for $1, consumers will feel deceived if charged $2 when they order one at the restaurant. They reasonably expected the truth, and their expectations were violated.

Truth in the
Mass Communication Landscape

Professional communicators struggle with truth on a daily basis. Print, online, and broadcast journalists work with tight deadlines, difficult sources, and hard-to-find documents in their efforts to uncover the truth. Often they wrestle with their own biases to produce factual articles. Public relations practitioners strive to balance the desires of their clients with their need to maintain professional integrity, as well as the trust of those they deal with in the media. Advertisers try to market products creatively while at the same time trying to build trust and confidence among consumers. Professional communicators can find guidelines in practitioner codes of ethics for addressing problems they may encounter in striving for truthful representation of their responsibilities.

Advertising

Professional associations consistently call on advertisers to avoid false or misleading statements. These include manipulative price claims such as the so-called *bait and switch*, a tactic where a business attracts customers by offering a low-priced item with the intention of switching them to a more expensive purchase. Often this involves advertising an item that the business does not have or which the business has in only very limited stock. When the customer arrives, the item is sold out, and the more profitable item is offered instead.

Advertisers should not use *testimonials*, endorsements of a product or service, unless the advertisement accurately reflects the genuine opinion of the person making the endorsement. Thus, a celebrity endorser not only should have used the product being sold but also should offer an honest appraisal of that product. Moreover, special care should be used to ensure that statements provided by scientific or other authorities are accurately reported in the advertisement and that the opinions are adequately supported by others in the same profession.

Advertisers must also take care with *advertorials*, advertisements that look like news stories or news editorials. Consumers perceive the truthfulness of persuasive communication, such as advertisements, more skeptically than informative communication, such as news stories. Attempting to blur the line between the types of communication is a deceptive practice. Typically, advertorials look and feel different from editorial material. In every case, the advertorial should clearly be marked as an advertisement to avoid deceiving the reader/viewer.

A more troublesome problem for advertisers is the desire for accuracy in advertising. The American Advertising Federation suggests that advertising should be held to the same standards of accuracy as journalism. The American Association of Advertising Agencies admonishes its members to avoid "exaggerations, visual or verbal."[19] This presents an enormous challenge for advertisers. Many, frankly, regularly fail to adhere to the standards. In 2022, a class-action federal lawsuit alleged Burger King misled customers by inflating the size of its burgers in images. The lawsuit claimed the trademark Whopper was 35% larger in images than what was served in restaurants.[20] Food companies use words like "sustainable," "humane," and "natural" to attract consumers concerned about the environment and animal welfare.[21] The lack of clear-cut definitions for such terms resulted in one lawyer advising his clients not to use them to avoid litigation.

Public Relations

Public relations often straddles a line between advocacy and objectivity. While professionals advocate for their clients, they realize that their work must avoid questionable practices to maintain public trust. With that in mind, professional organizations in public relations encourage members to ensure that the information they disseminate is accurate. Members should attempt to correct any inaccurate information as quickly as possible.

The public relations industry has taken an ethical stance against efforts to mislead the audience about the nature of clients or causes being represented. This includes *astroturfing*, false "grass roots" efforts that pretend to have risen from the work of dedicated individuals but in reality represent the efforts of large, undisclosed special interest groups. It can also utilize the deceptive practice of paying "volunteers" to show up at meetings or protests.

Whitewashing describes covering up damaging information by presenting a biased version of the facts. A variation that public relations professionals should take care to avoid is *greenwashing*, a process that uses deception to portray an organization as environmentally friendly when the real intent involves increasing profit or manipulating public opinion to attract consumers who want to buy goods or services from companies that care about the environment. The term was coined by environmentalist Jay Westerveld in response to efforts by hotel chains to encourage guests to reuse towels in the name of saving the environment.[22] In reality, Westerveld said, the effort aimed to increase the profit of the hotel chains much more than it did anything to benefit the environment. To avoid ethical issues over greenwashing, claims should be clear and easy to understand; avoid using terms with no clear meaning, such as "eco-friendly." Similarly, do not use images that are misleading and give an unjustified green impression (i.e., trees or flowers that are unconnected to the product). Be honest about a brand's sustainability practices.

Journalism

The traditional view of journalism holds it up as a profession dealing in facts and objectivity, guarding against bias and manipulation. Print, online, and broadcast journalists confront many of the problems faced by the other mass communication professions. Journalists should actively seek out sources and verify the accuracy of information before disseminating information to the public. Photojournalists should work to ensure that their work is free from staging, Photoshopping, and other deceptive practices that alter their images or the way those images are viewed by the audience.

Summary

Almost all professional organizations in the field of mass communication claim to value truth. However, truth means different things to different people. *Correspondence theory* says that truth corresponds to reality, something that is factually knowable. *Coherence theory* holds that truth is not a measure of how much a statement corresponds to the "real world" but rather how much it coheres to the established system of beliefs. *Social construction theory* argues that what we call "truth" is a construct of the societies in which we live.

Different ways to uncover truth are linked with each of the theories. Correspondence theory utilizes *facts*, statements about reality that can be verified in the real world. Professional journalism organizations, in particular, revere facts. They encourage their members to seek out facts and report them accurately and without bias. Coherence theory relies on *inferences*—logical conclusions that we deduce from observations. *Judgments* are subjective personal opinions. Social construction theory uses judgments, similar to inferences but based on society's assignment of meaning.

While we might disagree as to what constitutes "truth," we almost universally agree that truth is a virtue. By contrast, deception is broadly viewed as a vice. *Deception* can be divided into two categories. *Manipulation* involves communication that can mislead others into believing something the communicator knows is not true. *Fabrication*, commonly called "lying," involves communicating false information.

For some, deception is only unethical when the person being deceived has a reasonable expectation of the truth. This, in turn, depends on the context of the communication, the relationship between the communicators, and the nature of the truth.

Truth is a goal for most professional organizations in mass communication, but it remains an elusive goal. It can be difficult to agree on the meaning of truth or even on what constitutes truth. Practitioners confront questions of truth on a daily basis. Codes of ethics in the various communication fields provide some guidance in terms of ethical ideals and minimum expectations. But in the end it falls to the individual to render ethical judgments on a case by case basis.

Notes

[1] Society of Professional Journalists. (2014, September 6). SPJ code of ethics. http://spj.org/ethicscode.asp

[2] Radio Television Digital News Association (RTDNA). (2015, June 11). *Code of ethics and professional conduct.* https://www.rtdna.org/ethics

[3] International Association of Business Communicators. (2022). IABC code of ethics for professional communicators. https://www.iabc.com/About/Purpose/Code-of-Ethics

[4] Institute for Advertising Ethics. (2020). *Principles and practices for advertising ethics.* https://www.iaethics.org/principles-and-practices

[5] Schmidt, C. (2022, December 21). Evanston sends first monthly cash transfers to pilot program participants. *Chicago Tribune*, p. 4.

[6] Coherence theory actually goes much deeper than this, with many supporters arguing that truth is a subjectivity that exists only within a belief system. For a good overview, see Dorsey, D. (2006). A coherence theory of truth in ethics. *Philosophical Studies, 127*(3), 493–523.

[7] Ruth Ann Smith and others have amply documented the impact of advertising on consumer inference. Smith, R. A. (2013). The effects of visual and verbal advertising information on consumers' inferences. *Journal of Advertising, 20*(4), 13–24.

[8] Kardes, F. R. (1988). Spontaneous inference processes in advertising: The effects of conclusion omission and involvement on persuasion. *Journal of Consumer Research, 15*(2), 225–233.

[9] Lasorsa, D. L. and Lewis, S. C. (2010). Reports, inferences and judgments in deceptive and legitimate news stories. *Journalism & Mass Communication Quarterly, 87*(2), 378–392.

[10] Gunter, A. C. (1998). The persuasive press inference: Effects of mass media on perceived public opinion. *Communication Research, 25*(5), 486–504.

[11] A state judge later issued an injunction blocking essential parts of the law.

[12] Pahousevideo. (June 25, 2012). Turzai: Voter ID will allow Romney to win PA [Video file]. http://www.youtube.com/watch?v=EuOT1bRYdK8

[13] See for example, Noah, T. (2012, August 15). Pennsylvania voter ID: Ask not why. *The New Republic.* https://newrepublic.com/article/106234/pennsylvania-voter-id-ask-not-why

[14] Weinger, M. (2012, June 25). Mike Turzai: Voter ID helps GOP win state. *POLITICO.* http://www.politico.com/news/stories/0612/77811.html

[15] Caddell, J. W. (2004). Deception 101—Primer on deception. Strategic Studies Institute. https://irp.fas.org/eprint/deception.pdf

[16] Sissela Bok covers the distinction between fiction and lying well. Bok, S. (1999). *Lying: Moral choice in public and private life.* Pantheon Books, 207.

17 Garrett, T. M., Baillie, H. W., and Garrett, R. M. (1989). *Health care ethics: Principles and problems*. Prentice Hall, 97.

18 Ibid.

19 American Association of Advertising Agencies. (2016, October 14). 4A's standards of practice. https://www.aaaa.org/4as-standards-practice/

20 Wile, R., (2022, April 11). Burger King accused of false advertising in lawsuit alleging Whoppers are too small. NBCnews.com

21 Jacobs, A. (2021, September 7). Lawsuits over "misleading" food labels surge as groups cite lax U.S. oversight. *The New York Times*.

22 Edwards, C. (2022, August 5). What is greenwashing? *Business News Daily*. https://www.businessnewsdaily.com/10946-greenwashing.html

9 Case Study

Truth and Accuracy

You are a budding reporter for Channel 26 News in Franklin, a city of 200,000 located in the Midwest. Your assignment editor, Hal Bruntz, has sent you out to cover the opening of "Extreme Glory"—a highly anticipated action movie about a group of heroic soldiers fighting the war in Afghanistan. He has arranged a 10 a.m. meeting with Janella Matava, manager of the local 8-screen Prism House Theater. Matava will give you a CD with some clips from the movie that you can splice into your story.

Also at the theater will be Maj. Rick Beaucen, a local veteran of the Afghanistan war who served in the unit on which the film is based. The news producer has scheduled three minutes for your story on the "News 26 at Noon," which means that you will have to be back at the station no later than 11 a.m. to put your package together. It presents a challenge but also something of a break. It's the first time you have been given three minutes for a story. Up until now, everything you've done has been a standard 30–45 second voiceover with only the occasional standup.

The plan is simple. Head out to the theater, interview the theater manager, interview Beaucen, get an interior shot of preparations for the movie, grab a shot of the crowd buying tickets, then head back to the station and put it all together for the noon news.

When you and your camera operator arrive at the theater, you are greeted by the manager, who takes you past the lines of people waiting to get tickets and back to her office where you meet Beaucen. The interviews go smoothly. The theater manager seems a bit nervous on camera and doesn't really offer much that you can use. Beaucen is a bit long-winded, but he gives some good insight into the war and the film. You figure you can use his stuff, run a short bite from the manager, then fill in the time by interviewing some people in line and doing a standup with the crowds outside.

You thank Matava and Beaucen, then head back out to the lobby only to discover that the lines and the crowd are gone. Matava sees the look on your face and asks what's wrong. You explain that you had planned to use shots of the people standing in line and maybe even interview one or two for the story. Matava replies that the special early show was scheduled for 10:15 a.m. It's 10:30 now. Everyone has already been seated, and the movie has started. None of the other movies will open until the normal matinee time around 1 p.m.

At this point, panic starts to set in. You realize your plans to tell the story of a very popular movie opening won't work with video of an empty lobby. Matava offers to help though. She says she can get a group of theater employees to take off their uniforms and pretend to be customers. The guy working the box office window can go through the motions of selling tickets, and you can get your video.

Unsure of what to do, you call your assignment editor. When Bruntz gets on the line, you explain the problem. Without some crowd shots, you don't have enough to fill the full three minutes at this point. And without some decent visuals, creating a good standup will be difficult.

"I see what you're saying," Bruntz replies. "Look, I'm not going to tell you what to do. I have three minutes set aside for you. I can cut it down a bit if you can't fill it, but I'd really like to have that story. Personally, I don't think getting some folks there to line up for tickets is such a big deal. They're probably going to be going to the movie later anyway. And it's not like this story will have a big impact on our viewers either way. It's your call though."

Bruntz is on the line waiting for an answer. What will you decide to do?

10

Conflicts of Interest

In this chapter, you will learn about:
- Defining a conflict of interest
- Primary and secondary interests
- The problem with appearance of a conflict
- The three major types of conflicting interests
- How to handle conflicts of interest

Most human beings maintain a wide variety of loyalties or interests. We have divergent degrees of loyalty to ourselves, our families, our friends, our neighbors, and to others. We have some loyalty to the assorted organizations to which we might belong, such as social clubs, political organizations, or religious/faith groups. If we are employed, we also have loyalties to our coworkers, our employer, our profession, and the public. Depending on our chosen career path, we might have additional loyalties to clients past and present, to news sources, to readers, or to customers.

Professional Conflicts of Interest

A *conflict of interest* arises when our loyalties (interests) clash, usually forcing us to choose one loyalty over another. Conflicts of interest can be personal, such as when a sibling starts trouble with a friend. However, here we will focus on *professional conflicts of interest*, those that arise when a professional interest conflicts with a personal interest. In such cases, scholars generally refer to the professional interest as the *primary interest* and the personal interest as the *secondary interest*. In general, things like maintaining a client's confidentiality, respecting a customer's privacy, serving the public's needs, and telling the truth are primary interests. Meanwhile, personal relationships, outside work, and involvement in external organizations would be considered secondary interests.

Secondary interests do not lack innate value. Activity such as involvement in an external organization can constitute a rewarding experience for the individual, the organization, and the community. However, when one's personal interests conflict with one's professional obligations, that conflict can give rise to an ethical dilemma. Imagine a situation where a public relations professional plays an active role in their local gun control organization's efforts to protest a firearms manufacturer. If that manufacturer seeks public relations support from her firm, it creates a potential conflict of interest between her obligations as a professional and her personal allegiance to the local organization.

Personal Interests as Secondary

It is no coincidence that personal interests are classified as "secondary" interests. When making ethical decisions in the workplace, one is typically expected to place professional interests ahead of personal ones. The Society of Professional Journalists' Code of Ethics states this quite succinctly: "Journalists should be free of obligation to any interest other than the public's right to know."[1] But what does one do when the interests of one's profession conflict with one's obligations as a human being?

Consider the case of Kevin Carter, a South African photojournalist who won a 1994 Pulitzer Prize for his photograph of an emaciated Sudanese girl being stalked by a vulture while struggling to make her way to a food center during a famine. Carter set up his camera and prepared to take a shot. He waited patiently for the bird to spread its wings. After watching the vulture stalk the child for 20 minutes, he gave up and snapped the photo. Only then did he chase the bird away. As the child continued her journey to the food station, Carter sat under a tree smoking a cigarette, talking to God, and crying. He later said that he never knew what became of the girl or if she ever made it to the food center.[2]

Should journalists become involved in the events they cover, at times putting aside their work and helping their fellow human beings, or is it their duty to maintain an objective distance and document what they experience? The answer may be that it depends on the circumstances. As Poynter Institute ethicist Bob Steele notes, "There were, ideally, lots of other people there to give aid, medicines, care, but nobody is going to replace the role of the journalist."[3] While horrifying, the photo generated tremendous public attention for the plight of the Sudanese people. Carter gathered and provided information that made it easier for people to understand and render financial support, potentially helping millions of people. But did he exploit the young Sudanese girl and degrade her humanity to do so?

Such conflicts can be difficult to resolve, as Lauren Pond notes:

> As photojournalists, we have a unique responsibility to record history and share stories in as unbiased and unobtrusive a way as possible. But when someone is hurt and suffering, we have to balance our instincts as professionals with basic human decency and care.[4]

When individuals do decide to put aside their role as journalists to directly help people in trouble, they run into an entirely new set of ethical problems. Consider CNN's Anderson Cooper, who was reporting on the aftermath of an earthquake in Haiti when he saw a boy apparently hit in the head with a piece of concrete. The boy was bleeding profusely and Cooper did not see anyone coming to his aid, so he decided to run to the boy, pick him off the ground and carry him approximately 100 feet to safety.[5]

Cooper's actions received prominent coverage on CNN. But some journalists and media scholars worried that he had created a conflict of interest by getting involved in the story he was reporting. There were multiple debates about journalistic ethics in the coverage of relief efforts in Haiti. Sanjay Gupta is the chief medical correspondent for CNN and a practicing neurosurgeon. CNN showed a four-minute video of him examining a 15-day-old baby with a minor head injury whose mother had died in the earthquake. Bob Steele again weighed in:

> There definitely are cases where a journalist who is qualified can and should provide medical assistance when the need is immediate and profound. If it's imperative that he intervene and help medically, then take him out of his journalistic role and do that. But don't have him covering the same stories in which he's a participant. It muddles the journalistic reporting. It clouds the lens in terms of independent observation and reporting.[6]

Critics said the resulting coverage looked more like marketing for CNN than justifiable news about the earthquake in Haiti. Such coverage raised questions about CNN's credibility in providing reliable information about the disaster and its aftermath.

Avoiding Even the Appearance of a Conflict

Mass communication professionals are counseled to avoid not only conflicts of interest but even the appearance of a conflict of interest. As AdExchanger editor David Kaplan observes, "when it comes to the appearance of a conflict of interest—if it looks like a conflict, you've got a conflict."[7] Kaplan was writing about Laura Desmond—CEO of media and marketing services agency StarCom MediaVest Group (SMG)—who was forced to resign her position on the board of directors of Tremor Video, a leader in high tech video advertising.

When Tremor made the decision to go public with its stock, Desmond's position on the board meant that she would receive stock options worth nearly $300,000. SMG did a lot of business with Tremor Video. In fact, it spent more than $18 million with Tremor that year, making it one of the firm's largest clients.

In theory, Desmond could use her position as CEO of SMG to steer even more business toward Tremor Video, in turn making her Tremor stock options worth more money. In other words, she would be in a position to make decisions for her company based on what was good for her personally and not necessarily what was good for the company. The fact that she had removed herself from any SMG decisions relative to Tremor Video did not matter in the eyes of her critics. As Jim Edwards of the Business Insider wrote: "Desmond has a vested interest in the success of Tremor. This does not look good. It may not be a conflict of interest. But it has the appearance of a conflict of interest. And people in the adbiz ought to care about appearances."[8] In the end, resigning her position was the only way for Desmond to remove the appearance of a conflict and therefore the ethical problem.

Types of Conflict

Conflicts of interest tend to fall into three general categories: conflicting personal relationships, conflicting group loyalties ,and financial conflicts.

Conflicting Personal Relationships

A *conflicting personal relationship* is one that places or appears to place one's personal loyalty to others in conflict with one's professional responsibilities. Conflicts can take as many forms as there are different kinds of personal relationships. However, the most common conflicts are those of relatives, friends, and lovers.

Nepotism is the practice of favoring relatives over others for opportunities in the workplace. For example, two major shareholders filed a lawsuit in 2011 against Rupert Murdoch, chairman and CEO of News Corp., one of the world's largest media groups with holdings that include Fox News and the *Wall Street Journal*. The suit followed Murdoch's decision to have News Corp. buy the Shine Group, a London-based television production company owned by his daughter, Elisabeth, for an estimated $675 million. Elisabeth Murdoch stood to make more than $300 million from the sale.

In their lawsuit, shareholders charged that Murdoch and others "treated News Corp like a wholly-owned family candy store" and "imposed rampant nepotism" within the business.[9] Columnist Allan Sloan wrote that Murdoch had questionably involved family members at many levels of News Corp. but that the purchase of Shine went too far in blurring the lines between public and family business:

> It's one thing to have News Corp. employ family members, and for Rupert Murdoch to let it be known he wants to be succeeded by someone named Murdoch. But it's a whole different thing to use assets of a company 88% owned by the public to buy businesses owned by Murdoch children.[10]

The case was eventually settled for $139 million, with no admission of wrongdoing on Murdoch's part.[11]

Other kinds of personal relationships can create conflicts of interest as well. Dating at work, for example, can be a problem in any business. Imagine that you begin a dating relationship with a coworker, or worse yet a subordinate. What happens if you have the opportunity to grant that individual something professionally beneficial such as a raise, a recommendation, a lucrative client, or some other perk? Do you give it to them? If you do, no matter how clearly it might be deserved, some of your colleagues will believe that it was the result of your personal relationship rather than your professional one. This injures not only your own credibility but also that of your partner. So, should you deny that individual a professional benefit that might otherwise be deserved? That hardly seems fair to the person or, for that matter, in the best interest of the business. Again, no matter how objective and fair you believe yourself to be, others will see personal interests driving professional decision making.

In mass communication professions, this can apply to people outside your firm as well: a journalist dating a source, a public relations professional becoming romantically involved with a client, an advertising executive going out with a media buyer from a firm with which the company does business. All these situations represent potential ethical pitfalls. To a lesser extent, so do friendships, which can give rise to the same kinds of personal/professional conflicts, either real or perceived. Common sense must be exercised. If a relationship—anything from a Facebook friend to a close family relative—could be perceived as creating a potential conflict of interest, then it must be dealt with as such.

Conflicting Group Loyalties

Like personal loyalties, group loyalties can create potential ethical problems when they conflict with one's professional responsibilities. Group loyalties can take many different forms. For example:

- An advertising professional's religious beliefs might conflict with the ability to work on a holy day or to promote a given product or service.
- A journalist's strong support of environmental groups might interfere with coverage of business and the environment.
- Sports writers must decide whether loyalty to the home team should be placed ahead of efforts to maintain journalistic objectivity.

The stronger the sense of loyalty one possesses for an external group, the greater the potential for an ethical problem.

Conflicts of interest can also arise when professional loyalty to one group conflicts with a professional loyalty to another group, such as when a public relations professional represents opposing parties in a dispute. Consider the case of Mark Penn, former world-wide CEO of public relations powerhouse Burson-Marsteller. In 2007, Penn took over as chief strategist for Sen. Hillary Rodham Clinton's presidential campaign. Although many viewed it as a conflict of interest, Penn stayed on as head of Burson-Marsteller while working on the Clinton campaign. Technically, Penn was not actually on Clinton's staff. Instead, Clinton retained his polling firm, which was a unit within Burson-Marsteller; the campaign paid millions of dollars for the services of the polling firm.[12] As Fred Wertheimer, president of the ethics-minded Democracy 21 group, told Bloomberg news: "That individuals and groups are serving today as both consultants to campaigns and as lobbyists or PR folks for private clients is a modern-day phenomenon that has inherent conflicts of interest. . . . It is a very unhealthy practice."[13] Penn illustrated the problem himself when he wrote in his internal blog at Burson that working with Clinton was "good for business."[14]

The problem with such conflicting relationships is that they sometimes place loyalty to one group at odds with loyalty to another. In Penn's case, this became apparent in April 2008 when the *Wall Street Journal* reported that the CEO/strategist had met with Colombia's ambassador to the United States in order to discuss how to promote a free trade agreement between the two nations.[15] At the time Penn was representing Burson-Marsteller, which had received a $300,000 contract from the Colombian Embassy to promote the trade arrangement. However, Sen. Clinton was on record as opposing any such trade deal.

In his role as CEO of Burson-Marsteller, Penn had a duty to do everything he could to promote the trade agreement for his Colombian client. At the same time, he was responsible for representing the interests of Sen. Clinton, who very publicly opposed the agreement. In such a situation, one might reasonably ask whose interests Penn served more. The Colombian government fired Penn's firm one day after the story appeared in the *Wall Street Journal*. A day after that, Penn resigned as Clinton's chief strategist as a direct consequence of the conflict of interest.[16] Penn continued to head Burson-Marsteller until stepping down in 2012.[17]

Financial Conflicts

Financial conflicts arise when an external reward that has monetary value or represents personal gain for an individual could be seen to interfere with that individual's professional loyalty or duty. There are four major sources of financial conflicts of interest: inappropriate compensation, gifts and perks, ownership, and awards.

Inappropriate compensation refers to external rewards in the form of monetary gain provided outside of the norms of professional conduct. Any form of compensation from anyone other than your employer can potentially create a conflict of interest. Some forms of inappropriate compensation are clearly unethical—such as a producer who accepts a bribe to cover up a news story or an advertising executive who sells proprietary information to a client's competitor. Others can seem more innocent, yet still present serious danger. For example, a journalist who agrees to do public relations work on the side might consider that extra money to be fairly earned. But it could present a conflict of interest if that work could be seen to bias that journalist's news coverage. A public relations professional who purchases stock based on information gained from a client could face both ethical and legal troubles.

The problem of inappropriate compensation lay at the root of the payola scandal that struck the music industry in the 1950s. *Payola* refers to the practice of providing a covert incentive, often in the form of a cash payment, to a disc jockey in exchange for that individual's agreement to play a specific song on the radio. The practice of music industry officials bribing individuals to play or otherwise promote specific songs is older than broadcasting itself.[18] However, the problem rose to national prominence in the late 1950s when Congress launched an investigation into the practice. Many disc jockeys, including top names such as Alan Freed and Dick Clark, eventually became ensnared in the scandal. Congressional investigations resulted in payola becoming a crime unless it was publicly disclosed to listeners. Although no individuals have ever been officially charged under the payola statutes, the laws have been credited with reducing inappropriate payments in the music industry.[19]

Payola, like most other forms of inappropriate compensation, creates a conflict between the desire for financial benefit and professional responsibility. A DJ might play a song because of the personal reward rather than a responsibility to play music that the audience might find appealing. The same can be true when the professional offers inappropriate compensation to others. The International Public Relations Association counsels its members to "neither directly nor indirectly offer nor give any financial or other inducement to public representatives or the media, or other stakeholders."[20]

The practice is frowned on in journalism circles as well. *Checkbook journalism* refers to paying sources for information. While many codes of ethics prohibit such practices, the National Press Photographers Association perhaps states it most plainly: "Do not pay sources or subjects or reward them materially for information or participation."[21] Sources who are paid for their information could be enticed to provide exaggerated information as a result of the payment. They might conclude that if a journalist is willing to pay for one story, she might be willing to pay even more for another story—even if that means the source must make up the details in an effort to be paid. Clearly, these concerns could reduce the reliability of information obtained as the result of payment.

Gifts and perks create ethical problems in much the same way as inappropriate financial compensation. Journalists are often offered free trips, concert tickets, test products and other valuable gifts in exchange for coverage. Such special favors are generally refused. As the Associated Press Managing Editors note in their Statement of Ethical Principles: "Expenses in connection with news reporting should be paid by the newspaper."[22] The same is true in business communication. The International Association of Business Communicators advises: "Do not accept undisclosed gifts or payments for professional services from anyone other than a client or employer."[23] Even gifts from a client could present an issue if they entice communicators to favor that client over another served by their agency.

Stock or Other Financial Ownership

Imagine being the client of a public relations account executive who holds a large amount of stock in your major competitor. Might it be fair to wonder whether that individual truly wants you to succeed if your success could seriously damage the value of that stock? Stock ownership can create a conflict between your own financial interests and the interests of your profession, the business you work for, or both.

The New York Times prohibits most business financial staff members from owning stock in any company (other than the newspaper).[24] Why? Because knowing what news will be reported about a publicly traded company can be very lucrative. For example, when Steve Jobs resigned as CEO of Apple in 2011, that company's stock fell virtually overnight. A savvy investor, say a financial editor, who knew about Jobs' resignation before it appeared in the news could have made a substantial financial gain by short selling Apple stock.[25]

Awards

Nearly every field of mass communication has a plethora of awards designed to recognize the work of its professionals. Journalism has the Pulitzer. Advertising has the ADDY. Public relations has the SABRE awards. Television has the Emmy. Radio has the Marconi. Blogging has the Bloggies. And every field has many, many others. Some awards come with financial compensation of thousands of dollars. Even if an award does not come with a financial bonus, it could lead to promotions or other career opportunities for the recipient.

While awards themselves do not present an ethical problem for mass communication professionals, placing the desire for an award above one's responsibility as a professional can lead to trouble. As noted in chapter 6, the APME warns against self-serving journalism and writing stories primarily for the purpose of winning awards and prizes.[26]

The pursuit of rewards creates problems in the field of advertising as well. Al and Laura Ries argue in their book *The Fall of Advertising & the Rise of PR* that too many advertising executives care more about winning awards for their agencies than they do about properly serving their clients—citing research that shows some agencies spend more on award areas than on independent research.[27] Ian Perrin, CEO of the ZO media agency, says that the obsession with awards has damaged the industry in the eyes of its clients. Such obsession contradicts ethical codes that counsel mass communication professionals to give paramount attention to the needs of the public and/or their clients rather than self-serving interest in winning awards.

Dealing with Conflicts of Interest

Conflicts of interest, both real and perceived, can damage your credibility as a professional. They can taint the reliability of the information that you provide to the public or to your clients. They can even corrupt you personally. As such, ethical conflicts of interest must be dealt with. But how? There are five primary techniques for dealing with conflicts of interest: (1) avoid them; (2) remove them; (3) disclose them; (4) monitor them; and (5) recuse yourself from the situation.

Avoid

The first option for dealing with conflicts of interest is to avoid them. An advertising executive can maintain a policy of not hiring relatives. A public relations consultant can refuse to take on a client whose interests conflict with the consultant's religious beliefs. A photographer can turn down an all-expenses-paid trip.

Avoiding a conflict of interest requires that one first recognize the conflict, which means being constantly on the lookout for potential conflicts of interest, real or perceived. Even then, it is not always possible. Suppose a journalist's significant other wins a promotion at work, placing that individual in a position to be covered by the journalist. The decision to avoid that conflict could be out of the journalist's hands.

Remove

The second option for handling conflicts of interest is to remove them. A public relations professional can sell off stock in a company before accepting its rival as a client. Easy enough, but in the example of the journalist whose significant other wins a promotion, should the journalist break off the relationship? Placing one's profession so firmly ahead of one's personal life seems unjust and requiring the journalist to do so unethical.

Disclose

When an ethical conflict of interest cannot be avoided or easily removed, it must be disclosed. Many conflicts of interest arise from those involved being unaware of the conflict. When a sports reporter makes a favorable comment about a player on a local high school baseball team, viewers might feel betrayed if the reporter fails to mention that the player is the reporter's nephew. If the reporter acknowledges the family relationship, viewers have information that allows them to judge the truthfulness of the comment.

Monitor

If a potential conflict of interest has been disclosed, it must also be monitored. One mention of a reporter's baseball playing nephew might be acceptable and even desirable. But if that same reporter continues to report positive news about that nephew, increasingly at the expense of other players, it could create an ethical problem for the reporter and the news station. Disclosure encourages colleagues and supervisors to monitor potential conflicts of interest to ensure that personal interests don't get in the way of professional ones.

Recuse

When all else fails, those involved in a potential conflict of interest must recuse themselves from the situation. Like removal, recusal gets rid of the conflict. However, it does so by removing one's professional responsibility from the conflicting situation. An advertising executive whose environmental activism creates a potential conflict with a client might agree to have no contact with that client and no access to the client's information. Photojournalists who have done private work for a business might agree not to cover that business in their role as a journalist.

Summary

A *conflict of interest* arises when our loyalties (interests) clash, usually forcing us to choose one loyalty over another. In clashes between professional and personal interests, scholars generally refer to the professional interest as the *primary interest* and the personal interest as the *secondary interest*. While codes of ethics usually call for primary or professional interests to come first, there are times when many in the public would prefer that individuals put their duty as human beings ahead of their duty as mass communication professionals.

When it comes to conflicts of interest, we are counseled to avoid even the appearance of a conflict. The perception of a conflict can cause as much damage to credibility and reliability as an actual conflict. If a journalist writes a flattering article about a business owned by a close relative, the perception of conflict damages that journalist's credibility and reputation even if personal interests had no influence on the story.

Conflicts of interest can be grouped into three general categories: conflicting personal relationships, conflicting group loyalties, and financial conflicts. Conflicting personal relationships can include nepotism, friendships, and romantic relationships. Conflicting group loyalties occur when devotion to an external group interferes with one's professional duty. Financial conflicts arise when an external reward that has monetary value or represents personal gain for an individual could be perceived as interfering with that individual's professional loyalty or duty.

There are five options for handling ethical conflicts of interest. Avoid them by recognizing and circumventing such conflicts. Remove them by disassociating yourself from the personal conflict. Disclose them to your colleagues and other affected parties. Monitor them so disclosed conflicts do not worsen. Finally, one can recuse oneself by disassociating oneself from the professional conflict. For example, a reporter could change beats, or an advertising executive could switch clients.

NOTES

[1]   Society of Professional Journalists. (2012). SPJ code of ethics. http://spj.org/ethicscode.asp

[2]   Smith, R. (2009, April 14). One image of agony resonates in two lives. *The New York Times*. Carter committed suicide three months after receiving the Pulitzer Prize. The criticism and negative coverage of his actions in Sudan combined with memories of other disturbing events he had covered may have contributed to his suicide.

[3]   Cited in Stamets, R. (1994, April 14). Were his priorities out of focus? *Tampa Bay Times*.

[4]   Pond was writing of her experience watching and photographing a Pentecostal man, surrounded by his parishioners, die from a rattlesnake bite instead of calling paramedics against his and his family's wishes. Pond, L. (2012, May 31). Why I watched a snake-handling pastor die for his faith. *The Washington Post*. https://www.washingtonpost.com/lifestyle/style/why-i-watched-a-snake-handling-pastor-die-for-his-faith/2012/05/31/gJQA3fRP5U_story.html

[5]   Cooper details his version of events on his blog. Cooper, A. (2010, January 18). In the midst of looting chaos. http://ac360.blogs.cnn.com/2010/01/18/anderson-in-the-midst-of-looting-chaos

[6]   Quoted in Brainard, C. (2010, January 20). Reporters doubling as docs in Haiti. *Columbia Journalism Review*. https://archives.cjr.org/the_observatory/reporters_doubling_as_docs_in_1.php

[7]   Kaplan, D. (2013, September 30). Agencies, ad tech vendors and avoiding appearance of conflict. *AdExchanger*. http://www.adexchanger.com/agencies/agencies-ad-tech-vendors-and-avoiding-appearance-of-conflict/

[8]   Edwards, J. (2013, June 18). Starcom CEO's personal stake in IPO shows the ad industry doesn't understand conflicts of interest. Business Insider. http://www.businessinsider.com/laura-desmonds-personal-stake-in-tremor-ipo-2013-6

[9]   *The Amalgamated Bank et al v K. Rupert Murdoch et al.* (2011). http://lawprofessors.typepad.com/files/murdoch-shine-complaint.pdf

[10] Sloan, A. (2011, Feb. 24). Missing from Murdoch's family deals: News Corp. shareholders. *Fortune*.

[11] Ironically, the $139 million settlement was paid out to News Corporation because shareholders effectively sue on behalf of the corporation. In the end, News Corporation and attorneys for the plaintiff and the defendant benefited from the settlement. cf. James., M. (2013, April 23). News Corp. agrees to $139-million settlement of suit against board. *Los Angeles Times*.

[12] Kornblut, A. (2007, April 30). Clinton's PowerPointer. *The Washington Post*.

[13] Burger, T. & Jensen, K. (2007, May 24). Clinton aide Penn mixes campaign role, advocacy for companies. *Bloomberg*. http://www.bloomberg.com/apps/news?pid=newsarchive&sid=aYaUqMqpWpW4&refer=home

14 Tumulty, K. (2008, April 8). Clinton's Mark Penn problem. *Time.*
    https://content.time.com/time/politics/article/0,8599,1728992-1,00.html
15 Ibid.
16 Kornblut, A. & Balz, D. (2008, April 7). Clinton's chief strategist steps down. *The Washington Post.*
17 Penn ran into another high-profile conflict of interest one year later, ironically with the same newspaper that had exposed problems with the Colombian free trade agreement. Penn was writing a regular column for the *Wall Street Journal* when it was revealed that Josh Gottheimer (the executive vice president of Burson-Marsteller) was using information in Penn's column to generate new business for the firm. The newspaper rejected the conflict of interest claim because Penn indicated that he had no advance knowledge that his column would be used by the firm and that there was no inappropriate coordination of their efforts. cf. Perez-Pena, R. (2009, August 27). *Wall St. Journal* gives an ethics green light to a P.R. executive's column. *The New York Times.*
18 Segrave, K. (1994). *Payola in the music industry: A history, 1880–1991.* McFarland & Co Inc.
19 Coase, R. H. (1979). Payola in radio and television broadcasting. *Journal of Law and Economics, 22*(2), 269–328.
20 International Public Relations Association. (2020) IPRA code of conduct.
    https://www.ipra.org/member-services/code-of-conduct/
21 National press Photographers Association. (n.d.) NPPA code of ethics.
    http://nppa.org/code-ethics
22 Associated Press Managing Editors. (1994). APME statement of ethical principles.
    http://www.columbia.edu/itc/journalism/j6075/edit/ethiccodes/APME191.html
23 International Association of Business Communicators. (2022). IABC code of ethics for professional communicators. https://www.iabc.com/About/Purpose/Code-of-Ethics
24 *New York Times* (2019). Ethical journalism: A handbook of values and practices for the news and opinion departments.
    https://www.nytimes.com/editorial-standards/ethical-journalism.html#
25 A "short sale" is a stock deal in which the seller borrows stock and sells it, with the idea that the seller will return the same amount of stock at a later date. If you borrow a stock and sell it for $100 a share, then the stock drops to $93 a share next day, you can repurchase it at the lower rate and theoretically make $7 for every share you borrowed. If the stock rises in value, you could stand to lose money instead, because you would still need to purchase the stock in order to return it.
26 Associated Press Managing Editors (1994).
27 Ries, A., & Ries, L. (2004). *The fall of advertising and the rise of PR.* HarperBusiness.

10 Case Study

Public Relations:
Client/Personal/Public Conflict

You are a communications associate with the Eckles Group, the largest public relations agency in the city of Fairview. You moved to the city two years ago to take a position with the firm right out of college. You are anticipating a promotion to junior account executive soon. Not only have you been successful at the company but also as an active member of the community. Perhaps nowhere is this more evident than your work with "Save Fort Pilton"—a local nonprofit organization focused on preserving a deteriorating Civil War era structure and battlefield on the outskirts of Fairview. You have been running a public relations campaign on behalf of the organization for more than a year, and it has finally started to generate enough donations that saving the fort now looks like a real possibility.

On a sunny day in June, you sit in on a lunchtime meeting with the Feckner Corporation—a hot new online entertainment company that plans to open a large regional office in Fairview within the year. Feckner executives are looking for public relations representation, and Eckles Group owner Donna Eckles wants the account. The meeting seems to go well; your supervisor, Nelson Cuddy, asks you to stay for a moment after the meeting.

"We really need this client," Cuddy says as he closes the door. "Not only are they going to be a major employer locally and not only do they offer us a terrific opportunity to expand more into the online environment but there's also a good chance that if we prove ourselves, we could make a bid for the national account."

You agree. The Feckner Corporation seems like a real player in online entertainment. The company has undergone rapid growth over the past 18 months, and the planned expansion into Fairview presents a unique opportunity for the Eckles Group.

"There's one issue though, and I hope this isn't a problem," Cuddy says, taking a seat across the table from you. "I know you've been doing a lot of pro bono work for that Fort Pilton group, and that's great. But . . . well . . . the land that Feckner's looking at for their new facility overlaps a good portion of the old battlefield."

This is bad news, and you tell Cuddy as much. "Save Fort Pilton" has been working hard to get enough money to buy up all of the old battlefield grounds in order to preserve history and perhaps create a visitor site. Just when the group has begun to experience some success, this will be a major disappointment.

Unfortunately, Cuddy explains, the area around the old fort is the best land available. It has sat undeveloped for years, so Feckner believes it can be had cheaply if they move fast. And they *really* want it. He acknowledges that this would be a blow to volunteers and a public relations problem for Feckner, but it would also be an economic boon for the community and your firm. You realize that your help could even put you over the top in your quest for a promotion.

"Look, I know this is an important issue to you, but Donna and I were hoping that maybe you could help us out here," says Cuddy. "We need to know what your group is thinking. What are their plans? Who are their big donors? We're not looking for anything confidential here. But we need to plan a campaign that's really going to win us this client, and we think your experience with the Fort Pilton group can give us the edge we need."

The request is troubling. You have been involved with "Save Fort Pilton" because you believe in the cause. The people you have met in the organization have become friends, and they are as committed to preserving the fort as you are. They trust you and would no doubt feel betrayed if they found out you decided to help develop the old battlefield for a corporation rather than as a historic site. On the other hand, you have a professional obligation to your boss and to a potential client important to your company. You also have a financial obligation to yourself and your family.

After considering all this, you express concern that this conflict of interest might make it very difficult for you to work with Feckner on this project.

Cuddy seems prepared for the question.

"There's no real conflict of interest," he says. "A conflict occurs when you put your personal interests above the interests of the company. That's not the case here. In fact, we're asking you to put the interest of the company ahead of your own interest. So, what do you say? Will you help us out?"

You can ask for a little time to think things over if you want. But Cuddy needs an answer before close of business today. What will you decide to do?

11

Privacy

In this chapter, you will learn about:
- Privacy as a human right
- Legal vs. ethical privacy considerations
- The four civil wrongs of privacy
- Types of persons and their privacy
- Digital privacy
- Values in handling privacy ethics

On July 20, 2021, a monsignor serving as general secretary of the U.S. Conference of Catholic bishops resigned his post after information about impending media reports alleging improper behavior surfaced. Hours after the announcement, The Pillar, a self-described Catholic media project focused on investigative journalism that launched in January 2021, published an article based on commercially available app signal data it had obtained.[1] The article stated the signals indicated Burrill frequented gay bars and used the LGBTQ dating app Grindr.[2]

The monsignor's resignation made headlines around the world. For some it was a story about "holding the powerful to account."[3] Others questioned the ethics of the article. Todd Gitlin, a Columbia University journalism professor, said the article was "scummy" and that hacking devices to obtain information "is illicit, indefensible, and all-around contrary to journalistic ethics." Rick Edmonds, a media business analyst for the Poynter Institute, said: "The article raises a number of questions about cyber security and personal privacy and presents an alarming question of whether you can be tracked wherever you go."[4] Still others noted that the *New York Times* had used smartphone data to track individuals involved in the U.S. Capitol riot but also pointed to the fact that the newspaper only identified one individual, who had agreed to be named for the story.[5]

At the bottom of all these anxieties lies one issue—privacy. Should professional communicators use electronic data to track the behavior of individuals? Should they out the sexual orientation of individuals without their permission? Does it matter if the individuals are prominent people? What about if they belong to organizations that advocate for issues related to sexuality? Does it matter that data is legally or illegally obtained—or does that depend on the situation? The rise of the information society during the past 25 years has driven worries about privacy to the forefront of professional communication ethics.

Privacy as a Human Right

We weren't always so concerned about privacy, which in ancient times existed philosophically primarily as a Western concept. Buddhism, for example, rejects the existence of a self.[6] Early Confucian texts view privacy as a hindrance to the formation of an ideal society,[7] a belief espoused independently by Plato.[8] Aristotle discussed privacy indirectly, differentiating family life from political (public) life. Here the idea of privacy had a negative connotation. The private life was one of "privation" where one was "deprived" of the free association with others that one found in political life.[9]

The political philosopher Hannah Arendt argues that the rise of modern society has blurred the lines between the private and the political such that,

> we call private today a sphere of intimacy whose beginnings we may be able to trace back to late Roman, though hardly to any period of Greek antiquity, but whose peculiar manifoldness and variety were certainly unknown to any period prior to the modern age.[10]

Arendt viewed the modern age as an age defined in part by advances in technology, which is not coincidental with regard to increasing concerns about privacy.

Privacy consultant Jan Holvast observes that the "history of privacy makes clear that there is a strong relationship between privacy and the development of technology."[11] In Aristotle's time, privacy would have been threatened by eavesdropping and gossip. Centuries passed before society developed communication by written letters, which gave rise to the danger of intercepted messages. Again, more time passed before the printing press provided publishers of magazines and newspapers with the ability to publish private information for a wide audience. Even so, concerns for privacy remained low enough that a right to privacy does not explicitly appear in the U.S. Constitution.[12]

Over the next century, we developed the ability to record sound, to capture images in photographs, and to communicate almost immediately over great distances. At the same time, newspaper and magazine readership became much more widespread. This perfect storm of new media and mass communication led to all manner of harm, as attorneys Samuel Warren and Louis Brandeis recognized in their call for recognition of the right to privacy.

> The press is overstepping in every direction the obvious bounds of propriety and of decency. Gossip is no longer the resource of the idle and of the vicious, but has become a trade, which is pursued with industry as well as effrontery. To satisfy a prurient taste the details of sexual relations are . . . broadcast in the columns of the daily papers. To occupy the indolent, column upon column is filled with idle gossip, which can only be procured by intrusion upon the domestic circle.[13]

Technology that makes it possible to magnify the reach of one's words also magnifies the harm that could be caused by those words.

Warren and Brandeis described privacy as "the general right of the individual to be let alone."[14] Without legal protection, privacy remained almost exclusively a matter of ethics and personal conscience. Nearly 40 years after he had cowritten the call for a right to privacy, Brandeis wrote the dissenting opinion in a U.S. Supreme Court case where his concerns about invasive technology had proven prophetic. In that case, the government had admitted wiretapping eight phone lines to record conversations among individuals who were suspected of violating prohibition laws. The individuals had not been arrested or indicted, nor had the government obtained any judicial order for the surveillance. However, the Court ruled that the wiretaps did not violate the plaintiffs' Constitutional protection from illegal search and seizure because wiretapping did not represent a physical search, nothing physical was seized, and agents did not go onto the plaintiff's property. In his dissent from that opinion, Justice Brandeis wrote that time works changes and "subtler and more far-reaching means of invading privacy have become available to the government"—and these new technologies were even worse than previous "puny instruments of tyranny," such as physical search and seizure, because they enabled the government to invade the privacy of many individuals at once, even those not suspected of crimes.[15]

Four "Civil Wrongs" of Privacy

When it comes to the ethics of privacy, professional communicators rely on law for guidance perhaps more than in any other area of ethics. Our professions do not usually call on us to violate the truth, breech confidentiality, and so on. But we often must obtain information and communicate publicly about matters that others might view as private. Concepts of legal privacy can help us frame our discussion not only of what we *cannot* legally do but also of what we *should not* ethically do when it comes to privacy.

The legal right to privacy owes much to the work of Warren and Brandeis. Seventy years later, William Prosser restructured invasions of privacy into four *torts* (civil wrongs) actionable in court.[16] His categories can serve as a framework for discussing the ethics of privacy in professional communication.

Intrusion into Seclusion. When we enter property that is not open to the public without permission, we are trespassing. If we gather information while there, we are likely also violating the privacy of the owner and any individuals who have a right to be there. This covers not only land and buildings but personal property such as packages and backpacks. It also extends to audio/video recording or other eavesdropping technology that does not involve physical intrusion. Note that intrusion covers the gathering of information whether or not we intend to disseminate it. We potentially make the invasion even more harmful when we disseminate that information.

In the modern era, the civil wrong of intrusion applies equally to private spaces online. This raises questions about what might be considered "private space" online. Certainly, one's email account would qualify. What about Instagram posts limited to friends? Is a Facebook post defaulting to a "public" audience fair game? Can we gather information from a public Reddit group? What about creating an account to access a forum where people discuss child abuse? Is there a difference between using the information we gather for purposes of market research or quoting someone's "public" speech for an article on our blog? These are ethical discussions informed by our recognition of an individual's desire for privacy and our ethical and legal needs to balance that against other considerations.

Public Disclosure of Private Facts. Factually true details of one's past or present life may be embarrassing and potentially harmful to one's reputation. Prosser argued that the publication of such facts constituted a civil wrong when they were: (1) disclosed to the public, as opposed to an individual or small group; (2) sufficiently private; and 3) likely to be deemed offensive to a reasonable person.

In the United States, what we do in public spaces or in full view of others generally does not merit legal privacy protection. As we will see, information about individuals who have chosen to lead public lives—such as actors, musicians, politicians, sports figures and social media influencers—also receives limited protection. The same holds true for information related to criminal proceedings, at least in the United States. However, some countries do have laws prohibiting the naming of crime victims or the accused, prior to their being found guilty.

Professional communicators might have a legal right to publish information, but questions remain as to whether publication could be ethically justified. For example, most U.S. states permit the media to name victims of sex crimes. Most media outlets choose not to do so for ethical reasons. However, they frequently do name the accused, long before the courts decide that individual's guilt or innocence. Professional media typically may legally identify a juvenile accused of committing a crime, provided that they have lawfully obtained the juvenile's name.[17] Likewise, we could use public databases to identify the shortest driver in the state or the teacher with the most parking tickets. In each case, ethics compels us to ask whether we *should* do so.

Placing a Person in False Light. False light is the civil wrong of using accurate facts in such a way that they paint a false picture of an individual that causes harm. Suppose your campus newspaper runs a story that children who recently visited campus have complained that someone touched them inappropriately during their visit. Suppose further that they illustrate that story with a photo of you volunteering at the event and playing with the children. You might reasonably object that, while the photo is accurate, its context within the story makes it falsely seem as though you had inappropriate contact with the children. Professional communicators must always be on guard to ensure that the information published is not only factually accurate but also provided in a context that does not mislead the audience.

Technology adds new twists to claims of false light in the era of Photoshop. In 2017, a tattoo model filed a $5 million lawsuit against rapper Cardi B charging misappropriation of likeness and false light invasion of privacy.[18] The cover photo for a mixtape that helped launch her career depicted a man with a full back tattoo of a tiger battling a snake; the man is performing a sex act on the rapper. The cover designer did a Google search and found a photo of Brophy's back tattoo. The designer used Photoshop to apply the image to the back of the model on the cover. Brophy contended that the tattoo was unique and that it led people to believe that it was his image, which in turn harmed him and his family. The trial took place five years after the initial filing and lasted two and one-half days. Cardi B contended that the mixtape image was not Brophy's. On October 21, 2022, the jury sided with Cardi B.[19]

Appropriation of One's Image or Likeness. The Cardi B lawsuit touches on another area of privacy—the unauthorized use of a person's name, likeness, or comparable unique symbols of one's identity that results in harm to that person. In addition, individuals have a *right of publicity*, which prohibits the unauthorized use of their names or likenesses for financial gain. Prosser originally argued that, as with one's person or property, one should have exclusive control over one's own name and likeness.[20] Prosser's notion of appropriation grew into two distinct concepts: misappropriation (requiring a demonstration of harm) and publicity (requiring use for financial gain.). Some states now have different laws governing misappropriation and publicity. In some cases, a state might require that individuals be a celebrity or that they in some other way earn money from their name or likeness in order to make a claim under the publicity tort.[21]

In the Cardi B case, the model argues that his tattoo constitutes a uniquely identifiable part of his body and so represents a unique symbol of his identity. He contends that the use of identity in this manner has caused him harm (misappropriation) and that it has been used without authorization for another's financial gain (publicity).

Laws differentiate the types of harm caused by violations of one's privacy, but ethical concerns remain about how we should act when deciding what to do. Since the 1960s, privacy has entailed a set of freedoms. On the one hand, privacy entails an interest in avoiding disclosure of personal matters—often meaning the freedom to withdraw. On the other it involves the power to control publicity about oneself—the freedom to project one's identity in society. After the Supreme Court ruling in *NCAA v. Alston* that found NCAA rules limiting the education-related benefits for student athletes violated federal antitrust laws, the NCAA in July 2021 changed its regulations to allow student athletes to earn compensation for their name, image, and likeness (NIL). Student athletes were allowed to profit from their public personas—and to prevent others from profiting from unauthorized appropriation (the right to publicity).

Types of Persons and Their Privacy

Another area where Prosser's concept of the right to privacy helps to clarify ethical discussion is that of public vs. private figures. Prosser defined public figures as those who by their own choice have entered a position in the public eye and, more broadly, as anyone who has simply "arrived" at such a position.[22] He argued that,

> such public figures are held to have lost, to some extent at least, their right of privacy. Three reasons are given, more or less indiscriminately, in the decisions: that they have sought

publicity and consented to it, and so cannot complain of it; that their personalities and their affairs already have become public, and can no longer be regarded as their own private business; and that the press has a privilege, guaranteed by the Constitution, to inform the public about those who have become legitimate matters of public interest.[23]

The question arises as to who might constitute a public figure. Here we might benefit from definitions arising from another area of law—that pertaining to *libel*, the publication of false information that harms the reputation of an identifiable person or persons.

From an *ethical* perspective, we can distinguish at least five types of persons whose privacy could be compromised by the actions of professional communicators.

1. *Private figures.* Most of us are private figures—regular citizens who have not actively sought or gained fame through our actions or our career choices. We retain the highest degree of control over our identities and therefore the protection of our privacy. This does not mean that other categories of people surrender all their rights to privacy. However, their status as non-private figures factors into discussions related to their personal information.

2. *Public officials.* At the opposite end of the privacy spectrum are individuals who have or appear to have power over governmental matters. This includes any elected officials, including the president of the United States. Some spouses, although not elected to office, might also reasonably be viewed as having power over some governmental matters. Public officials also include the heads of various governmental departments—from federal government offices down to the local police chief. In general, we view personal details about public officials as newsworthy and open to public scrutiny in ways that do not apply to private figures.

3. *General-Purpose Public Figures.* This category includes celebrities such actors, musicians, social media influencers, sports figures, and other individuals who have deliberately placed themselves in the public eye. In so doing, they might be viewed as having surrendered some of their right to privacy. Aspects of their lives could reasonably be seen as newsworthy in ways that would not apply to private figures.

4. *Limited-Purpose Public Figures.* These individuals have entered into some public controversy or a limited position of authority in the public eye, but they have not achieved the same degree of name recognition as general-purpose public figures. They retain a high degree of privacy on matters

beyond what placed them in the public eye. For example, scientists who speak out on climate change might reasonably be seen as opening themselves up to an examination of their scientific work as a whole and their personal lives, limited specifically to climate change (e.g., their own carbon footprint). In all other aspects of their lives, they generally merit treatment as private figures.[24]

5. *Accidental Public Figures*. Private figures sometimes take an action that makes them newsworthy, even though they did not seek to enter the public eye. Take, for example, "Alex from Target." At age 16, he was working a checkout counter at Target when someone quietly snapped a photo of him and put it on the Internet.[25] The photo went viral, with people on social media raving over his youthful good looks. Alex did not take part or even know about the photo or its posting. Ethically speaking, he was an accidental public figure made famous through no fault of his own and therefore owed all the privacy due a private figure. Subsequently, he agreed to be flown to Los Angeles to appear on *The Ellen DeGeneres Show* and consciously entered the public eye, surrendering some of his rights to privacy. However, social media pandemonium can become so out of control that it prevents a rational approach to privacy and ethics. Screaming teenage girls chased Alex when he appeared in public, there were insults and death threats on social media, and the family's personal information (social security numbers, bank accounts, and phone records) were posted online.[26]

Digital Privacy

The four torts of privacy do not address all the issues of privacy. In fact, some have argued that the focus on Prosser's conception of privacy has at times made the law less able to adapt to new circumstances and new technologies.[27] For example, we might ask which privacy torts cover *doxing*, the publication of one's personal information (e.g., address, phone number, employer) online, often for the purpose of encouraging persecution of the individual whose information has been shared. One might argue that doxing constitutes a form of misappropriation or nonspecific invasion of privacy; however, the courts tend to deal with it as a form of harassment or victimization. While these distinctions are important in legal matters, in ethics the fact that an action potentially causes harm carries more value than how we might categorize it.

From a professional communication standpoint, we must also consider privacy concerns arising from the collection of personal data online. The amount of information gathered from individuals can be staggering. One data privacy story highlighted the example of a middle school math teacher identified through cellphone data that tracked her to a Weight Watchers meeting, to her dermatologist's office, while she was hiking, and staying at her ex-boyfriend's home.[28] People grant access to their location to apps that, for example, provide traffic information, weather, or local news. Frequently those apps do not reveal that they can share and sell the data gathered. As we saw in the introduction to this chapter, data obtained from cell phones and apps can be used to harm the individuals from whom it was gathered.

From an ethical standpoint, we need to be concerned about multiple details related to the gathering and use of online data. Some of the concerns are summarized below.

- *Purpose.* Is the data used to benefit the individual from whom it was obtained, or is it used or sold for the benefit of others?
- *Disclosure.* Is the data gathered overtly, with the full knowledge and consent of the user, or covertly without the user's knowledge?
- *Identifiability.* Is the data individualized, containing identifiable personal data, or is it aggregated or redacted so that it cannot be connected to any single individual?
- *Ownership.* Does the user retain ownership and control over their data, or does the gathering or purchasing agency claim ownership?
- *Compensation.* If the agency claims ownership, did the user agree to the sharing of ownership and receive compensation for the data?

Research shows that the reputations of professional communicators and the companies involved can be at stake.[29]

Handling Privacy Ethics

When handling privacy from an ethical perspective, we benefit from the law's ability to identify issues and inform our discussion. But ethics is a matter separate from law, and it requires its own rational analysis. Usually, this involves deciding whether we ought *not* make public something that we legally *may* make public.

Ethics demands respect for humanity and the interests of people who do not want disclosure of private information. Professional communicators, however, must also consider the public's right to know in certain situations. In making decisions about whether private information should be made public, there are three overriding concerns—autonomy, fairness, and transparency.

As we have seen, an individual's reasonable expectation of privacy varies with the degree to which their actions have placed them in the public eye. It is a matter of *autonomy*—the right to govern oneself. Public officials and public figures consciously surrender their privacy to some degree, but private figures typically do not.

Imagine you are the head of public relations for your firm, and you discover that an employee has cancer. Wanting to create good publicity and help the employee with expenses, you create a GoFundMe-style fundraiser. If you have done this without first consulting that employee, you might have violated their privacy. Not everyone wants to make their cancer status public nor to have money raised on their behalf. You violate others' autonomy by disclosing their private information and using their name without their advance approval. Regardless of your benevolent motives, it is their decision to make, not yours.

Fairness means treating people impartially, without any inherent bias or favoritism. Decisions related to protecting privacy can easily lead to unethical treatment of individuals when we fail to ensure fair treatment of all. We must treat all people equally in light of their status as private or public figures, without regard for our personal feelings.

Imagine you are a crime blogger covering a police report about a drug bust. The suspects call you to proclaim their innocence, asking that you keep their names off of your blog because they don't want it to interfere with their college admission applications. Do you base your decision on whether or not you believe them? If that's the case, you will probably introduce your personal biases into the decision of whose information becomes public and whose does not. Do you make case-by-case decisions about whether to publish the addresses of burglary victims and what was stolen from them? By what criteria do you do so? Do you agree to withhold victim information at the requests of arresting officers? What criteria do they use when they make such requests? These types of individual decisions can lead to unfair and unjust results.

We can attempt to ensure fairness by creating rules in advance and then following those rules when making decisions about private information. For example, "we do not publish the names or street addresses of crime victims." Of course, we might find ourselves deciding to break those rules in certain circumstances, perhaps creating new rules or amendments in the process. But we do so through an organized process intended to ensure fairness.

Maintaining *transparency* is important. Transparency includes being honest and forthright with ourselves, our colleagues, our customers, and the public about the actions we take and the ethical reasoning behind them. If you sell information provided by your customers, transparency demands that you ensure that they know what you are doing and why. If you withhold the names of victims at the request of the arresting officers, make plain your reasoning for doing so. Any policy you or your company follow that affects stakeholders in an ethical situation should be communicated fully to ensure that all involved share the same ethical expectations.

Summary

The concept of privacy as a human right has a long-standing history, with its philosophical roots dating back to the ancient Greeks. The advance of technology has played a significant role in the heightened sense of a need for privacy. The perfect storm of new media and mass communication prompted Warren and Brandeis to articulate the need for legal protection of privacy—one's right to be left alone. William Prosser categorized four civil wrongs of the invasion of privacy: (1) intrusion, (2) disclosure, (3) false light, and (4) appropriation.

The publication of private information can be more or less ethically permissible based on the public or private status of the person involved. We have a special responsibility to protect the personal information of private figures. In contrast, we have a wide degree of latitude when publishing information about public figures who have voluntarily entered the public eye. Limited purpose public figures are individuals who enter the public spotlight in a limited way or on a specific issue; they surrender their privacy as it relates to that issue. Some individuals accidentally draw public attention; accidental public figures typically receive the same respect as private figures.

Digital privacy has grown in importance along with the rise of the web and social media this century. Gathering personal data from online and other media users raises a number of questions, including who owns the data, the purpose for which the data will be used, whether the users consented to the gathering and use, whether the user is identifiable, and whether users are compensated for their data. These issues affect the privacy of personal information for users and the reputations of professional communicators and the companies for which they work.

Professional communicators should acknowledge and support the autonomy of individuals—the right to control their personal information. In addition, fairness requires that all people be treated equally, without personal bias or favoritism. Finally, motives and the ethical decisions made with regard to privacy should be transparent.

NOTES

1. Data from mobile devices is portrayed as anonymous by substituting unique numerical identifiers for users' names and phone numbers. However, when phone location and app usage is recorded, people with information about residences, workplaces, and other data points can connect the numerical identifier data to a specific individual. Steinfels, P. (2021, August 16). The deep strangeness of the Catholic church's latest scandal. *The Atlantic*. The cost to identify a single individual from a data set that could have signals from millions of users is very costly—experts estimate hundreds of thousands of dollars. The Pillar did not identify the source of the data, the cost to obtain, or who paid the fees.

2. White, C. (2021, July 28). New Catholic website "The Pillar" operates on shaky journalistic foundation. *National Catholic Reporter*. https://www.ncronline.org/news/new-catholic-website-pillar-operates-shaky-journalistic-foundation

3. Hennessey, M. (2021, 2 Aug.). Catholic journalists expose a scandal, and liberals scoff. *Wall Street Journal Opinion*. https://www.wsj.com/articles/catholic-church-scandal-jeffrey-burrill-pillar-grindr-11627915562

4. Gitlin and Edmonds quoted in White (2021).

5. Boorstein, M., Iati, M and Izadi, E. (2021, July 24). A Catholic newsletter promised investigative journalism. Then it outed a priest using Grindr data. *The WashingtonPost*. https://www.washingtonpost.com/religion/catholic-priest-grindr-pillar/2021/07/24/b2772f02-ecb6-11eb-8950-d73b3e93ff7f_story.html

6. An interesting argument for a Buddhist conception of privacy can be found in Hongladarom S. (2016) *A Buddhist theory of privacy*. Springer.

7. Whitman, C. B. (1985). Privacy in Confucian and Taoist thought. In D. Munro (Ed.), *Individualism and holism: Studies in Confucian and Taoist values* (pp. 85–100). University of Michigan Center for Chinese Studies. https://repository.law.umich.edu/cgi/viewcontent.cgi?article=1020&context=book_chapters

8. Arruzza, C. (2011). The private and the common in Plato's *Republic*. *History of Political Thought, 32*(2), 215–233.

9. Arendt, H. (1998). *The human condition*. University of Chicago Press (Original work published 1958), p. 38.

10. Ibid.

11. Holvast, J. (2007). History of privacy. In K. de Leeuw & J. Bergstra (Eds.), *The history of information security: A comprehensive handbook* (737–770). Elsevier, p. 737.

12. Several amendments to the Constitution imply privacy rights. For example, the First Amendment secures the freedom to choose any religious belief and to keep the choice private; the Third Amendment protects privacy in the home; the Fourth Amendment protects the right of privacy against unlawful search/seizure by the government; the Fifth Amendment justifies the protection of private information under its right against self-discrimination; the Ninth Amendment interpreted as justifying a broad reading of the Bill of Rights protects a fundamental right to privacy not specifically stated in the first eight amendments; the Fourteenth Amendment prohibits states from passing legislation that infringes on personal autonomy protections in the first thirteen amendments. Findlaw Staff (2022, October 18). Is there a "right to privacy" amendment? Findlaw. https://www.findlaw.com/injury/torts-and-personal-injuries/is-there-a-right-to-privacy-amendment.html

13. Warren, S.D. and Brandeis, L.A. (1890). The right to privacy. *Harvard Law Review, 4*(5), 193–220, p. 196. https://doi.org/10.2307/1321160

14 Ibid., p. 205.

15 *Olmstead et al. v. United States*, 277 U.S. 438 (1928). The case was reversed by *Katz v. U.S.* (1967).

16 Prosser, W. (1960). The torts of privacy. *California Law Review, 383*(48), 392–398, p. 389.

17 In general, police are prohibited from releasing the names of juveniles. However, journalists have other ways of obtaining that information.

18 Weiss, D. C. (2020, Dec. 8). Judge allows lawsuit against Cardi B over "humiliating" use of tattoo on album cover. *ABAJournal.*

19 Landrum, J. (2022, October 21). Cardi B absolved in racy mixtape artwork lawsuit. ABC News.

20 Prosser, W. (1960), p. 406.

21 Noa Dreymann provides an excellent discussion of publicity law applied to celebrities and non-celebrities in Dreymann, N. (2017). John Doe's right of publicity. *Berkeley Technology Law Journal, 32*, 673–712. She argues that the right of publicity has increasingly and wrongfully been limited to celebrities when it should afford protection to to non-celebrities as well.

22 Prosser, W. (1960), pp. 410–411.

23 Ibid., p. 411.

24 The more individuals enter the public arena, the more privacy they surrender. Those who voluntarily appear on talk shows or who testify before Congress usually become correspondingly more open to public scrutiny.

25 Kaufman, L. (2014, Nov. 5). Known as "Alex from Target," teenage clerk rises to star on Twitter and talk shows. *The New York Times.* https://www.nytimes.com/2014/11/06/business/media/teenage-clerk-rises-from-target-to-star-on-twitter-and-talk-shows-.html

26 Bilton, N. (2014, November 12). Alex from Target: The other side of fame. *The New York Times.*

27 See, for example, Richards & Solove. (2010).

28 Singer, N. (2018, Dec. 10). Your apps know where you were last night, and they're not keeping it secret. *The Irish Times.* https://www.irishtimes.com/business/technology/your-apps-know-where-you-were-last-night-and-they-re-not-keeping-it-secret-1.3726102

29 See, for example, Aguirre, E., Mahr, D., Grewal, D., de Ruyter, K. and Wetzels, M. (2015). Unraveling the personalization paradox: The effect of information collection and trust-building strategies on online advertisement effectiveness. *Journal of Retailing, 91*(1), pp. 34–49. doi: 10.1016/j.jretai.2014.09.005

11 Case Study

Advertising:
Privacy and Marketing Technology

You are the president of Tatum and Harper Advertising in New York City. Your company has been attempting to make a name for itself in the rapidly growing field of online marketing. To that end, you have been considering ways to gather better information about customers and potential customers online.

Your research has led you to a newly developed computer program that tracks consumer behavior online. The software, HappyBuddy Helper, offers a wide variety of tools for tracking online behavior—from examining how customers use your clients' websites to gathering specific details about customers, their interests, purchases, and practically everything they do online.

The program requires that those being tracked download and run a bit of software code. To encourage this, customers and potential customers are given the opportunity to enter a contest online. Entering requires that the user complete a form and accept the "terms and conditions" of the contest. One of these conditions is that they agree to download and run HappyBuddy Helper.

You need to decide which level of tracking you want to purchase. The options, which gather progressively more information, are:

Level 1: Data from the contest form is used to fully identify the user. Whenever customers visit one of your clients' websites, HappyBuddy tracks what pages they visit, what products they view, and so forth. On subsequent visits, HappyBuddy can customize websites to make it easier for customers to find and see the types of things in which indicated an interest.

Level 2: HappyBuddy runs in the background whenever the customer launches a web browser. It lists every site that the user visits and whether or not the site belongs to a present client. It also lists the order in which those sites were visited and the length of time the customer spent on each Web page. This information is sent to your firm whenever the user logs onto the computer.

Level 3: Every time a user completes a form online, HappyBuddy copies the information and sends it to your firm. This will include data such as name, address, phone number, age, income, and so forth. It could also include answers to a variety of questions such as color preferences or the kinds of purchases the user has made within the past year.

Level 4: HappyBuddy takes control of the user's web cam when it is not in use. The program uses the web cam to monitor the user's activities in order to help determine how closely they are looking at the sites they are visiting and what other activities they might be engaged in. This could be used to identify products currently possessed by the user, as well as potentially employ eye-tracking software to investigate how users interact with web pages.

The possibility of acquiring HappyBuddy Helper has generated excitement and concern among members of your team.

Julie Bailey, vice president of marketing services, is impressed with the quality and quantity of information that can be gathered by the software. It might be cliché, but it is also true that "information is power." And this is potentially a lot of information. "The sheer volume of data gathered by the program could provide Tatum and Harper with the information it needs to customize client websites, help manage product development, and market products to entirely new customer bases in entirely new ways," she says. "We could even take it a step further and combine it with everything from driving data to grocery store purchases to create a complete profile of every single customer and potential customer for our clients' products and services. Wow!"

Jerry Bowman, vice president of account services, believes that access to this information could prove very useful in winning over new clients and providing better service to existing clients. "With this information in our hands, we know more about our clients' customers than the clients do," says Bowman. "Heck, we know more about the customers than they know about themselves."

Roseann Donato, vice president of management services, isn't so sure about all this information gathering. "Some of this is pretty intrusive," she says. "Is it really okay for us to be spying on people this way? And what are we using the information for? If it's to benefit the customers, then we might be okay in some instances. But if we're using the information to take advantage of the customers' weaknesses or overall psychology, even in the interest of our clients, then I'm not so sure we *should* be doing this even if we can."

The decision is ultimately yours to make. Will you go ahead with the HappyBuddy Helper software purchase? If so, what level of tracking will you implement and why?

12

Confidentiality

In this chapter, you will learn about:
- Confidentiality as distinct from privacy
- Implicit and explicit promises of confidentiality
- Factors affecting the reasonable expectation of confidentiality
- Legal protections for confidentiality
- Ethical obligations of confidentiality
- Confidentiality owed clients and employers
- Source and information confidentiality in journalism

Mass communication professionals are in the business of information. Information can be valuable—sometimes very valuable indeed: tomorrow's winning lottery numbers; the closing number of the stock market one week from today; the location of buried treasure; the exact value of an old painting you see at a yard sale; the exact specifications of the next generation mobile phone; adverse health information pertaining to the CEO of a multibillion-dollar tech firm. The right information in the right hands can be worth millions or even billions of dollars.

Information can also be dangerous: military troop transport schedules; top secret aircraft plans; a list of police informants or undercover officers; the name of a government whistleblower; information on how to engineer a deadly virus. Certain information in the wrong hands can get people hurt or even killed.

As a communication professional, you will encounter information every day. Most of that information is common or easily obtained by those who are interested. Anyone can request a police report, check out the advertising rates in local media, view information about a public corporation, or take a photo in a public place, at least in the United States. But communication professionals also regularly encounter information that can be valuable and/or dangerous. That is when confidentiality becomes an ethical issue.

Confidentiality and Privacy

Confidentiality refers to the promise to retain as secret any information that the source does not want identified. It differs from *privacy*, the right of an individual or group of individuals to maintain control over their bodies, their property, and certain information about themselves. Privacy is an innate right of individuals. By contrast, confidentiality arises from promises made by the communication professional.

Promises of confidentiality can be either explicit or implied. An *explicit promise of confidentiality* is one that is overtly stated in order to gain access to information. A public relations manager might be required to sign an agreement that all client information should be maintained as confidential. The agreement is an overt promise of confidentiality. Likewise, a journalist who agrees to protect a source's identity has explicitly granted confidentiality and becomes ethically obligated to ensure the source remains anonymous.

An *implied promise of confidentiality* arises from creating or permitting a reasonable expectation of confidentiality without an overt promise. As with the expectation of truth, this expectation of implied confidentiality arises from: (1) the setting of the communication; (2) the relationship of the communicators; and (3) the nature of the information being communicated.[1]

The setting of the communication. An informal setting, such as a chance meeting at a coffee shop, might be more likely to imply confidentiality than a formal setting, such as a meeting at the office. If you have a casual conversation with a reporter at a bar, you would probably be surprised to find your statements in a news report the next day. By contrast, if the reporter makes an appointment and visits you during normal business hours, you will have a lower expectation of confidentiality. Comments made publicly, especially those at government meetings, have no implied confidentiality. This is true even when the speaker attempts to assert such confidentiality through statements such as "now, this is off the record." Everything that happens in public or during a government meeting is considered on the record.

The relationship of the communicators. The closer the relationship, working or nonworking, the more likely that confidentiality could be implied. For example, a conversation between friends might be more likely to imply confidentiality than a conversation between a journalist and a source. The character of some relationships, such as advertiser/client, implies confidentiality. Other relationships, such as reporter/source, do not imply confidentiality provided that the journalist has first identified himself or herself as a journalist. An overt confidentiality agreement, written or verbal, is usually required in order to reasonably expect that information will be safeguarded by the journalist.

The nature of the information being communicated. Some information inherently implies a level of confidentiality. The more intimate, embarrassing, incriminating or dangerous the information, the greater the implication of confidentiality. A client who expresses a preference for tea over coffee has a lower expectation of confidentiality than one discussing plans to release a new product in the coming year.

In situations where a promise of confidentiality could reasonably be implied, responsibility for clarifying the situation rests with both parties. However, a special burden is placed on the individual who might be judged as violating implied confidentiality. If the communication professional intends to share the information with others, it must be made clear that no implication of confidentiality exists. This could be as overt as a reporter asking, "We're on the record here, right?" or seeking permission to get the individual to speak on camera. Depending on the situation, it can be as subtle as a journalist obviously beginning to take notes or a public relations practitioner inviting a coworker into the conversation. No matter the technique used, the individual providing information must be reasonably aware that the information can be shared or made public.

Legal Protections of Confidentiality

Society recognizes the value of confidentiality, so much so that it provides a level of legal protection for confidentiality in some situations. Explicit promises of confidentiality can be viewed as contracts that receive protection under contract law. If advertising executives sign a confidentiality agreement and then provide confidential information to a third party, they might be sued for violating a contract. The same applies to a reporter who violates a promise— a verbal contract—not to reveal the name of a source. However, a court can overrule these explicit promises of confidentiality. In such cases, information about a client or source can be revealed to the court without legal penalty.

The explicit or implied confidentiality of some relationships are protected even in courts of law. For example, spouses cannot be forced to reveal confidential information received from one another. The government cannot compel a lawyer to divulge confidential information about a client without that client's consent. Priest/penitent and doctor/patient relationships also benefit from a level of legal protection. Communication in these types of relationships is considered *privileged*—confidential communication about which one cannot be compelled to testify in a court of law. Such privileges are far from absolute, but they do provide a level of protection for confidentiality.

While mass communication professionals can be obligated both ethically and legally by explicit promises of confidentiality, they do not enjoy a high degree of protection from being forced to reveal confidential information in a court of law. The nature of business, as well as the government's right and responsibility to oversee commercial transactions, results in almost no privilege for client communication in advertising and public relations. However, journalists do enjoy limited privilege in their work. This comes in the form of *shield laws*, state legislation aimed at giving reporters some protection from being legally compelled to reveal privileged information in court.

Shield laws typically allow journalists to maintain as confidential the identity of anonymous sources. In some cases, the laws also offer protection for nonconfidential material such as photographs, video, or other information that a reporter has gathered but not used in a news report. For example, law enforcement officials might want to view unused video of a riot to identify suspects in the theft of electronics from a local retail outlet. Journalists typically object to such a high level of cooperation so that they do not risk being seen as an arm of law enforcement while reporting on potentially illegal activities. Shields laws can give them some level of protection in these cases.

Note that the "reporter privilege" granted by shield laws is far from absolute. First, despite pleas from journalists, the federal government does not have a shield law.[2] Wyoming is the only state without a shield law.[3] Shield laws vary in the other states, providing either an absolute or qualified privilege to refuse to disclose sources or information obtained in the course of news gathering. In general, the courts honor journalistic privilege except when: (1) there is probable cause that the journalist has information related to the commission of a crime; (2) the information "cannot be obtained by alternative means less destructive of First Amendment rights;" and (3) the government has a "compelling and overriding interest in the information."[4]

Ethical Obligations of Confidentiality

Remember that the law and ethics are different. What is legal might not be ethical, and what is ethical might not be legal. But it is important to be familiar with the law in order to understand the limitation of confidentiality promises made to clients and sources. The courts have the legal right to compel advertising and public relations professionals to divulge confidential information given or received from their clients. Because the government will generally take precautions to safeguard against the public release of any confidential or proprietary information, this does not usually present an ethical problem. However, clients should be aware that ethical obligations do not supersede legal obligations when under subpoena by a court of law.

In some states and in some circumstances, courts may also compel journalists to surrender confidential information or the names of confidential sources. Failure to comply with a court's demands could result in contempt of court charges and jail time for the journalist. Perhaps the most famous such case involved Judith Miller, a *New York Times* reporter who refused to testify concerning the name of a government official who had told her the name of an undercover CIA operative. Miller spent 85 days in jail before she testified after receiving a telephone call from her source releasing her from her confidentiality agreement.

Journalists must consider legal requirements before making promises of confidentiality. In cases where their source has knowledge related to the commission of a crime, the journalist may be legally obligated to divulge the source's name in a court of law. The source has a right to know whether the journalist intends to comply with any legal obligation to reveal the information, or whether the journalist is willing to maintain source confidentiality beyond the limits of the law. Absent an agreement that protects confidentiality only to the legal limits, journalists are generally considered to have an ethical obligation to maintain confidentiality with their sources even if it means going to jail.

It should be noted that confidentiality agreements can be nullified in cases where maintaining such agreements clearly runs counter to a compelling public need. For example, confidentiality does not apply to the intent to commit a felony crime, especially one that would result in death or serious injury. If a journalist promises confidentiality to a whistleblower and during the course of the interview that whistleblower confesses the intent to kill his coworkers, the journalist does *not* have a professional ethical obligation to keep that information secret.

Confidentiality in Advertising and Public Relations

Professionals in advertising and public relations owe an implicit ethical duty of confidentiality to clients and to employers in addition to any explicit promises of confidentiality that they make. This duty applies to all clients and employers—past, present, and prospective, including pro bono work. Confidential information from a past client should not be used to benefit a present client nor to win over a prospective one. Information may be shared as part of a consultation with other professionals—provided they are similarly bound by a promise of confidentiality to the employer/client who is aware that the information will be shared. Confidential information also may be shared ethically in cases where there is a compelling public need to do so, such as the need to prevent physical harm to the public. However, the decision to share confidential information should not be an individual decision, except in those very rare situations where clear and immediate danger requires such a decision.

Clients. A client's information must be protected for the good of the client. In situations where confidential information should be shared outside of the individuals assigned to a project—including suppliers and contractors—the client should first provide consent. A client's confidential information exists to benefit the client, not the professional, the agency, or outside interests.

Employers. Professionals in advertising and public relations have the same obligation to protect employer confidentiality as they do to protect client confidentiality. This does not mean that skills, techniques, tactics, and other nonproprietary aspects of professional development cannot be learned and brought to the benefit of other employers. It does mean that the confidential and/or proprietary information of an employer, such as specific plans to reach into new markets or to obtain new clients, remains the property of that employer and is not shared to benefit the employee or other agencies.

Confidentiality in Journalism

Confidentiality in journalism falls into two broad categories: source confidentiality and information confidentiality.

Source Confidentiality (Anonymous Sources)

Source confidentiality refers to a journalist's promise to maintain the confidentiality of information gathered from a news source and/or the source's identity. The Society of Professional Journalists notes that few ethical issues in journalism are more connected to the law than the use of anonymous sources.[5] Both keeping a promise not to identify a source and breaking such a promise could result in legal proceedings. Anonymous sources are sometimes the only means of breaking a story that has important consequences for readers, but anonymous sources can also mire journalists in ethical dilemmas.

Journalists prefer *not* to make promises of confidentiality to sources. Information from anonymous sources possesses less inherent credibility than information from named sources. Credibility is an absolute necessity for journalists; readers must believe the journalist's information is accurate and fair.[6] Readers can't evaluate the possible motives of unnamed sources. The sources themselves are less accountable for what they say. Moreover, granting confidentiality to a source places a burden on the journalist to protect that source's identity. As a result, journalism organizations recommend that sources be identified whenever possible.

Despite the desire of journalists to identify every source in every story, sometimes a source may require a promise of anonymity before speaking with a journalist. Remember that a promise of anonymity is just that—a promise. It cannot be forced on the journalist, nor can it be demanded after the fact. For example, there are times when a source might offer up information that he or she did not intend to divulge and then say "Now, all that was off the record." Not so. Indeed, a journalist will often respond "My question was on the record." In such cases, the journalist is not ethically compelled to maintain confidentiality. However, he or she might decide that it is in everyone's best interest to do so, particularly when interviewing a source who has little experience dealing with the press.

In cases when a source demands anonymity before agreeing to provide information, the need for anonymity must be balanced against the public's need for the information. Confidentiality should be reserved for stories of overriding public importance.[7] Before promising anonymity, a journalist should consider several questions.

1. Does the value of the information warrant granting anonymity to the source? Journalists will often ask the source to clarify the kind of information that will be discussed before deciding whether to grant anonymity.

2. Does the source have an actual *need* to remain anonymous? Many sources desire anonymity, but not all have a real need to remain unnamed. Journalists usually reserve anonymity for those sources who fear for their lives, their jobs, or their safety.

3. Does the source have personal or professional motives for releasing the information? Does the information enhance the reputation of the source while undermining that of others? Personal agendas reduce the credibility of the source. Public interest outweighs personal or professional interest in issues where the source desires anonymity. For example, political sources who offer negative information about their

own candidates would be more likely to receive anonymity than those who offer negative information about candidates in the opposing party.

4. Does the source have direct knowledge of a crime or did the source commit a crime to gain the information he or she intends to provide? A source who wants to blow the whistle on a company's illegal activities has knowledge of a crime. A source who takes documents from the company and delivers them to the journalist has likely committed a crime. In either case, a court could demand that the journalist reveal the information or go to jail for contempt of court. Journalists need to discuss how far they will go to protect a source's anonymity.

When a journalist agrees to promise confidentiality to a source, conditions of the agreement should be clarified so that both parties know what to expect. Given that sources, especially inexperienced sources, can be confused about promises of anonymity, responsibility for guaranteeing clarity lies with the journalist. While a confidentiality agreement can take any form to which the two parties agree, there are several common types of source confidentiality.

Without attribution usually means that the journalist will withhold the name and identification of the source but can use quotations and attribute them in a manner agreeable to both the source and journalist. For example, a statement might be attributed to "a source within city hall" or "a source in the mayor's office."

Off the record means that the journalist will not directly quote or paraphrase a source's statements. However, general information from the interview could be used in a news story or to confirm what other sources have said.

Deep background is a creation of *Washington Post* reporter Bob Woodward, as described in the book *All the President's Men*. A source working on deep background provides general guidance to a journalist, but information from that source cannot be used directly in any way, even to confirm what other sources have said.

Information Confidentiality

Information confidentiality refers to information obtained through a pledge of confidentiality made by someone other than the journalist. This can involve everything from corporate secrets to classified government documents to confidential communications.

Take classified government documents, for example. Journalists covering the U.S. Department of State, national security, the military and other intelligence areas often seek access to classified government documents. When they manage to gain access to those documents, they must decide whether or not the material should be shared with the public. It's not always as straightforward a decision as one might think. Not all classified information presents a clear danger. Indeed, much of it can be rather mundane and even trivial.[8] As national security reporter Walter Pincus writes:

> [E]ven secrets uncovered might not merit being put in public print, on television, or on the Internet. Much as reporters ought to realize that everything an official says publicly might not deserve to be published, just discovering something that is being kept secret, even by government officials, doesn't mean it needs to be exposed.[9]

In other cases, the information can harm national security interests and put lives in danger.[10] In those cases, journalists usually refrain from publishing. However, some experts believe that journalists might lack the information or knowledge to guarantee that the information they publish won't jeopardize security or safety. In the age of massive databases and worldwide digital distribution, journalists increasingly face questions about truth versus the potential harm caused by revealing confidential government information.

In 2006 Australian activist Julian Assange founded WikiLeaks, an advocacy journalism website that provides a place for sources to leak confidential information to the press and the public. The site claims that "we accept (but do not solicit) anonymous sources of information."[11] Approximately four years after its founding, WikiLeaks obtained nearly 250,000 confidential U.S. State Department diplomatic cables related to the wars in Iraq and Afghanistan.[12] The site subsequently provided much of that information to several newspapers and itself published a small selection of the documents.[13] The release of that information created immediate controversy, raising questions about how much the information endangered U.S. interests and the safety of individuals. Some journalists wondered whether WikiLeaks had done more to increase government secrecy than it had to combat it.[14]

WikiLeaks raises a number of important questions for traditional journalists. Many of these questions involve legal aspects of the case, such as whether laws designed to protect traditional U.S. journalists should apply to foreign advocacy journalists. But ethical questions abound as well. What is a journalist? What obligations do journalists have to their nation and its people? In an increasingly "flat"[15] world, how do journalists cooperate with so-called "citizen journalists" from other countries? The public interest has long been an argument to permit the release of confidential government information. But when asking what constitutes the best interest of the public, journalists increasingly need to ask whose interests and which publics they serve.

In 2011, Assange announced plans to expand WikiLeaks into the realm of corporate secrets, beginning with a major American bank

thought to be Bank of America.[16] Although the leak did not material-
ize and has even been called a hoax,[17] it does raise the issue of journalism and corporate confidentiality. Like classified government
documents, much of a corporation's confidential communication no
doubt involves rather trivial and uninteresting material. Some of
it contains proprietary information and trade secrets protected by
law. While it might be newsworthy to reveal the recipe for Coca-
Cola or the 11 secret herbs and spices in Kentucky Fried Chicken,
journalists would have to weigh the benefits of doing so against the
right of corporations to protect such secrets.

Journalists have a responsibility to consider the ethical rami-
fications of revealing classified government documents, corporate
secrets, or other information thought to be confidential. Journalists
typically have a duty to pass information along to the people and let
them decide what to do with it. In the words of the American Society
of News Editors: "The primary purpose of gathering and distribut-
ing news and opinion is to serve the general welfare by informing
the people and enabling them to make judgments on the issues of
the time."[18] Many journalists weigh this duty against another, more
consequentialist, duty to minimize harm.[19] Subjects of a news story
could be endangered if their names are revealed, or a business could
lose its competitive edge if confidential information is published.
What is the balance between the public's need for information and
protecting the confidentiality of sources? Confidential relationships
should not be breeched without due ethical consideration.

Summary

Confidentiality differs from privacy. The former refers to promises made to protect a source, while the latter refers to the right of
individuals to control information about themselves. Promises of
confidentiality can be either explicit—overtly stated—or implied—
creating a reasonable expectation of confidentiality.

Society recognizes the value of confidentiality and provides legal
protection in some situations. Explicit promises of confidentiality
can be viewed as contracts, which can be protected under contract
law. Some communication is considered *privileged*, such as between
spouses or between doctors and patients. One cannot be compelled
to reveal privileged information in a court of law. While the courts
recognize almost no privilege for client communication in advertising and public relations, journalists enjoy limited privilege in their
work. This comes in the form of *shield laws*, state legislation aimed
at giving reporters some protection from being compelled to reveal
confidential information in court.

Professionals in advertising and public relations owe an implicit ethical duty of confidentiality to clients and to employers. Confidentiality in journalism takes two forms: source confidentiality and information confidentiality. Journalists must decide whether to promise confidentiality to a source as well as weighing a duty to inform the public or to safeguard corporate or government secrets.

NOTES

[1]   Garrett, T. M., Baillie, H. W., and Garrett, R. M. (1989). *Health care ethics: Principles and problems*. Prentice Hall, 97.

[2]   Attridge, M. (2022, April 27). House tries again on federal law to protect journalists and sources. Capital News Service.

[3]   Brown, F. & SPJ Ethics Committee. (2020). *Media ethics: A guide for professional conduct* (5th ed). Society of Professional Journalists.

[4]   *Branzburg v. Hayes*, 408 U.S. 743 (1972).

[5]   Farrell, M. (n.d.). Anonymous sources. Society of Professional Journalists Ethics Committee Position Papers. https://www.spj.org/ethics-papers-anonymity.asp

[6]   Ibid.

[7]   Ibid.

[8]   Bender, B. (2022, August 23). White House launches new war on secrecy. Politico.

[9]   Pincus, W. (2008). Secrets and the press. *Nieman Reports*. https://niemanreports.org/articles/secrets-and-the-press/

[10]   Preston, P. (2010, July 31). WikiLeaks' Afghan story raises dilemma over safety of sources. *The Guardian*.

[11]   WikiLeaks (2011, May 7). What is Wikileaks? http://wikileaks.org/About.html. This is an important distinction. In the United States, journalists can be held legally accountable if they encourage individuals to break the law by leaking classified documents. However, the courts have tended to be more lenient when journalists have not broken the law nor encouraged others to do so in order to obtain confidential documents. cf. *Pearson v. Dodd*, 410 F.2d 701 (D.C. Cir.), cert denied, 395 U.S. 947 (1969).

[12]   Savage, C. (2022, November 28). Major news outlets urge U.S. to drop its charges against Assange. *The New York Times*.

[13]   Greenwald, G. (2010, December 10). The media's authoritarianism and WikiLeaks. *Salon*.

[14]   Calabresi, M. (2010, December 2). WikiLeaks war on secrecy: Truth's consequences. *Time*.

[15]   Friedman, T. L. (2005). *The world is flat: A brief history of the twenty-first century*. Farrar, Straus and Giroux.

[16]   Greenberg, A. (2010, November 29). WikiLeaks' Julian Assange wants to spill your corporate secrets. *Forbes*.

[17]   Carney, J. (2011, April 26). The great Wikileaks Bank of America hoax. CNBC.

[18]   American Society of News Editors. (2002). *ASNE statement of principles*. http://www.unm.edu/~pubboard/ASNE%20Statement%20of%20Principles.pdf

[19]   Society of Professional Journalists. (2014, September 6). SPJ code of ethics. http://spj.org/ethicscode.asp

12 Case Study

Journalism:
Source Anonymity

You are a reporter for the *Burlington Guardian*, a large weekly newspaper serving Burlington (pop. 33,614) and surrounding suburbs. Your paper has been covering an explosion and fire that killed three employees and injured 14 others at a local chemical plant. Pentarage Synthetics, which owns the plant, indicated that the explosion was triggered when a cloud of monomer vinyl chloride ignited inside the plant.

Two days after the explosion Lonnie Harton, a system operator at the plant, calls you at the office. He asks you to meet him this evening at a diner in Avondale, about 30 minutes outside Burlington. He claims to have information regarding the explosion but says he is afraid of being found out by his employers. You agree and meet Harton at the diner just after 7 p.m.

After introductions, Harton gets right down to business. "Look all this if off the record, but . . ."

You stop him right there. Before you agree to any kind of confidentiality, you tell him that you need to have some idea about what he has. Harton then pulls out a small pile of papers. He explains that these papers show how Pentarage Synthetics has been cutting corners on safety to reduce processing costs at the Burlington plant for years. But before he turns them over to you, he needs to know that you will keep his identity secret.

The material seems like it would be useful, so you agree in principle. You explain that "off the record" can mean a variety of different things. Harton responds that he wants his name kept out of the papers. He seems scared, and he doesn't want you to use his job title or anything else that could identify him. But he does agree to allow you to attribute the papers to "a source within the plant." With the agreement in place, Harton turns over the papers. These prove to be a proverbial treasure trove. With help from Harton, you can see that the papers show Pentarage had been skimping on safety at the plant for years.

After returning to the office, you scan the documents into PDF format and email them to a chemistry professor who works as an independent analyst. He confirms Harton's interpretation of the documents. With the

documents, as well as the information from Harton and the chemistry professor, you go to press with the story. The next day, it's the talk of the
town. The district attorney announces that her office will be launching an
investigation into the chemical plant. Officials from the state Department of
Environmental Resources and the U.S. Environmental Protection Agency
have agreed to get involved as well.

The next day, a man shows up at your office just before lunch and asks
to speak with you. He identifies himself as Chris Strite, a detective, and
explains that company officials believe the documents you based your story
on have been forged, probably by a disgruntled employee. The officials
said their documents show that the company has operated within accepted
industry limits going back several years. To help clear things up, Strite asks
you to turn over the documents so that authorities can compare your documents to what the company provided. Strite also asks for the name of your
source, so that he can be questioned about the possible forgery.

You offer to speak with your source about the issue, but it will take
some time. You cannot very well just pick up the phone and give him a
call. Strite says that you do not have time. Officials need the information
as soon as possible.

"I'll give you until 3 o'clock," says Strite. "After that I'm going to have
to get a warrant. And just so you know, any warrant won't just include
the company documents. We'll have to take your computers here and at
home, as well as your cell phone and all your files. And don't try dumping
them or deleting anything, because you'll be arrested for destroying evidence and impeding a lawful investigation."

*You have three hours before Detective Strite returns.
What will you decide to do?*

13

Visual Ethics

In this chapter, you will learn about:
- Deepfake ethical concerns
- Truth in visual communication
- Staging and photoshopping
- Ethics and body image
- Visual privacy
- Dangers of submitted content

When videos seemingly featuring Tom Cruise swept across Tik Tok in spring of 2021, they quickly made news. It wasn't because of anything that the actor said or did because Tom Cruise wasn't in the videos. Visual effects artist Chris Ume uploaded *deepfakes*, videos created by using advanced technology to apply another person's face and voice so seamlessly that it can be almost impossible for the average viewer to tell the difference. Ume explained that he made the videos to have fun and raise awareness about the power of these new technologies.

While it's not easy to create truly good deepfake videos, at least not yet, they have the potential to be incredibly powerful and even dangerous depending on how or why they are used. Cybercriminals might use deepfakes to bypass biosecurity measures or to blackmail people.[1] One could send a deepfake showing sobbing loved ones pleading that you pay a ransom for their return. Officials worry that deepfakes could pose a threat to national security[2] or to the democratic process.[3] It's enough of a problem that Ume has called for laws to protect people from the misuse of artificial intelligence and deepfakes.[4] As he told the *Daily Mail*, "This type of tech is coming, and you can't stop it."[5]

Deepfakes offer so many possibilities to professional communicators that they could become a standard tool in the future. Marketers envision being able to craft a hyper-personalized advertising campaign that uses data gathered from the online activities of people to not only customize the ads presented to them but also to change who is in those ads, what that person says, and even what language they speak.[6] A single influencer can only make so many ads, but thousands of deepfakes could be personalized for maximum effect. That kind of power allows marketers to connect people to products and services that are a perfect fit, but it could also lead to manipulation on a scale that we can barely comprehend.

Truth in Visual Communication

Deepfakes illustrate many of the reasons why visual ethics merits its own separate discussion. We have evolved to place a lot of credence in what we see. Seeing something triggers an array of thoughts confirming the reality of a situation, making visual memories, and providing evidence for the reasoned decisions that we make.[7] Visual evidence increases one's ability to persuade an audience.[8] If it is true that seeing *is* believing, then altering what an audience sees could potentially alter beliefs about reality. This places an enormous responsibility on professional communicators.

Remember that the audience's expectations play an important role when it comes to truth. Fiction is not a lie because we know it does not purport to be truth. When the audience expects truth, however, fiction can become believable. In 1938, radio had recently become a primary supplier of information and entertainment.[9] On October 30 that year, some radio listeners heard what they thought were news bulletins about a Martian invasion. The first act in the adaptation of *War of the Worlds* for a Mercury Theatre radio play was written as late-breaking news bulletins.[10] Efforts to make the show sound realistic were wildly successful, and some of the audience who tuned in after the opening announcements didn't realize they were listening to a dramatization. In professional communication, we must be sure to keep the audience's expectation of truth in mind so that the visual images we present do not intentionally or unintentionally deceive them.

Consider how audience expectations differ when engaging with a visual image in journalism compared to advertising. In advertising, we expect the image to present the product, service, or individual in the best light possible. There's even an entire subgenre of advertising known as "mini-film advertising" where plots carry a narrative through several commercials. We expect that the subjects in advertisements are actors delivering lines and that the imagery has been planned, edited, and augmented to sell something. No reasonable person believes that Red Bull will make you grow actual wings.[11] We grant advertising a fair amount of creative license when it comes to storytelling. Visually, many commercials bear more resemblance to fiction than fact.

In contrast, audiences presume journalists work to provide the truth. Studies suggest that audiences expect a journalist to act as a detached observer.[12] They want journalists to provide them with facts without opinion and bias.[13] When audiences see visuals in journalism, they expect that those images have not been appreciably altered from reality. Research shows that news subjects believe that journalists should prioritize accuracy when visually rendering events.[14] Different people may have differing perceptions of accuracy. When subjects voice an expectation of accuracy, they may mean that they hope to be portrayed as they see themselves. "Visual journalists need to interact—nonverbally and verbally—with those they cover to increase the nuance and accuracy of the depictions produced.[15] While accuracy may be multidimensional, striving for accuracy is a must.

If journalism represents one end of the spectrum and advertising the other, public relations and marketing lie in between. In general, audience expectations depend upon how and where a visual is used. If providing a visual image for a brochure, an illustration for a corporate website and so on, expectations would lean more toward those of advertising. The rules would be relaxed a bit because the audience would tend to expect illustration rather than accuracy. However, when visual images could be understood to depict real situations or appear in a context that suggests a high degree of accuracy, such as press releases, the rules of journalism would apply.

Staging

One concern in journalistic images is the practice of *staging*, arranging the subjects or background in a photograph in order to achieve a certain effect. Staging involves the photographer manipulating the image prior to taking the photo. Physically moving objects in the photo or directing the people or animals in a photo constitutes staging, which most find ethically suspect.

One of the most iconic photographs of the 20th century shows U.S. marines raising the American flag during the Battle of Iwo Jima in World War II. On February 23, 1945, a Marine combat patrol climbed and captured the strategic Mount Suribachi. Shortly thereafter, they raised an American flag. Staff Sergeant Louis Lowery, a photographer for the Marine Corps' *Leatherneck* magazine, took a photo of the men raising the flag.[16] American troops nearby cheered when they saw the flag, and their reaction prompted an officer to order that another, larger flag be raised that could be seen across the island. Associated Press photographer Joe Rosenthal was climbing the hill and arrived in time to snap a single shot of the second flag raising without even looking through the viewfinder. Not sure whether he would have a useable image, Rosenthal took an obviously staged shot of 18 Marines looking at the camera and cheering. This later became known as the "gung-ho" photograph.[17]

Rosenthal sent his film to Guam to be developed and radiofaxed to AP in San Francisco.[18] Before he even saw the results, Rosenthal's photograph of the second flag raising appeared in newspapers worldwide. It became the most recognizable image of World War II, and one of the most reproduced of all time. It won the Pulitzer Prize in 1945, and the U.S. Marine Corps War Memorial sculpture is based on the photograph. The photo was remarkable in its artistic composition and depiction of the courage and spirit of the soldiers.

When Lowery saw Rosenthal's picture, he alleged it had been staged. Someone asked Rosenthal if he had posed the picture. Thinking the question referred to the gung-ho photo, he said "yes." When he realized the question related to a different photo, he tried to correct his answer, but rumors continued to swirl. Fortunately, Marine Sergeant Bill Genaust filmed the event, and his video confirms that the photo was not staged.[19]

Comparing Lowery's photograph with Rosenthal's offers some insight into why people might have assumed Rosenthal staged his photo. Lowery's composition shows a Marine holding a rifle in the foreground, and the flag flapping in the breeze in the background. It was serviceable but not memorable.[20] It didn't have the powerful visual message and excellent composition of Rosenthal's image, which had wonderful lighting, a strong diagonal made by the flag staff, and a pyramid shape of Marines pushing the flag up.

Natural photographs are unstaged; photographers have no role in arranging the subjects or background of a photograph. The subjects in the iconic Iwo Jima photograph were not performing for the camera; they were not instructed how to behave. The National Press Photographers Association tells members to "not intentionally contribute to, alter, or seek to alter or influence events."[21] Photographs of events, even preplanned events, are generally considered ethical for all professional communication provided that they do not attempt to deceive the viewer as to the events themselves.

Staged photographs are set up to one degree or another by the photographer, who either changes naturally occurring objects or directs the subjects in the photo. *Overtly staged photos* do not attempt to hide the fact that they are staged. Subjects look directly at and pose for the camera. Joe Rosenthal's "gung-ho" shot is a fine example of an overtly staged photograph. It makes no attempt to deceive the viewer. By contrast, *covertly staged photographs* attempt to deceive the viewer by presenting staged reality as though it were a naturally occurring event. In contexts where the audience has a reasonable expectation of photographic truth, such as journalism, covertly staged photographs are widely considered unethical.

Photoshopping

Photoshopping refers to using computer software to alter the content of photographs. The term derives from Adobe Photoshop, the industry standard photo editing software that enables users to manipulate and combine photographs, graphical images, and text. However, it can also refer to the use of apps such as Facetune, which is used for editing selfies on social media. Such software can transform bland photographs into brilliant studio-quality shots or turn images of actual events into lies so believable that they can even fool professionals.

So, how much is too much? As with staging, journalism tends to take a fairly strong stance on the use of Photoshop and other editing software. The NPPA code of ethics says that members should "not manipulate images or add or alter sound in any way that can mislead viewers or misrepresent subjects."[22] For the most, that prohibits adding/removing anything within the frame. Many would add to that list of prohibitions the practice of altering shadows or colors within a photograph. Cropping, the act of trimming a photograph, usually meets with approval provided that it does not alter the context of a photograph. But most other edits are suspect.

Traditional photojournalists tend to have a zero-tolerance policy for anything that could not have been accomplished in a darkroom. Cropping and lightening or darkening an image slightly for clarity would be okay. Most other changes would not. Non-journalistic professional communicators tend to be less absolutist when it comes to the ethics of photoshopping, which makes it more difficult to draw the line between ethical and unethical behavior. Consider the widespread practice of touching up celebrity photographs before sharing them online. At what point does it become deceptive? Can we whiten someone's teeth? Lighten or darken their skin? "Airbrush" blemishes off their skin? Make them appear thinner? Add or remove people from the photograph?

As with staging, the context of advertising provides the most flexibility when it comes to photoshopping. The culture clash between advertising and journalism on this issue can be dramatic. In the mid-1990s a photographer from a midsized southern newspaper was assigned to take a photo of a ribbon-cutting ceremony at the opening of a local business. The shoot went well, and the photo ran in the newspaper without a problem. However, the business owner liked the photo so much that he wanted to use it in an ad for his new business. He had one request though. He wanted to digitally add a relative who could not attend the ceremony. This was not a problem for the advertising staff, which made the adjustment and ran the ad. But that level of digital manipulation was a serious ethical violation in the eyes of the photographer who took the picture, as well as the rest of the news photography staff. They went so far as to threaten a walkout over the issue until management came up with a compromise. From that point forward, any photo that might eventually appear in an ad would be assigned two photographers, one from the journalism side and one from the advertising side. The journalist's photo could not be altered other than to achieve better focus or contrast. The advertising photographer's image could be altered as much as he or she desired.

Audiences expect a certain blend of fact and fiction in advertising. Provided the audience can clearly identify visuals as part of an advertisement, they will not be deceived into thinking a perfect setting with perfect people eating a perfect meal is real. But what of a celebrity photograph shared via Instagram or Twitter? What about images sent to the media for publication? Are those all deceptive because they present a false depiction of reality? Or is some amount of photoshopping acceptable because "everybody does it"— therefore the audience should expect that the photos they see are no more real than a movie or an advertisement?

In 2020, Khloe Kardashian caused an uproar among her fans and others when she uploaded a photo on Instagram in which she appeared so different from her usual look that some shocked fans wondered if she had undergone significant plastic surgery. Others were hoping she photoshopped her image.[23] For many, the answer became clear after a viewer of *Keeping Up With the Kardashians* saw her on the show wearing the same clothing and accessories she had donned for the Instagram post but with her face looking completely different.[24] After closer inspection, fans noticed flaws in the Instagram photo, including a missing beauty mark and a necklace seeming to hang from only half a chain. It seemed clear that the photo had been digitally altered.

Other Issues in Visual Ethics

Much of the ethical focus on visual communication revolves around concern for the truth. However, a number of other issues arise as well.

Body Image

While some of Kardashian's Instagram followers said they were deceived by the photo on her Instagram account, others were more concerned that Khloe felt the need to enhance her photo.[25] Still others worried about the impact on her fans, especially young women presented with an impossible standard of beauty. Jasmine Fardouly, a researcher on social influences on young people's mental and physical health, observed that Kardashian and other social media influencers "who edit their appearances actively promote an ideal that is not attainable—for them or their followers."[26] The impossible standard exists only within Photoshop.

A meta-analysis of research on *body image* demonstrated that mass media negatively affect the degree of satisfaction with the audience's body image, sometimes to the degree of provoking depression or eating disorders.[27] Photographs were found to have an adverse effect on women and men of all age groups and in multiple cultures. However, the issue of body image has been studied more closely with regard to women than men. Attractive images posted to Instagram, and specifically images of celebrities, have a negative impact on young women's body image.[28] The effect is particularly strong among those who already suffer from reduced self-esteem.[29] Even when Instagram photos can be seen to have been manipulated through Photoshop or other editing software, they still increased the negative effect of self-comparison.[30] The impact was found to be true in peer as well as celebrity photos.

Concerns about the negative effects of photoshopping on audience members prompted a British Member of Parliament in 2020 to propose a law requiring advertisers, broadcasters, and publishers to display a warning notice on digitally-altered images.[31] Legislation in France requires advertisers to label edited images as retouched. Norway passed a law in June 2021 requiring advertisers and social media influencers to disclose when images are altered.[32] Unfortunately, studies suggest that the warning labels have little or no effect in reducing the negative impact of photoshopped images.[33] In fact, a meta-analysis of research into the effect of photoshopping laws suggested that such laws could even be detrimental because they actually encourage more self-comparison with the photoshopped images.[34] One group of researchers concluded that improving body images "requires the fashion, advertising and media industries to stop photoshopping women's bodies to make them appear thinner."[35]

Privacy

Technology has enabled photos and video to become pervasive in our society. Nearly everyone in the United States now has a readily accessible camera and video recorder. As a result, moments that once might have been considered private now have the potential to become embarrassing public events. Some countries, such as France, have laws that prohibit individuals from taking any person's photograph without their permission, even in public spaces. Privacy laws in the United States do not extend into the public sphere, except in places like restrooms where one has a reasonable expectation of privacy. What you say or do in public *is* public. And anyone has the right to take a photograph of anything that is in plain view.

Despite that, the Reporters Committee for Freedom of the Press notes that privacy law can change frequently and usually without much notice.[36] Laws can vary from state to state, and photographers who knowingly or unknowingly cross the line could find themselves in civil court. A few questions highlight the ethical/legal issues involved in photographing subjects and help professional communicators avoid problems.

Did you obtain the subjects' permission, before or after taking the photograph? When autonomous adults grant you permission to take their photograph, you are typically not violating their right to privacy. Your request should include an explanation of how the photos or video will be used so that the subject can provide informed consent. In commercial communication, such as advertising, marketing, and public relations, such consent should be in writing.

Do the subjects have a reasonable expectation of privacy? Recall that intrusion covers various types of trespass but also covert surveillance such as hidden cameras. As a rule, the photographer should be physically present when recording an event. Technology that extends one's perception, such as a telephoto lens, could be seen as suspect when it allows a photographer or videographer to record something that could not otherwise be seen with the naked eye.

Are the subjects or the actions in the photograph newsworthy or of artistic value? In general, matters of legitimate concern to the public enjoy less privacy protection from an ethical standpoint. Likewise, individuals such as politicians and celebrities, might reasonably be viewed as having surrendered a great deal of their privacy by virtue of their position in the public eye. However, ethically this should not be seen as freedom to violate their privacy without legitimate reason to do so.

Does the photograph or cutline (caption) place the subject in a false light? Context can be especially important in photographs. Failure to understand or explain the context of an image can violate the subjects' privacy by placing them in a false light. Imagine you take a photo of a someone entering a pornography store and then publish it. Without any context, one might reasonably assume the individuals to be customers. However, other explanations could apply. Perhaps they were looking for a lost friend, asking to use the restroom in an emergency, or looking to avoid someone following them. Failing to give subjects the opportunity to clarify what they were doing and why runs a serious risk of portraying them in a false light.

As a general rule of thumb, openness about your identity and motives, together with providing the subjects of your photography or videography an opportunity to explain or respond to your work before it becomes public, will help address or alleviate many privacy concerns in visual communication.

Submitted Content

In 2008, Agence France-Presse (AFP), the world's oldest news agency, circulated a photo showing the simultaneous launch of four missiles by Iran. News organizations around the world, including BBC News, MSNBC, the *Los Angeles Times*, the *Financial Times*, the *Chicago Tribune*, ran the photograph on front pages, websites, and news programs. Unfortunately, it was a fake. The truth came out after bloggers and others pointed out that the fourth missile appeared to have been added digitally by copying and pasting elements of the other three. The Associated Press soon disseminated a photo showing the launch of three missiles. The lesson for the media, according to a *New York Times* assistant managing editor is the need for "eternal vigilance."[37]

Concerns about staging, photoshopping, invasions of privacy, and so on apply to content submitted by others as much or even more than your own work. When you air or publish visual images, you are as accountable to the public for those images as if you had taken them yourself. Too often, professional communicators lack the time, resources, personnel, or even the forethought to properly vet the content that comes to them. The AFP eventually revealed that the source of the image was Sepah News, the official news site of the Iranian Revolutionary Guard. Had organizations been aware of the source, they could have recognized that the photograph was provided by propagandists for a foreign power's military. Instead, organizations who obtained the photograph from AFT relied on the credibility of that organization. News organizations that seek video footage and photos from outside sources must remain vigilant about possible Photoshop enhancement.

Summary

Humans have evolved to believe what we see, which places a special responsibility on professional communicators when it comes to visual communication. We have the ability to alter the perception of reality with technology such as *deepfakes*. While this shows promise for tailoring messages to individual audience members, it could also lead to massive manipulation.

Audience expectations play an important role when it comes to truth, particularly in visual communication. We may understand that the subjects in advertisements are actors performing on a stage, but we expect journalistic images to conform to reality. Any deliberate attempts to alter the contents of a news photograph are viewed as a form of deception. Marketing and public relations tend to fall somewhere between those two extremes, depending on the purpose and use of visual images.

The two primary issues when it comes to truth in visual communication are staging and photoshopping. *Staging*, arranging the subjects or background in a photograph in order to achieve a certain effect, involves the photographer manipulating the image prior to taking the photo. *Natural photographs* are unstaged. *Photoshopping* refers to using computer software, such as Adobe Photoshop or Facetune, to alter the content of photographs. Digital manipulation of imagery is common and acceptable in advertising, provided it does not alter important facts—for example, distorting the size of a product. In journalistic and other settings where audiences have an expectation of truth, digital editing should be kept to a minimum.

Another concern with photoshopping is the impact that it has on the degree of satisfaction audience members have regarding *body image*. Research has repeatedly shown that photoshopped images of attractive people negatively affect the audience, sometimes to the degree of provoking depression or eating disorders. Even in images that have not been photoshopped, professional communicators should use caution and keep in mind the impact those images could have on the audience.

Technology has enabled photos and video to become pervasive in our society, and this has increased concerns about privacy. Some countries have laws that prohibit individuals from taking any person's photograph without their permission, even in public spaces. Although the United States does not, ethical professional communicators take steps to ensure that they do not violate the privacy of individuals who can be identified in photographs and videos. Openness about identity and motives plus providing subjects an opportunity to explain the context of a photograph before it becomes public will help address privacy concerns in circumstances that raise ethical questions.

Finally, photographs and video submitted by outside sources should receive extra attention to ensure that it meets ethical standards. Organizations and individuals should take steps to verify that the image has not been staged or photoshopped, as well as to confirm that the context of the photograph properly conveys the truth of the situation. Airing or publishing visual images—whether taken personally or acquired from another source—imposes public accountability.

NOTES

[1] Bracken, B. (2021, May 3). Deepfake attacks are about to surge, experts warn. Threatpost. https://threatpost.com/deepfake-attacks-surge-experts-warn/165798/
[2] Perkins, T. (2021, June 3). Deepfakes could pose a threat to national security, but experts are split on how to handle it. Broadband Breakfast. https://broadbandbreakfast.com/2021/06/deepfakes-could-pose-a-threat-to-national-security-but-experts-are-split-on-how-to-handle-it/
[3] Puutio, A. & Timis, D.A. (2020, Oct. 5). Deepfake democracy: Here's how modern elections could be decided by fake news. World Economic Forum. https://www.weforum.org/agenda/2020/10/deepfake-democracy-could-modern-elections-fall-prey-to-fiction/
[4] Kahn, J. (2021, March 5). Deepfake master behind those viral Tom Cruise videos says the technology should be regulated. *Fortune.* https://fortune.com/2021/03/05/tom-cruise-deepfake-creator-technology-should-be-regulated/
[5] Greep, M. (2021, March 17). Visual effects artist behind realistic "deepfake" TikTok videos of Tom Cruise warns people to get used to the "highly believable" technology, saying it's already too late to "stop it coming." *Daily Mail.* https://www.dailymail.co.uk/femail/article-9371273/Creator-alarming-Tom-Cruise-deepfake-videos-circulating-TikTok-warns-stop-tech.html
[6] Patel, N. (n.d.). How could deepfakes change marketing? *Neilpatel.com.* https://neilpatel.com/blog/deepfakes-marketing/
[7] Millar, A. (2011). How visual perception yields reasons for belief. *Philosophical Issues, 21,* 332–351.
[8] See, for example, McCabe, D. P., & Castel, A. D. (2008). Seeing is believing: The effect of brain images on judgments of scientific reasoning. *Cognition, 107*(1), 343–352.
[9] Yogerst, C. (2022, October 28). Orson Welles' *War of the Worlds* broadcast: Its ominous echoes for a fractured media. *Hollywood Reporter.*
[10] Schwartz, A. B. (2015, May 6). The infamous *War of the Worlds* radio broadcast was a magnificent fluke. *Smithsonian Magazine.*
[11] You may have heard the story about the man who sued because, contrary to its slogan, Red Bull did not give him wings. While that's amusing, it's also not true despite many headlines that imply the contrary. In actuality, his lawsuit claimed that Red Bull consistently and falsely implied that it provided a higher boost of energy than a cup of coffee. The company settled the claim for $13 million. See, for example, Brant, E. (2014, Oct. 9). So Red Bull doesn't actually "give you wings." *BBC News.* https://www.bbc.com/news/newsbeat-29550003
[12] Riedl, A. and Eberl, J. (2022). Audience expectations of journalism: What's politics got to do with it? *Journalism, 23*(8), 1682–1699.

13   The Media Insight Project. (2018, June 18). What the public expects from the press (and what journalists think). American Press Institute. https://www.americanpressinstitute.org/publications/reports/survey-research/public-expects-from-press/

14   Thomson, T. J. (2019). In front of the lens: The expectations, experiences, and reactions of visual journalism's subjects. *Journalism & Communication Monographs, 21*(1), 4–65, p. 46.

15   Ibid., p. 51.

16   Newcott, B. (2020, February 21). Was this iconic World War II photo staged? *National Geographic.*

17   CNN updated a 2016 article with an array of 11 photographs from Iwo Jima. The first is Rosenthal's Pulitzer-prize winning photo; the second is Lowery's photo; the ninth is Rosenthal's gung-ho photo. View the photos at: https://www.cnn.com/2015/02/18/world/gallery/cnnphotos-iwo-jima/index.html

18   Patterson, T. (2016, February 23). The inside story of the famous Iwo Jima photo. CNN.

19   Video available at https://www.youtube.com/watch?v=MLCupx1UExg

20   Patterson (2016).

21   National Press Photographers Association. (n.d.). *NPPA Code of Ethics.* http://nppa.org/code-ethics.

22   National Press Photographers Association.

23   Michaels, W. (2020, May 23). Fans are confused by Khloé Kardashian's face in her new Instagram pics. Showbiz Cheatsheet.

24   Greenwald, M. (2020, August 18). Khloe Kardashian under fire over "scary" photoshop fail: "So unnecessary." Yahoo.

25   Ibid.

26   Fitzsimmons, B. (2021, April 6). Opinion: The Kardashians have created a body and beauty standard even they can't live up to. MamaMia. https://www.mamamia.com.au/khloe-kardashian-unedited-photo/

27   Huang, Q., Peng, W., & Ahn, S. (2021). When media become the mirror: A meta-analysis on media and body image. *Media Psychology, 24*(4), 437–489.

28   Brown, Z., & Tiggemann, M. (2016). Attractive celebrity and peer images on Instagram: Effect on women's mood and body image. *Body image, 19,* 37–43.

29   Ahadzadeh, A. S., Sharif, S. P., & Ong, F. S. (2017). Self-schema and self-discrepancy mediate the influence of Instagram usage on body image satisfaction among youth. *Computers in Human Behavior, 68,* 8–16.

30   Kleemans, M., Daalmans, S., Carbaat, I., & Anschütz, D. (2018). Picture perfect: The direct effect of manipulated Instagram photos on body image in adolescent girls. *Media Psychology, 21*(1), 93–110.

31   Gallagher, S. (2020, September 14). MP calls for warning notices to be added to photoshopped images of bodies in adverts and on social media. Independent. https://www.independent.co.uk/life-style/luke-evans-mp-photoshop-images-social-media-adverts-b436112.html

32   Press-Reynolds, K. (2021, July 2). Influencers in Norway will soon have to disclose when paid posts include edited or manipulated body photos. Insider. https://www.insider.com/norway-law-social-media-influencers-advertisers-disclose-edited-images-2021-7

33   See, for example, Frederick, D. A., Sandhu, G., Scott, T., & Akbari, Y. (2016). Reducing the negative effects of media exposure on body image: Testing the effectiveness of subvertising and disclaimer labels. *Body image, 17,* 171–174; or Bury, B., Tiggemann, M., & Slater, A. (2016). The effect of digital alteration disclaimer labels on social comparison and body image: Instructions and individual differences. *Body Image, 17,* 136–142.

34   Danthinne, E. S., Giorgianni, F. E., & Rodgers, R. F. (2020). Labels to prevent the detrimental effects of media on body image: A systematic review and meta-analysis. *International Journal of Eating Disorders, 53*(5), 647–661.

35 Bromberg, M., & Halliwell, C. (2016). "All about that bass" and photoshopping a model's waist: Introducing body image law. *U. Notre Dame Austl. L. Rev.*, *18*, 1, p. 19.
36 The Reporters Committee for Freedom of the Press. (2007). *Photographers' guide to privacy.* https://www.rcfp.org/wp-content/uploads/imported/PHOTOG.pdf
37 Folkenflick, D. (2008). On the smoky trail of a faked missile photo. NPR. https://www.npr.org/templates/story/story.php?storyId=92454193

13 Case Study

Public Relations:
Projecting Diversity

As the marketing director for the Fairfield Group, a firm of about 50 employees that provides various professional services to business clients, you have been tasked with representing the company at a job fair this Sunday. The annual event attracts hundreds of local job seekers as well as thousands more online. It's an important opportunity not only to attract new talent but also to maintain and improve your corporate image.

The firm's chief executive officer, Erica Mueller, has recently begun encouraging your team to pursue more diversity within the workplace. Although she believes that it's the right thing to do from a human perspective, she also judges that it will help the business better attract and serve clients. However, she insists that she does not want the firm to hire people solely because they fill a diversity quota. Instead, she says, she wants to make sure that the hiring process works to be broad and inclusive in order to attract a wide range of candidates from many different backgrounds.

On Friday afternoon, your marketing assistant, Ted Miles, comes to you with copies of the poster and brochures that you will be using at the job fair, as well as a mock-up of the website you will be launching for the event. Prominent among all that literature is a promotional photo of the firm, but you don't recognize some of the people present. After a moment you realize that the woman farthest right in the photo is Amie Norris, one of your front-end Web developers. But her skin tone is all wrong.

"Ted . . . what happened to Amie's skin in this photo? And who's the guy sitting at the head of the table on the left? I don't recognize him. Is he new?"

Ted shows you the original photo of the team meeting, noting that it only features white employees. He says that everyone thought that, given the push for diversity, they should have people of color in the photo. Unfortunately, by the time they realized their mistake, it was too late to reshoot the photo. So instead, Ted used Photoshop to change Amie's skin tone and add in the headshot of a model that he found on pixabay.com.

"Couldn't you find anyone from the firm to be in the photo instead of Photoshopping it?" you ask Ted. "We can always just reshoot it. What about James or Tanisha?"

He responds that Tanisha is out of town on vacation until Monday, and James said he didn't feel comfortable being included in a promotional photo just because of his race. Ted adds that he was lucky enough that Amie gave him the okay to darken her skin tone for the photo.

"There's a reason the boss wants to make this place more diverse," he says. "And seeing all those white faces isn't exactly putting out the welcome mat to that broad, diverse audience she wants to attract. This ad might help us achieve the kind of diversity that we all want for the firm."

Even so, you hesitate.

"Look, the photo is pretty obviously staged," Ted continues. "Our advertisements and other marketing material use Photoshop all the time to change the way things look. This is pretty much the same thing. And we're doing it for a good reason, right?"

Ted is standing there looking at you expectantly. What will you decide to do?

14

Framing an Ethical Future

The Markula Center for Applied Ethics notes that we not only have an image of ourselves acting ethically but also images of what an ethical community, an ethical business, an ethical government, or an ethical society should be. "Ethics really has to do with all these levels—acting ethically as individuals, creating ethical organizations and governments, and making our society as a whole more ethical in the way it treats everyone."[1] Ethics refers to standards and practices that tell us how to behave, and it is also concerned with our character. Effective ethical behavior requires knowledge, skills, and habits.

A reflective, systematic approach to ethics by everyone benefits society. Media have a powerful influence on society, and communication professionals provide information that influences how people think. Pew Research Center's mission, for example, is to generate "a foundation of facts that enriches the public dialogue and supports sound decision making. . . . Fact-based information is the fuel democracies run on—the raw material from which societies identify problems and construct solutions."[2] Ethical decisions made by media practitioners have significant consequences.

Media Literacy

Media consumers also have a responsibility; they must utilize critical thinking skills in assessing the media consumed. Media literacy is a requirement for informed consumers. While stories of mass hysteria over the *War of the Worlds* broadcast (see chapter 13) were

189

overblown, some listeners were confused. "Then, as now, media literacy is a key facet toward intelligent public engagement."[3] Sifting through attention-seeking information to find facts requires work. Constantly evolving technologies create ethical dilemmas, adding to the need for consumers to remain vigilant.

Generative AI innovations "change how we create and consume media, disrupting the creative marketplace and communication industries."[4] ChatGPT is a text-to-text artificial intelligence language processing algorithm that produces answers to any question within seconds. It generates text from an enormous dataset—from news articles to novels to poems to song lyrics. Its proficiency raises concerns about journalists, poets, and novelists replacing their own efforts with chatbot generated offerings.[5]

ChatGPT was released by Open AI in November 2022. Google offers LaMDA, a rival chatbot; Silicon Valley startups are also working on other offerings. A significant concern is students using the algorithm for their assignments. In response, university professors, department chairs, and administrators nationwide have redesigned courses.[6] Potential alternatives to essay assignments are oral exams, group work, and handwritten papers. Instructors are phasing out take-home, open-book assignments, which are vulnerable to the use of chatbots. The University at Buffalo in New York and Furman University in Greenville, South Carolina plan to include a discussion of generative artificial intelligence in required courses to teach incoming students about academic integrity.

Software such as Rewordify helps job seekers create resumes tailored to specific jobs. The job seeker enters a job posting, and the software determines the most relevant keywords to insert in a resume.[7] Text-to-image generative AI, such as Microsoft Designer or Dall-E, creates images based on verbal prompts. AI-powered photos could easily lead to disinformation, facilitating the creation of deepfakes.[8] Policy and regulations lag behind innovation. Personal ethics become ever more necessary. Andrew DeVigal lists questions for communication professionals to consider.

- How do publications label and define generative AI content?
- When is it appropriate to publish generative AI images, and when is it not?
- What's the balance in the creative process between using the assistance of generative AI versus using generative AI to create?
- What ethical and legal boundaries do we need to consider when using and publishing generative AI content?
- What safeguards should be in place to prevent the abuse of news photography?

Diversity

Diversity is an important element in discussions about ethics that has only recently been included in media codes[9]. Diversity needs to be addressed in multiple areas: accuracy and fairness (avoiding stereotypes, reflecting multicultural society); the composition of news organizations and who is making decisions; the development of story ideas and who does the reporting; inclusiveness in choosing sources, using people of different races, genders, ages, sexual orientation, socioeconomic status, religions, and geographic location in reporting; and giving voice to the voiceless.

A diverse staff is more likely to produce a wider range of stories and perspectives.[10] Two-thirds of journalists surveyed said their organization has enough gender diversity among its employees, and 58% say there is enough age diversity. The percentages decrease for sexual orientation diversity (43%), socioeconomic status diversity (34%), and racial and ethnic diversity (32%). Younger and female journalists are more likely than their older and male peers to think there is not enough diversity in their organizations.

Diversity in sources more reliably reflects the world, making journalism more accessible and better.[11] Ethical reporting means including the voices of individuals most affected by the issue discussed in the story. The need for diversity isn't limited to topics about race or sexual orientation. Different ages, genders, etc. may have different perspectives on whatever is being reported.

Producing news that is relevant for a multiracial and multigenerational audience may require a cultural shift in how journalism is done.[12] Does reporting center on the people affected by issues, or is it driven by the voices of experts and officials? If the issue is the product of systemic inequality, is historical context provided? Diversity in newsrooms lags other organizations. Newsroom employees are more likely to be white and male (86.9%) than U.S. workers in general.[13] The changing landscape of the news business has resulted in diverse journalists making different choices. The traditional, mainstream news organizations once considered the industry's top employers face competition for talent from digital start-ups, nonprofit news organizations, and new media ventures pioneered by BIPOC entrepreneurs.

A Personal Code of Ethics

This book provides background and frameworks for analyzing ethical dilemmas. Awareness about philosophical approaches to ethics provides a foundation for recognizing potential ethical problems, analyzing possibilities, and formulating an ethical response. There are no simple, black-and-white answers to what we should do or what our responsibilities are in a specific situation. Different individuals evaluating the same situation could reach different, defensible decisions.

> In the most basic terms, the best way to arrive at an ethical decision is to ask the right questions. If you can do that, and if your answers to those questions make sense to you—and if you can then explain your reasoning sensibly to other people—you've done what you needed to do to reach a sound, defensible ethical decision. That's true even if someone else, given the same set of circumstances, might arrive at the opposite decision and consider it just as defensible.[14]

For example, a reporter could decide that accuracy is the most important value, while someone in public relations might stress loyalty.

Chapters 2 through 5 discussed philosophical approaches to ethical behavior. You may believe strongly that consequences are more important than duty or that a virtuous character leads to ethical actions and justice. Whatever your priorities, your ethical decisions should be rational, and you should be able to justify your decisions.

> Ethics is less about the conflict between right and wrong than it is about the conflict between equally compelling (or equally unattractive) alternatives and the choices that must be made between them. Ethics is just as often about the choices between good and better or poor and worse as about right and wrong.[15]

The Online News Association has a website to help members build their own ethics codes. The project began with the recognition that the journalism profession encompassed so many people and technologies that no single ethics code could reflect the needs of everyone.[16] We encourage you to develop your own framework for doing ethics. We hope the philosophies, models, justifications, and codes presented in these chapters motivate you to frame an ethical process to guide your future actions. Your personal code won't solve every dilemma, but it will be a framework for deliberation. Ethics is a journey, with new input gained from each experience and application.

Making ethical decisions requires reflective thinking and analytical skills to evaluate complex situations and to decide between competing choices. Frameworks provide a procedure to approach problems methodically. Chapter 7 provided two justification models for ethical decisions: the Bok model and the Potter Box. There are many models and guidelines you might find useful in formulating your personal code. As one example, the Josephson Institute of Ethics suggests seven steps to making better ethical decisions.[17]

1. *Stop and think*. Analyze calmly rather than rushing to a decision. Ask yourself questions at every step.

2. *Clarify goals*. What aspect of the issue creates an ethical concern? What is most important to you?

3. *Determine facts*. Do you have enough information? Consider what you know and what you need to learn. Are you considering facts or assumptions? Are there different perspectives? Evaluate the reliability of the information you receive. What are the motivations of the people who provided the information?

4. *Develop options*. Are there professional guidelines (codes of ethics) that are useful in deciding possible courses of action? Can you learn from precedents related to this issue? Were people with different perspectives included in the decision-making process?

5. *Consider consequences*. Who will be affected by your decision, both short-term and long-term? What stakeholders do you need to consider? How would you feel if you were one of the stakeholders? Has harm been minimized? Have you considered alternatives with different consequences?

6. *Choose*. Have you talked with people whose judgment you respect to help make your decision? Would your family and friends approve of your course of action? Are you willing for your decision to be applied universally? Can you justify your thinking in reaching your decision?

7. *Monitor and modify*. Difficult decisions have varying responses. Monitor the effects of your decision. Are there unintended consequences? Use the information learned in making future decisions.

Compare the Josephson process with the six steps recommended by Chris Roberts and Jay Black.[18]

1. *What's your problem?* What makes the situation an ethical dilemma? Look at the problem in detail and from different points of view to understand all aspects.

2. *Why not follow the rules?* Are there precedents, guidelines, or codes that apply? Are they applicable to all cultures, organizations, individuals? What are the weaknesses?

3. *Who wins, who loses?* Identify stakeholders and loyalties. Who benefits, who could be hurt?

4. *What's it worth?* What value is most important to you that you are unwilling to compromise?

5. *What do philosophers say?* What principles do you follow? Where do you place the importance of consequences versus duty and/or character?

6. *How's your decision going to look?* Was your process and the decision logical? Your justification process should be transparent, and you should be accountable.

We'll review one final ethical model, TARES. Sherry Baker and David Martinson developed five principles for ethical persuasion.[19]

1. **T**ruthfulness of the message. Is the communication accurate? Does it mislead others to believe what I do not believe?

2. **A**uthenticity of the persuader. Does the message compromise my integrity? How do I feel about my involvement?

3. **R**espect for the persuadee. Is the appeal self-serving? Is the persuadee regarded as rational and autonomous?

4. **E**quity of the persuasive appeal. Would I want someone to make this appeal to me? Is it clearly persuasive or disguised as information?

5. **S**ocial responsibility for the common good.

Decision-making models are tools for enhancing analytical skills. Whatever model one chooses, going through the steps focuses thinking on the process of making an ethical decision. After recognizing the need to choose between alternatives, frame the issues by identifying relevant values and ranking their importance. What is causing the problem? Who will be affected? Use careful reasoning to evaluate the alternatives. Make sure you can explain the choice you make.

We hope the chapters in this book help you analyze issues from different perspectives. Looking at issues from different vantage points enhances effective decision making. The Socratic method of asking questions hones critical thinking, and discussing potential answers with others builds skills and insights. Think carefully about your actions, your responsibility to others, and the results of your decisions. Complex situations call for nuanced responses. The ultimate test of any ethics code is the behavior that results from the application of abstract principles to specific situations.

To conclude our exploration of ethics, we revisit the reasons for studying ethics from chapter 1. The philosophical foundations of ethics form the basis for ethical reasoning. A better understanding of how to examine ethical issues objectively contributes to both individual and professional growth. The book addressed making ethical choices in various professions, providing examples of some of the choices professionals face. Recognizing the existence of ethical dilemmas, identifying the values underlying ethical conflicts, acknowledging the people affected and obligations owed, applying reasoned principles, and accepting responsibility are key elements in ethical decision making.

NOTES

[1] Markula Center for Applied Ethics (2021, November 5). A framework for ethical decision making. Santa Clara University. https://www.scu.edu/ethics/ethics-resources/a-framework-for-ethical-decision-making/

[2] Pew Research Center (2022). Our mission and code of ethics. https://www.pewresearch.org/about/our-mission/

[3] Yogerst, C. (2022, October 28). Orson Welles' *War of the Worlds* broadcast: Its ominous echoes for a fractured media. *Hollywood Reporter.* https://www.hollywoodreporter.com/business/digital/orson-welles-war-of-the-worlds-broadcast-its-ominous-echoes-for-a-fractured-media-1235250796/

[4] DeVigal A. (2022, November 11). A news photo editor's nightmare is an art director's dream. Poynter. https://www.poynter.org/reporting-editing/2022/a-news-photo-editors-nightmare-is-an-art-directors-dream/

[5] Warner, J. (2023, January 8). Will artificial intelligence like ChatGPT render writers obsolete? *Chicago Tribune,* sec. 4, p. 6.

[6] Huang, K. (2023, January 20). Cheating in class at new level. *Chicago Tribune,* sec. 2, p. 2.

[7] Svei, D. (2023, January 8). Use these 5 resume trends to your advantage. *Chicago Tribune,* sec. 2, p. 9.

[8] DeVigal (2022).

[9] Brown, F. & Society of Professional Journalists' Ethics Committee (2020). *Media ethics: A guide for professional conduct* (5th ed.). Society of Professional Journalists.

[10] Gottfried, J., Mitchell, A., Jurkowitz, M., & Liedke, J. (2022, June 14). Journalists give industry mixed reviews on newsroom diversity, lowest marks in racial and ethnic diversity. https://www.pewresearch.org/journalism/2022/06/14/journalists-give-industry-mixed-reviews-on-newsroom-diversity-lowest-marks-in-racial-and-ethnic-diversity/

[11] Patel, N. R. (2022, April 7). 5 questions reporters and editors should ask to diversify their sources. Poynter. https://www.poynter.org/ethics-trust/2022/how-to-diversify-journalism-sources/

[12] Cheung, P. (2022, March 28). Journalism should take a cue from entertainment—diversity grows audiences. Poynter. https://www.poynter.org/commentary/2022/paul-cheung-journalism-diversity-entertainment-industry/

[13] Burns, G. (2022, February 1). News organizations are increasing diversity efforts, a Medill survey finds. Poynter. https://www.poynter.org/business-work/2022/news-media-diversity-equity-inclusion-2022/

[14] Brown (2020), pp. 9–10.

[15] Wilkins, L., Painter, C., & Patterson, P. (2022). *Media ethics: Issues and cases* (10th ed.). Rowman & Littlefield, p. 7.

[16] The Online News Association. (2023). A customized ethics code for every organization. ONAethics. https://ethics.journalists.org/about/

[17] Josephson Institute (2022). The seven-step path to better decisions. Has harm been minimized? Josephson Institute. https://josephsoninstitute.org/med-4sevensteppath/

[18] Roberts, C., & Black, J. (2022). *Doing ethics in media: Theories and practical applications* (2nd ed.). Routledge.

[19] Baker, S., & Martinson, D. L. (2011). The TARES test: Five principles for ethical persuasion. *Journal of Mass Media Ethics, 16*(2–3), 148–175.

Index